AF734541

ECONOMIC ISSUES, PROBLEMS AND PERSPECTIVES

EXCHANGE RATES: POLICIES, EFFECTS AND FLUCTUATIONS

ECONOMIC ISSUES, PROBLEMS AND PERSPECTIVES

Additional books in this series can be found on Nova's website under the Series tab.

Additional E-books in this series can be found on Nova's website under the E-book tab.

GLOBAL ECONOMIC STUDIES

Additional books in this series can be found on Nova's website under the Series tab.

Additional E-books in this series can be found on Nova's website under the E-book tab.

ECONOMIC ISSUES, PROBLEMS AND PERSPECTIVES

EXCHANGE RATES: POLICIES, EFFECTS AND FLUCTUATIONS

NATALIE B. PERKINS
EDITOR

Nova Science Publishers, Inc.
New York

Copyright © 2011 by Nova Science Publishers, Inc.

All rights reserved. No part of this book may be reproduced, stored in a retrieval system or transmitted in any form or by any means: electronic, electrostatic, magnetic, tape, mechanical photocopying, recording or otherwise without the written permission of the Publisher.

For permission to use material from this book please contact us:
Telephone 631-231-7269; Fax 631-231-8175
Web Site: http://www.novapublishers.com

NOTICE TO THE READER

The Publisher has taken reasonable care in the preparation of this book, but makes no expressed or implied warranty of any kind and assumes no responsibility for any errors or omissions. No liability is assumed for incidental or consequential damages in connection with or arising out of information contained in this book. The Publisher shall not be liable for any special, consequential, or exemplary damages resulting, in whole or in part, from the readers' use of, or reliance upon, this material. Any parts of this book based on government reports are so indicated and copyright is claimed for those parts to the extent applicable to compilations of such works.

Independent verification should be sought for any data, advice or recommendations contained in this book. In addition, no responsibility is assumed by the publisher for any injury and/or damage to persons or property arising from any methods, products, instructions, ideas or otherwise contained in this publication.

This publication is designed to provide accurate and authoritative information with regard to the subject matter covered herein. It is sold with the clear understanding that the Publisher is not engaged in rendering legal or any other professional services. If legal or any other expert assistance is required, the services of a competent person should be sought. FROM A DECLARATION OF PARTICIPANTS JOINTLY ADOPTED BY A COMMITTEE OF THE AMERICAN BAR ASSOCIATION AND A COMMITTEE OF PUBLISHERS.

Additional color graphics may be available in the e-book version of this book.

LIBRARY OF CONGRESS CATALOGING-IN-PUBLICATION DATA

Exchange rates : policies, effects and fluctuations / editor, Natalie B.
Perkins.
p. cm.
Includes index.
ISBN 978-1-61209-505-9 (hbk.)
1. Foreign exchange rates. I. Perkins, Natalie B.
HG3851.E939 2011
332.4'56--dc22

2010054289

Published by Nova Science Publishers, Inc. † New York

CONTENTS

PREFACE

In finance, the exchange rates between two currencies specifies how much one currency is worth in terms of the other. This new book presents topical research on the policies, effects and fluctuations of exchange rates. Topics discussed include the effects of exchange rate fluctuations on real output, the price level, and the real value of components of aggregate demand in Egypt and Turkey; the role of CEECs exchange rates in monetary policy rules; the competitiveness of exchange rate fluctuations in Middle Eastern countries; foreign exchange rate exposure of Chinese firms in the new exchange rate regime and exchange rate flexibility and real adjustments in emerging market economies.

Chapter 1 – This chapter examines the effects of exchange rate fluctuations on real output, the price level, and the real value of components of aggregate demand in Egypt and Turkey. Building on a theoretical model that decomposes movements in the exchange rate into anticipated and unanticipated components, the empirical investigation traces the effects through demand and supply channels. In Turkey, anticipated exchange rate appreciation has significant adverse effects, contracting the growth of real output and the demand for investment and exports, while raising price inflation. Random fluctuations, in Turkey, have asymmetric effects that highlight the importance of unanticipated depreciation in shrinking output growth and the growth of private consumption and investment, despite an increase in export growth. In Egypt, anticipated exchange rate appreciation decreases export growth. Given asymmetry, the net effect of unanticipated exchange rate fluctuations, in Egypt, decreases real output and consumption growth and increases export growth, on average over time.

Chapter 2 - The Central and Eastern European Countries (CEEC) which joined the European Union between 2004 and 2007 show an interesting evolution of their exchange rate regimes. Although they all started from a comparable situation and have the common long-term goal of joining European Monetary Union, they opted for different exchange rate policies. Furthermore, the exchange rate policies were subject to frequent changes and adjustments. The authors first describe the evolution of exchange rate arrangements in CEEC, and survey in this chapter various aspects of their exchange rate policy.

The authors start with the discussion of differences betthe authorsen de facto and de jure exchange rate regimes. Second, the authors analyze the impact of exchange rate policy on exchange rate volatility, focusing on structural breaks or volatility regimes. While the level of volatility shows the external dimension of monetary stability, the break points may help to understand the processes that lead to changes in exchange rate arrangements. Third, the authors highlight the role of CEEC's exchange rates in monetary policy rules. Finally they review the literature on central bank interventions in CEEC.

Chapter 3 - Many Middle Eastern countries are resource-constrained, i.e., they are running a current account deficit. The deficit in the current account indicates that aggregate demand exceeds aggregate supply. Alternatively, domestic investment cannot be financed using national savings, necessitating continued reliance on foreign resources to fill in the resource gap.

Given the resource deficit, many countries have taken a closer look into ways to revive the current account balance and supplement domestic resources. There are two policy tracks. First, domestic policies may aim at constraining aggregate demand, particularly domestic consumption, to provide more domestic resources to finance domestic investment. Under this agenda, constraining the budget deficit usually takes top priority. The second priority is to pursue reforms to expand productive capacity and increase aggregate supply. The former track (demand management) may be difficult to implement given priorities for fiscal spending and in light of constraints on government revenues. The second track (supply management) is even more difficult given resource constraints and the time necessary to stimulate output supply and implement structural reforms.

In addition to domestic policies, countries may pursue an exchange rate management policy in order to stimulate exports and constrain imports. Nonetheless, exchange rate policy may not yield the desired results. Export competitiveness may not be stimulated, despite exchange rate depreciation, absent measures to revive quality, improve productivity, and guarantee access to new external markets. Moreover, many Middle Eastern countries have suffered from the J-curve effect whereby depreciation, in the short-run, may increase the value of imports, absent domestic alternatives to substitute for necessary imports.

The purpose of this chapter is to study the significance of the exchange rate in a sample of countries in the Middle East. The authors estimate empirical models that explain real output growth, price inflation, and the growth in real components of aggregate demand. The empirical models account for major policy variables: government spending, the money supply, and the exchange rate. In addition, the authors account for FDI flows in the empirical models.

Chapter 4 - Within the framework of the classical North-South linkages, in this chapter, the authors analyze the role of imported raw materials from the South in the transmission of a Northern relative monetary shock to exchange rates changes and welfare. In this context, the authors find that a low substitutability between Northern inputs (labor) and imported raw materials from the South is a source of exchange rate volatility as well as differential welfare effects.

Chapter 5 - The purpose of this chapter is to investigate the foreign exchange rate exposure of Chinese firms in the managed floating system after China announced this regime switch on 21st July 2005. The sample includes 1,448 Chinese listed firms in the Shanghai Stock Exchange (SHSE) and Shenzhen Stock Exchange (SZSE) during the period of 22nd July 2005 – 18th October 2006. In addition to the analysis of the foreign exchange exposure on the firm level, the authors intend to shed more light on the cross-sectional distributions of exchange rate exposures of Chinese firms by share classes and ownership structures.

Chapter 6 - full information and a simple alternative asymmetric information approach, in which shocks are not known to any agents in the economy at the time of the monetary policy decision. The latter approach can be seen as incorporating, in a discrete-time context, the notion that there is an institutional constraint in the timing of interest rate decisions relative to the higher frequency of shocks and changes in prices, output and exchange rates. The authors also distinguish between cases of expansionary and contractionary depreciations. The authors find that full information results are not robust to the presence of the informational friction here considered. For economies exhibiting expansionary or strongly contractionary depreciations, such friction leads to an optimal deviation from the full information outcome, namely, that the monetary authority does not react on impact to shocks. In the case of mildly contractionary deprec iations, their asymmetric information model predicts a lack of response of the central bank to aggregate demand shocks, as opposed to an offsetting movement in interest rates under full information. Optimal policies are thus found to depend on the degree of informedness in the economy.

Chapter 7 - This chapter uses a long-run structural VAR approach to study the sources of real exchange rate fluctuations of yen-dollar rates. The authors begin by identifying two types of macroeconomic shock (real and nominal), in order to reveal the sources of movements in real exchange rates. The evidence presented indicates that real shocks play a dominant role in explaining the fluctuations of the real exchange rate. Next, the authors extend the model to identify three types of macroeconomic shock (real supply, real demand, and nominal), again to reveal the sources of movements in real exchange rates. The evidence from the extended model also indicates that real shocks (real demand and real supply) play a dominant role in explaining the fluctuations of the real exchange rate.

Chapter 8 - This chapter analyses the extent to which managed floating helps macroeconomic stabilisation and contributes to real adjustment, in the face of real external disturbances in emerging market economies. The authors find that optimal policy reactions, as opposed to "fear of floating", may explain why nominal exchange rates have exhibited lower variability than nominal interest rates in developing countries along the recent years. The authors show that for this to occur it is necessary that devaluation affects positively the aggregate demand. Furthermore, the authors demonstrate that even when the analysis is restricted to a financial context, which seems appropriate when output achieves its long run potential level, some institutional arrangements can be engineered to reduce the destabilising effects of controlled floating.

In: Exchange Rates: Policies, Effects and Fluctuations
Editor: Natalie B. Perkins, pp. 1-24
ISBN: 978-1-61209-505-9
© 2011 Nova Science Publishers, Inc.

Chapter 1

A Comparative Analysis of Exchange Rate Fluctuations and Economic Activity: The Cases of Egypt and Turkey

***Magda Kandil*[1*] *and Nazire Nergiz Dincer*[2†]**

[1] Western Hemisphere Department, International Monetary Fund, Washington, D.C., USA

[2] State Planning Organization, Ankara, Turkey

Abstract

This chapter examines the effects of exchange rate fluctuations on real output, the price level, and the real value of components of aggregate demand in Egypt and Turkey. Building on a theoretical model that decomposes movements in the exchange rate into anticipated and unanticipated components, the empirical investigation traces the effects through demand and supply channels. In Turkey, anticipated exchange rate appreciation has significant adverse effects, contracting the growth of real output and the demand for investment and exports, while raising price inflation. Random fluctuations, in Turkey, have asymmetric effects that highlight the importance of unanticipated depreciation in shrinking output growth and the growth of private consumption and investment, despite an increase in export growth. In Egypt, anticipated exchange rate appreciation decreases export growth. Given asymmetry, the net effect of unanticipated exchange rate fluctuations, in Egypt, decreases real output and consumption growth and increases export growth, on average over time.

---

* The views expressed in this paper are those of the authors and should not be attributed to the International Monetary Fund, its Executive Board, or its management. Email: mkandil@imf.org

† The views presented are those of the author and do not necessarily reflect the views of the SPO. Email: ndincer@dpt.gov.tr

I. INTRODUCTION

There has been an ongoing debate on the appropriate exchange rate policy in developing countries. A depreciation (or devaluation) of the domestic currency may stimulate economic activity through the initial increase in the price of foreign goods relative to home goods. By increasing the international competitiveness of domestic industries, exchange rate depreciation diverts spending from foreign goods to domestic goods. As illustrated in Guitian (1976) and Dornbusch (1988), the success of currency depreciation in promoting trade balance largely depends on switching demand in the proper direction and amount, as well as on the capacity of the home economy to meet the additional demand by supplying more goods[3].

While the traditional view indicates that currency depreciation is expansionary, the new structuralism school stresses some contractionary effects. Meade (1951) discusses this theoretical possibility. If the Marshall-Lerner condition is not satisfied, currency depreciation could produce contraction.[4] Hirschman (1949) points out that currency depreciation from an initial trade deficit reduces real national income and may lead to a fall in aggregate demand. Currency depreciation gives with one hand, by lowering export prices, while taking away with the other hand, by raising import prices. If trade is in balance and the terms of trade are not changed, these price changes offset each other. But if imports exceed exports, the net result is a reduction in real income within the country. Cooper (1971) confirms this point in a general equilibrium model.

Diaz-Alejandro (1963) introduced another argument for contraction following devaluation. Depreciation may raise the windfall profits in export and import-competing industries. If money wages lag the price increase and if the marginal propensity to save from profits is higher than propensity to save from wages, national savings will go up and real output will decrease. Krugman and Taylor (1978) and Barbone and Rivera-Batiz (1987) have formalized the same views.

Supply-side channels further complicate the effects of currency depreciation on economic performance. Bruno (1979) and van Wijnbergen (1989) postulate that in a typical semi-industrialized country where inputs for manufacturing are largely imported and cannot be easily produced domestically, firms' input costs will increase following a devaluation. As a result, the negative impact from the higher cost of imported inputs may dominate the production stimulus from lower relative prices for domestically traded goods. Gylfason and Schmid (1983) provide evidence that the final effect depends on the magnitude by which demand and supply curves shift because of devaluation.[5] The combined effects of demand

---

[3] Empirical support of this proposition for Group 7 countries over the 1960-89 periods is provided in Mendoza (1992).

[4] The Marshall-Lerner condition states that devaluation will improve the trade balance if the devaluing nation's demand elasticity for imports plus the foreign demand elasticity for the nation's exports exceed 1.

[5] Hanson (1983) provides theoretical evidence that the effect of currency depreciation on output depends on the assumptions regarding the labor market. Solimano (1986) studies the effect of devaluation by focusing on the structure of the trade sector. Agenor (1991) introduces a theoretical model for a small open economy and distinguishes between anticipated and unanticipated movement in the exchange rate. Examples of empirical investigations include Edwards (1986), Gylfason and Radetzki (1991), Roger and Wang (1995), Hoffmaister and Vegh (1996), Bahmani (1998), Kamin and Rogers (2000), and Kandil and Mirzaie (2002 and 2003).

and supply channels determine the net results of exchange rate fluctuations on real output and price.[6]

This chapter focuses on a comparative analysis of the relationship between exchange rate fluctuations and economic activity in Egypt and Turkey, building on a theoretical model that incorporates the process of forming rational forecasts of the exchange rate. Recent experiences of currency crises have brought to the forefront the importance of anchoring agents' forecasts in the design of an appropriate exchange rate policy. Hence, the theory aims to separate the effects of anticipated shifts in the exchange rate from unanticipated deviations around agents' forecasts.

The data under investigation are for Egypt and Turkey over the sample period 1980-2005. The real effective exchange rate is constructed as a weighted average of the log value of the real price of the domestic currency in terms of the currencies of its major trading partners. The weights represent the relative share of each trading partner in the total trade (exports and imports) for each country. Hence, the real exchange rate accounts for the relative prices in the domestic economy relative to the weighted average of foreign price in major trading partners. The relative price channel is important to the analysis of exchange rate fluctuations given the high inflationary experience in Egypt and Turkey.

The remainder of the chapter is organized as follows. Section II presents a theoretical background. Section III discusses developments in Egypt and Turkey. Section IV outlines the empirical models and presents empirical results. The conclusion is presented in Section V.

II. Theoretical Background

In the real world, stochastic uncertainty may arise on the demand or supply sides of the economy. The chapter builds on a macro-economic model that incorporates exchange rate fluctuations of the domestic currency (see Kandil and Mirzaie (2002)). Fluctuations are assumed to be realized around a steady-state trend that is consistent with variation in macro-economic fundamentals over time.

In theory, the combination of demand and supply channels indicates that real output depends on unanticipated movements in the exchange rate, the money supply, and government spending in the short-run.[7] These movements define fluctuations in economic variables around full-equilibrium. In addition, supply-side channels establish that output varies with anticipated changes in the exchange rate, which enters the full-equilibrium definition of real output.

The complexity of demand and supply channels may determine the results of exchange rate fluctuations.

The net effect of currency appreciation on output growth and price inflation is determined by the dominant effect of demand or supply channels.

---

[6] For an analytical overview, see Lizondo and Montiel (1989).

[7] Shocks are assumed to fluctuate in response to domestic economic conditions or in response to external vulnerability, e.g., capital mobility or fluctuations in foreign reserves.

III. Economic Developments in Turkey and Egypt

To provide a background for investigation, this section outlines developments over the sample period that shaped economic developments in Turkey and Egypt.

A. Economic Developments in Turkey

In 1980-83 Turkey was governed by a military regime. In that period, the deteriorated public balances were relieved by the tight fiscal policy and suppressed wages; price controls were gradually removed and interest rates were gradually liberalized. On the other hand, the government followed an exchange rate policy that aimed at preventing the real exchange rate from appreciating, thereby supporting the export-led growth strategy. The import regime was gradually liberalized[8]. Thereby, the 1980's were the years of integration with the world economy for Turkey.

In 1984, a new government came to power and followed similar policies to that of the military government till 1988, except that public expenditures increased, causing public deficits. Moreover, tax policy was changed in 1985, resulting in a further deterioration in the public balances for which domestic lending became an effective tool for financing the public deficit. Higher public deficit necessitated the launching of the stabilization program in 1988. Stabilization policies were successful in decreasing the deficit but it could not prevent inflation from increasing. Finally, 1989 was a year of a crisis; elections were held; wages increased by 42 percent, the inflation rate, which was around 40 percent in the 1980-88 periods, rose to near 80 percent; and a new phase for the Turkish economy started.

Overall, between 1980 and 1989, exchange rate policy supported real depreciations and, thereby, export-led-growth strategy. Moreover, imports were liberalized by removing quotas and decreasing the tariffs, thereby increasing the share of imports to GDP. Till 1989, the economy grew well and high export growth proved to be the engine of growth. Owing to tight fiscal policy and suppressed wages, consumption growth slowed to below overall economic growth, resulting in an increase in the growth of domestic savings. Higher savings were necessary to finance the growth in investment and boost export-led growth.

In 1989, the capital account was liberalized and in 1990 Turkey adopted a convertibility policy for the Turkish lira, and a new era started in the Turkish economy. High capital inflows that were realized in the 1988-90 period led to an appreciation of the Turkish lira. Furthermore, the policy of the government (higher spending and high interest rates to finance the deficit) prevented the exchange rate from depreciating. By 1990, the Central Bank of Turkey (CBRT) increased interest rates to attract more capital inflows. During this period, a primary deficit was observed and the public sector borrowing requirement was financed with short-term domestic borrowing. With the increase in interest rates, the domestic debt stock grew to such a level that a debt-rollover problem arose. The expectations for a devaluation increased at the end of 1993. In January 1994, the CBRT abandoned the exchange rate policy and devalued the nominal exchange rate by 14%. The devaluation of the currency continued until April 1994 and the total devaluation for this period reached 173% in nominal terms.

[8] Quotas were removed and tariffs were reduced.

Output declined by 6.2% in the same year. In April 1994, a new economic program with the IMF was brought into effect to overcome the financial crises.

On the growth side, 1990 was the year of the recovery. The liberalization of the capital account, coupled with higher government spending, contributed to economic growth. As a result of wage increases and real appreciation of the Turkish lira, consumption increased by 13 per cent. Overall, growth was around 9 percent in 1990. The same trend did not continue in 1991. During the Gulf crisis surrounding Iraq's invasion of Kuwait, the Turkish economy was adversely affected by regional conditions, which slowed down economic growth. To stimulate economic growth, a depreciation of the exchange rate was necessary, which boosted export-led growth in 1992. In 1993, the continued inflow of capital resulted in currency appreciation and supported economic growth, particularly the growth of domestic spending on consumption and investment. Nonetheless, the continued accumulation of public debt reached a level that became unsustainable, resulting in a financial crisis in 1994. Uncertainty surrounding the crisis led to a contraction of real output by six percent in 1994.

As Turkey engaged in the economic program with the IMF in 1994, a series of reforms and stabilization policies were in place and economic recovery was underway. Following integration into the Customs Union in 1996, trade liberalization was accelerated, resulting in an increase in both exports and imports. The continued increase in capital inflows in 1996-1997 provided external resources to finance the current account deficit. Concurrently, foreign reserve accumulation contributed to a loose monetary policy, which supported the growth of investment and the economy. Unfortunately, inflation increased as well.

Starting with the economic program in 1994, the exchange rate policy was designed to stabilize the real exchange rate. The CBRT depreciated the nominal exchange rate parallel to inflation expectations.

In 1998, the Russian crisis hit the Turkish economy and private investment and consumption, as well as capital inflows, decreased sharply. Nonetheless, Turkey experienced a positive growth rate, boosted by export growth and the increase in public spending on consumption and investment.

In 1999, the economy underwent through another recession due to the earthquake and the deterioration in public finance. In December 1999, Turkey adopted another disinflation program with the support of the IMF. The aim of the program was to decrease inflation to a single digit at the end of 2002. The exchange rate regime of the program was announced as the crawling peg regime. The CBRT declared an exchange rate basket path consisting of 1 US$+0.77 Euro, and announced a daily depreciation rate, which added up to a cumulative of 20 percent by the end of 2000.

The implementation of the 1999 program gave positive signals. The nominal Treasury bond auction interest rates fell from 96.4% in November 1999[9] to 34.1% in January 2000. Consistently, inflation expectations decreased. The economy realized high capital inflows, which supported a high growth rate that reached 4.8% in the first half of 2000. However, higher growth resulted in an increase in consumption and investment spending, which stimulated an increase in import growth. Subsequently, the current account deficit deteriorated and the external balance became fragile. Despite crawling depreciation, capital inflow and high domestic spending led to a real exchange rate appreciation, which adversely affected export growth. Subsequently, the banking sector increased its foreign currency

[9] There was no Treasury auction in December, 1999.

denominated debt to a level that became risky for the system. With the sudden capital outflow in November 2000, the banking sector crises broke out, which led to a significant loss of foreign reserves of the CBRT.

In February 2001, political instability further contributed to a deterioration of economic conditions. As the economic crisis deepened, the crawling exchange rate regime was abandoned. The nominal exchange rate depreciated 94% (the annual increase of the second quarter of 2001) and the output response was detrimental, declining by 9.4%.

In May 2001, a new program based on a floating exchange rate regime, tight fiscal policy and structural reforms was implemented. Signs of recovery were observed in 2002; output grew by 7.8%. The source of growth was exports and public expenditures[10]. In 2002-2004, it can be said that Turkey has managed to diversify exports, which resulted in a significant increase in export growth, despite real appreciation of the Turkish lira. In support of economic reform, fiscal policy was tight, which contributed to a reduction in the inflation rate and interest rates. Hence, the primary engines of growth between 2002 and 2005 were export growth and the growth of domestic private absorption (private investment and consumption).

B. Economic Developments in Egypt

The 1980's was a period of rising inflation, foreign exchange shortages, balance-of-payment deficits, declining growth and a massive foreign debt for Egypt. The 1985 was the year of high foreign debt with liquidity shortages. The only choice for Egypt was rescheduling. In 1987, the stand-by arrangement with the IMF resulted in progress in economic reform. Two months later, the Paris Club agreed to reschedule. After a promising start, the political will was not supportive enough to carry on the structural reform program. The result was a comprehensive Economic Reform and Structural Adjustment Program (ERSAP) in 1991, based on a fixed exchange rate regime. The program aimed to increase competitiveness of the economy through executing a sequence of structural adjustment measures, and to ensure that fiscal and current account deficits are brought under control. Achieving exchange rate stability and fiscal discipline were at the heart of the stabilization program.

On one hand, the program succeeded in bringing the inflation rate down to 2-4 percent, achieving a growth rate of about 5 percent during the mid-1990s, and reducing fiscal and current account deficits. During the period 1998–2000, the local currency came under notable pressure. In an attempt to defend the overvalued exchange rate, policymakers heavily relied on international reserves. Therefore, international reserves dropped by almost 25 percent. Consequently, a large amount of liquidity has been pulled out of the market. The situation was aggravated by the unfavorable external shocks in the late 1990s (Asian crisis in June 1997; Luxor incident in November 1997 and oil prices deterioration starting from late 1997).

On the other hand, the authorities' attempt to defend the exchange rate peg resulted in an excessively overvalued real exchange rate. There was a justified fear of floating since it was not announced that the fixed exchange rate regime was a temporary arrangement and that it would be abandoned according to a careful exit strategy once inflationary pressures were

[10] Although tight fiscal policy was targeted in 2002, public expenditures could not be prevented due to elections held at the end of 2002.

contained. The overvaluation of the Egyptian pound led to a current account deficit, albeit the rise in that deficit in the last three years of the 1990s was mainly due to an increase in investment rather than consumption. Moreover, although the current account deficit as a ratio of GDP was not considered too high by international standards, the fact that Egypt was unable to attract significant private capital flows made it difficult to finance a growing deficit.

Excessive intervention to defend the exchange rate peg, coupled with external shocks, led to a severe credit crunch in late 1990s, forcing a severe slowdown in the domestic economy, starting from the fiscal year 1999/2000. To make things worse, the accumulation of non-performing loans in the banking system further shrank domestic liquidity and necessitated a massive bailout by the government.

In an attempt to stimulate the economy, the government has allowed the budget deficit to increase to about 5-7 percent of GDP since the late 1990s. As the depletion of domestic liquidity continued to pose the risk of a prolonged recession, it became necessary to abandon the exchange rate peg. The Central Bank of Egypt slowly and gradually moved toward a more flexible exchange rate regime since July 2000. While this was the right path to pursue, the adoption of the policy change came too late, resulting in a massive depletion of foreign reserves and a prolonged recession.

Toward the end of 2002, the situation was characterized by an overvalued real exchange rate; a budget deficit of about 6 percent of GDP; a vulnerable current account situation (the current account still shows a volatile deficit once net exports of oil and private remittances are excluded); a critical level of international reserves; a fragile financial system, segmented consumption markets, and finally a protracted economic slowdown. As the system continued to deteriorate, the Prime Minister of Egypt announced the flotation of the pound on January 28, 2003.

Following a period of overshooting, under a flexible exchange rate system, the value of the Egyptian pound stabilized, having lost more than fifty percent of its value relative to the US dollar. Growth picked up momentarily, rising to an estimated 2.7% in fiscal year 2004. Economic growth was led by an increase in exports of goods and services, following the sharp decline of the pound that raised Egypt's export competitiveness. In fiscal year 2005, growth rose to an estimated 4% as the pound stabilized and business and consumer confidence strengthened following the appointment of the government of Mr. Nazif. An increase in each of tourism income, remittances, and exports improved the current account position, resulting in an increase in foreign reserves. As confidence was restored in the stability of the Egyptian pound, the focus of the new government has been on structural reform that would enhance private sector activity and stabilize an export-led growth of the Egyptian economy.

IV. Empirical Investigation

Developments in Egypt and Turkey over time clearly illustrate that changes in the exchange rate policy have played a major role in shaping up economic conditions. Our investigation will aim at providing a thorough analysis of the interaction between exchange rate fluctuations and the macro-economy in Egypt and Turkey. The empirical investigation analyzes annual time-series data of real output, the price level and specific demand components in Egypt and Turkey for the period 1980-2005. The data and sources are given in Appendix A.

The results of the unit root test suggest that all of the variables, except for prices, include a unit-root but their first differences are stationary, whereas the second difference of prices is stationary for Turkey[11]. Similarly, for Egypt, all the variables,except for prices and output, are first-difference stationary. Prices and output are second-difference stationary.

A. Empirical Models

To identify the anticipated and unanticipated components of the exchange rate, we construct a model for the real exchange rate. To decide on the explanatory variables in the equation, we follow a formal causality test in Granger sense for the theoretically related variables[12]. The exchange rate is defined as the real effective exchange rate, a weighted average of the real bilateral exchange rate with major trading partners. Using annual data, the change of the exchange rate is regressed on its lags as well as lagged values of all variables that may be relevant to movements in the exchange rate in theory.[13] Lag structure is determined by Akaike Information Criteria. The final exchange rate equation accounts for statistically significant lags and is presented in Table 1 for Egypt and Turkey[14].

The residual of the above equation is the unanticipated component of the exchange rate, i.e., the exchange rate shock. Coefficients on the right-hand side indicate determinants of movements in the exchange rate in Egypt and Turkey.

The real exchange rate is not characterized by a high degree of persistence in Turkey. In contrast, the lagged exchange rate is significant in Egypt, providing evidence of a higher degree of persistence. The signs, using the evidence for both countries, indicate that an improvement in the trade balance leads to an appreciation of the exchange rate. This relationship is statistically significant in Egypt.

The real exchange rate depreciates in a more open economy[15]. This relationship is statistically significant in Turkey. In 2004, the share of imports to GDP reached 35 percent in Turkey, while the share of exports to GDP reached 28 percent. Given the relatively higher share of imports, compared to exports, the increased openness depreciates the exchange rate significantly. Causality test results do not support the relevance of openness to movements in the exchange rate in Egypt.

The real exchange rate depreciates in a more open economy[16]. This relationship is statistically significant in Turkey. In 2004, the share of imports to GDP reached 35 percent in

---

[11] The results are available upon request.

[12] The results are available upon request.

[13] The lags include real growth, which proxies the effects of productivity on the exchange rate.

[14] The necessary diagnostic tests are performed for the exchange rate model and the following models. Results are available upon request.

[15] Openness is defined as the sum of exports and imports to GDP. If imports are more binding, the exchange rate depreciates in response to a higher degree of openness. In contrast, if exports are more binding, e.g., in Korea, Japan, and China, openness would lead to an appreciation of the exchange rate.

[16] Openness is defined as the sum of exports and imports to GDP. If imports are more binding, the exchange rate depreciates in response to a higher degree of openness. In contrast, if exports are more binding, e.g., in Korea, Japan, and China, openness would lead to an appreciation of the exchange rate.

Table 1. Real Exchange Rate Models (+)

	Turkey								
	constant	Drs_{t-1}	Drs_{t-2}	Dtb_{t-1}	Dtb_{t-2}	$Dopen_{t-1}$	$Dopen_{t-1}$	d1	d2
Drs_t	0.05	0.41	-0.10	1.40	1.14	-1.23*	0.13	0.20*	0.28*
	(1.20)	(1.49)	(-0.04)	(1.44)	(0.26)	(-2.43)	(0.33)	(2.04)	(2.71)
R^2	0.66								

	Egypt					
	constant	Drs_{t-1}	Dtb_{t-1}	Dgt_{t-1}	d1	d2
Drs_t	0.05*	0.37*	0.13*	0.71*	-0.44*	-0.41*
	(2.47)	(2.78)	(0.52)	(2.26)	(-4.81)	(-4.44)
R^2	0.74					

* indicates significance at the 5% level.

(+) Here, Drs_t is the first-difference of the real exchange rate. The change in the trade balance to nominal GDP is denoted by Dtb_t. The change in the ratio of the sum of exports and imports to GDP, which is an indicator for openness, is denoted by $Dopen_t$. For Turkey, d1 and d2 are the dummy variables that take 1 in 1989 and 1997, respectively and 0 elsewhere, whereas, for Egypt, d1 and d2 are the dummy variables that take 1 in 1985 and 2003, respectively and 0 elsewhere.

Turkey, while the share of exports to GDP reached 28 percent. Given the relatively higher share of imports, compared to exports, the increased openness depreciates the exchange rate significantly. Causality test results do not support the relevance of openness to movements in the exchange rate in Egypt.

In the case of Egypt, causality test results indicate that the share of government expenditures to GDP is an important determinant of the real exchange rate. An increase in the share of government spending to GDP increases the budget deficit, the current account deficit, and depreciates the nominal exchange rate. Nonetheless, higher government spending is inflationary. The latter channel is more dominant, resulting in an appreciation of the real effective exchange rate with respect to an increase in the share of government spending to GDP. In another direction, government spending may force an increase in the interest rate, attracting capital inflows. The result is an appreciation of the exchange rate in response to an increase in government spending relative to GDP.

The structural break points, captured by the dummies on the right-hand side, indicate a significant change in the real effective exchange rate that could not be explained by the explanatory variables.[17] In Turkey, the significance of the dummy variables in 1989 and 1997 support major structural breaks that resulted in a significant increase in the real effective exchange rate. Recall 1989 was a crisis year and the inflation rate rose by 80 percent. Inflation was also high in 1997 due to the significant capital inflow to finance the current account deficit. In Egypt, the dummy variables indicate significant reduction of the real effective exchange rate in 1985 and 2003. In 1985, Egypt suffered from high debt and shortage of foreign reserves, resulting in a depreciation of the exchange rate. In 2003, the Egyptian pound was formally floated, resulting in a significant depreciation following a prolonged period of a fixed exchange rate policy.

To analyze the asymmetric effects of exchange rate shocks on the relevant macroeconomic variables, we decompose the exchange rate shock (unanticipated change in the exchange rate) to its positive and negative components, as defined for joint estimation, following the suggestions of Cover (1992) as follows:

$$neg_t = -0.5 \{ abs(Drs_t) - Drs_t \}$$
$$pos_t = 0.5 \{ abs(Drs_t) + Drs_t \}$$

Drs_t is the exchange rate shock and neg_t and pos_t are the negative and positive components of the shock or, to express it differently, unexpected depreciation and appreciation of the exchange rate.

Over time, it is assumed that real output growth, price inflation and components of aggregate demand fluctuate in response to changes in aggregate domestic demand, and exchange rate shocks.[18] In addition, given the importance of fluctuations in the energy price to regional economic conditions, we account for changes in the energy price in the empirical model.

The model specification is based on the results of the test for non-stationarity of real output

[17] Dummies are introduced based on visual observation of major breaks in the dependent variables. If significant the estimated models account for these dummies.

[18] Government spending and the money supply isolate the direct effects from indirect effects attributed to changes in the exchange rate with domestic policies.

$$Dy_t = A_0 + A_1 Do_t + A_2 Dm_t + A_3 Dg_t + A_4 E_{t-1} Drs_t + A_8 \left(Drs_t - E_{t-1} Drs_t\right) + v_t^y \quad (1)$$

Given these results, the empirical model of real output is specified in first difference form where *D(.)* is the first-difference operator.[19] Accordingly, all variables in the model enter in first-difference form. The unexplained residual of the model is denoted by v_t^y.

Let o_t be the log value of the energy price. In an oil-importing country, output growth is expected to vary negatively with changes in the energy price. Accordingly, $A_1<0$. Nonetheless, Egypt and Turkey are surrounded by oil-producing countries (Iran and Arab Gulf countries). It is possible that the countries would enjoy a positive spillover effect from a boom in neighboring countries in the wake of an increase in the energy price. Two sources of domestic policies, government spending and the money supply, approximate demand shifts, where g_t and m_t denote the log values of government spending and the money supply.

Finally, anticipated appreciation of the real exchange rate determines the cost of the output supplied. Let rs_t be the log value of the real exchange rate.[20] Accordingly, a rise in the exchange rate indicates real appreciation of the domestic currency. As producers anticipate a lower cost of imported intermediate goods, in the face of currency appreciation, they increase the output supplied. Nonetheless, it is possible that anticipated appreciation may trigger anticipation of a loss in competitiveness and, therefore, a decline in external demand, forcing a reduction in output supply.

Unanticipated change in the exchange rate is likely, however, to determine both aggregate demand and supply. Unanticipated currency appreciation, a shock to the exchange rate, decreases the cost of buying intermediate goods, increasing the output supplied. Concurrently, appreciation decreases net exports and the demand for domestic currency. The final effect remains indeterminate on aggregate demand, output, and price.

To demonstrate fluctuations in the output price, an empirical model is specified as follows:

$$Dp_t = B_0 + B_1 Do_t + B_2 Dm_t + B_3 Dg_t + B_4 E_{t-1} Drs_t + B_5 \left(Drs_t - E_{t-1} Drs_t\right) + v_t^p \quad (2)$$

Based on test results, output price is evident to be non-stationary. Accordingly, the empirical model is specified in first-difference form.

Energy price shifts increase the cost of the output produced and, hence, prices. Nonetheless, a positive spillover effect of an increase in the energy price on output growth may have a deflationary effect on price. Demand shifts increase price inflation. Accordingly, $B_2, B_3 > 0$.

Given that the effect of anticipated currency appreciation maybe positive or negative on the output supplied, price inflation may increase or decrease. An unanticipated appreciation of the domestic currency (a positive shock to the exchange rate) may increase (cheaper cost of imported inputs) or decrease (Loss of competitiveness) the output supplied and may decrease (net exports effect) or increase (money demand effect) aggregate demand. The reduction in

[19] Given non-stationarity of dependent variables, the empirical models are estimated in first-difference form.

[20] This measure captures shifts attributed to the nominal exchange rate, *s*, and the foreign price of imports, *p**, in theory.

demand, coupled with an increase in supply, is deflationary while the other channels increase price inflation.

In addition to the empirical models for real output growth and price inflation, we replicate the same models to explain cyclical fluctuations in components of aggregate demand, real growth of private consumption, *Dc*, real growth of private investment, *Di,* real growth of exports, *Dx*, and real growth of imports, *Dim*.

In all empirical models for Turkey, we test the significance of structural break using four dummy variables: a dummy variable for the economic crisis in 1988, a dummy variable for the Gulf crisis in 1992, a dummy variable for integration in the Customs Union in 1996, and a dummy variable for the earthquake in 1999.

Similarly, we test the significance of structural break in the empirical models for Egypt. The results support the statistical significance of the dummy variable for the Gulf crisis in 1991 and a dummy variable for the Asian crisis and Luxor incidence in 1997.

B. Empirical Results

To analyze the asymmetric effects of exchange rate shocks on output, the price level, and components of aggregate demand, we estimate empirical models that control for other policy variables.

B1. Fluctuations in Real Output Growth

Table 2 indicates fluctuations in real output growth with policy variables and fluctuations in the exchange rate in Turkey and Egypt. The growth of government spending is significant in stimulating real output growth in the current period in Turkey. The growth of the money supply appears to be counter-cyclical. That is, additional liquidity maybe targeting a slowdown in the economy. Real output growth appears to pick up in response to lagged growth of the money supply.

It is interesting to note that an increase in the oil price has a positive effect on output growth in Turkey. This evidence indicates a positive spillover effect from neighboring oil-producing countries (Iran and Arab Gulf countries) on output growth in Turkey.

Anticipated appreciation of the exchange rate, current and lagged, has a negative effect on output growth in Turkey. This indicates a dominant effect of the demand channel on output growth. As producers anticipate exchange rate appreciation and loss of competitiveness, they shrink the output supply. Apparently, anticipated appreciation is more important compared to unanticipated appreciation, as the latter is not significant in explaining real output growth. Lagged unanticipated depreciation (a negative exchange rate shock) has a positive effect on output growth. Unexpected depreciation increases the cost of imported inputs, forcing reduction in the output supply, as was evident in 1994 and 2001. The significant Wald test statistic indicates asymmetric effects of unanticipated currency appreciation and depreciation on output growth in Turkey.

In the case of Turkey, there are two significant dummies in the output equation, indicating a reduction in output growth in 1988 and in 1999. The first observation surrounds the beginning of the stabilization program that led to a significant reduction in government spending to contain the budget deficit. The second observation marks the 1999 earthquake.

Similar to Turkey, the growth of government spending increases real output growth significantly in Egypt. Further, monetary growth stimulates real output growth with a lag in Egypt. Moreover, an increase in the oil price does not determine real output growth significantly in Egypt.

In contrast to the evidence for Turkey, producers, in Egypt, react to lagged anticipated appreciation. Anticipated appreciation decreases the cost of imported inputs and increases the output supply. Hence, the cost channel dominates the competitiveness channel in determining the output supply in Egypt, although the effect is not statistically significant.

The negative response indicates reduction, although statistically insignificant, in real output growth with respect to unanticipated currency appreciation in Egypt. The positive response indicates reduction, although statistically insignificant, with respect to unanticipated currency depreciation in Egypt. The difference between the responses to positive and negative shocks is statistically significant according to Wald test results. Accordingly, exchange rate variability has a net negative effect on real output growth in Egypt over time. The structural break dummy indicates a significant reduction in real output growth in Egypt during the Gulf crisis in 1991.

B2. Fluctuations in Price Inflation

The evidence for Turkey indicates that the growth of government spending (lagged) has a significant positive effect on price inflation. While contemporaneous growth of government spending increases output growth, capacity limitation necessitates an increase in price inflation in the following period.

The inflationary effects of monetary growth are evident and significant, both in the current and lagged period. Liquidity stimulates additional demand and fuels price inflation. Consistent with capacity limitations, monetary growth fuels price inflation, without stimulating output growth in the current period. Having relaxed capacity constraints in the following period, monetary growth stimulates output growth, with additional increase in price inflation.

The effects of an increase in the energy price are interesting in explaining price inflation. The positive spillover effect on output growth correlates with a contemporaneous reduction in price inflation. In the following period, higher oil price increases cost and, therefore, price inflation.

Anticipated exchange rate appreciation raises price inflation in Turkey. This may reflect a high degree of persistence in price inflation. Expected change in the real effective exchange rate is a function of its lags, which are, in turn, dependent on lagged price inflation. The positive effect of anticipated appreciation on price inflation indicates close adjustment of price inflation to its lagged values.

Unanticipated appreciation of the exchange rate slows down price inflation in the next period. This is evident by the negative and statistically significant response of price inflation to lagged exchange rate appreciation, as was evident in 1985, 1995, 1998, 2000, and 2004. Unanticipated appreciation slows down the demand for exports and decreases aggregate demand. Additionally, unanticipated appreciation decreases the cost of imported inputs and increases aggregate supply.[21] Wald test statistic indicates asymmetric effects of exchange rate shocks (positive and negative) on price inflation in Turkey.

Table 2. Models of output and prices for Turkey and Egypt

	Turkey		Egypt	
Variables	Dy_t	DP_t	Dy_t	DP_t
Constant	0.12*	0.05	0.02	0.01
	(5.66)	(1.28)	(1.08)	(0.41)
Dg_t	0.54*	-0.31	0.12*	-0.16*
	(6.34)	(-1.39)	(1.91)	(-1.97)
Dg_{t-1}	0.10	0.44*	0.06	-0.01
	(1.31)	(2.23)	(1.40)	(-0.21)
Dm_t	-0.30*	0.58*	-0.02	0.51*
	(-7.87)	(6.89)	(-0.23)	(4.16)
Dm_{t-1}	0.21*	0.21*	0.20	0.12
	(6.04)	(2.79)	(2.01)	(0.90)
Do_t	0.64*	-0.53*	-0.05	-0.14
	(11.19)	(-2.43)	(-0.72)	(-1.51)
Do_{t-1}	-0.13	0.71*	-0.07	-0.17
	(-1.56)	(3.24)	(-1.15)	(-1.33)
$E_{t-1}Drs_t$	-0.30*	0.65*	0.04	0.06
	(-5.12)	(4.51)	(0.87)	(0.91)
$E_{t-2}Drs_{t-1}$	-0.17*	-0.01	0.05	-0.07
	(-3.54)	(-0.07)	(1.61)	(-1.61)
pos_t	-0.33	-0.09	-0.26	0.21
	(-1.72)	(-0.24)	(-1.74)	(0.87)
pos_{t-1}	-0.09	-1.15*	-0.06	0.09
	(-0.60)	(-2.59)	(-0.41)	(0.40)
neg_t	0.19	0.39	0.05	0.31*
	(0.21)	(1.26)	(0.38)	(2.07)
neg_{t-1}	0.39*	0.18	0.13	0.14
	(11.13)	(0.98)	(0.97)	(0.74)

[21] The import price data exist since 1994 for Turkey. In the face of unanticipated currency appreciation, for the periods 1997, 1999-2000 and 2002-2003, import prices, mostly import prices of consumption goods decreased. Moreover, the composition of imports suggests consumption of imported goods increases with respect to unexpected appreciation. The share of consumption goods constitutes 13 percent of total imports in 2004. This share increases in the years when unexpected appreciation is observed.

Table 2. (Continued)

	Turkey		Egypt	
Variables	Dy_t	DP_t	Dy_t	DP_t
d1	-0.06*	0.16*	-0.05*	
	(-4.06)	(4.19)	(-3.00)	
d2		0.08*		
		(2.45)		
d3		-0.13*		
		(-3.71)		
d4	-0.15*			
	(-12.20)			
R^2	0.98	0.99	0.59	0.95
Asym	12.64*	5.16*	3.94*	0.11

Dy is real output growth and Dp is aggregate price inflation.

* indicates significance at the 5% level, Asym is the result of the Wald test where the null hypothesis is no asymmetry.

The explanatory variables of the model are the growth rates of g_t for government spending, m_t for the money supply, o_t for energy prices, $E_{t-1}Drs_t$ for expected change in the real exchange rate, pos_t for unanticipated exchange rate appreciation, neg_t for unanticipated exchange rate depreciation, and dummy variables for structural breaks, d1 for the economic crisis in 1988 , d2 for the Gulf crisis in 1992, d3 for integration in the Customs Union in 1996, and d4 for the earthquake in 1999. For Egypt, d1 is for the Gulf crisis in 1991 and d2 is for 1997 for the Luxor attack, the recession of the Arab countries and the Asian Crisis.

Structural break dummies for Turkey indicate a significant increase in price inflation in 1988 and in 1992 and a significant reduction in 1996. During the 1989 crisis, price inflation increased by 80 percent. During the 1991 Gulf crisis, the Turkish economy was adversely affected by regional conditions, which fueled price inflation. The integration into the Customs Union in 1996 resulted in removal of tariffs on imports, decreasing price inflation.

In contrast to the evidence for Turkey, an increase in government spending counters price inflation significantly in Egypt. Higher government spending increases subsidies to control price inflation for basic consumption items.[22] In consistency with the evidence for Turkey, monetary growth stimulates price inflation in Egypt as additional liquidity chases after a limited supply of goods. In contrast to the evidence for Turkey, there is no significant effect of a change in the oil price on price inflation in Egypt.

In contrast to the evidence for Turkey, anticipated exchange rate appreciation does not determine price inflation significantly in Egypt. Further, there is no evidence of a significant effect of unanticipated currency appreciation on price inflation in Egypt. There is a significant positive effect of unanticipated currency depreciation on price inflation in Egypt in the current period. Unanticipated depreciation of the real effective exchange rate accommodates a

[22] See, for example, Reuters Newsedge, June 20 2006, "Trimming subsidy spending, especially on energy, is crucial to curbing the budget deficit in Egypt. Nearly a fifth of government spending in 2006/07 has been set aside for energy subsidies."

contemporaneous reduction in price inflation, which was particularly evident in the nineties. Clearly, inflation is a dominant component of fluctuations in the real effective exchange rate over time. Wald test statistic is not statistically significant, however, to establish a clear effect of exchange rate variability on price inflation in light of asymmetry.

B3. Fluctuations in Consumption Growth

Table 3 indicates fluctuations in real consumption demand with policy variables and fluctuations in the exchange rate in Turkey and Egypt.

In Turkey, consistent with the effect of government spending on output growth, private consumption increases significantly with the growth of government spending. Failure of monetary growth to stimulate growth in the current period is further supported by the negative and significant sign on consumption. In the following period, growth picks up and, therefore, consumption demand. The positive spillover effect of an increase in the energy price on growth in Turkey is consistent with an increase in real consumption demand.

As for exchange rate fluctuations in Turkey, consumption does not vary significantly with anticipated changes in the exchange rate. Unanticipated appreciation is also insignificant on real consumption growth. Unanticipated depreciation (lagged) has a positive significant effect on growth and, therefore, consumption demand. Consumption decreases significantly with lagged unanticipated depreciation of the real effective exchange rate, as was evident in 1988, 1989, 1994, 1999, and 2001. In the face of unexpected depreciation, consumers decrease consumption of durable goods, especially imported luxury goods.[23]

The Wald test statistic indicates significant asymmetry in the response of consumption growth to positive and negative exchange rate shocks. Further, the dummy variable indicates significant reduction in consumption growth in 1999, around the earthquake.

In contrast to Turkey, the growth of government spending crowds out private consumption in Egypt. Higher government spending increases the deficit and raises the interest rate. Through this channel, private savings may increase, shrinking the growth of private consumption. Similar to the evidence for Turkey, monetary growth (lagged) increases liquidity and stimulates the growth of private consumption in Turkey. In contrast to the evidence in Turkey, there is no significant evidence of the change in oil price on private consumption in Egypt.

Similar to the evidence for Turkey, anticipated exchange rate appreciation does not determine the growth of private consumption significantly. Further, private consumption does not vary significantly with unanticipated currency appreciation. Unanticipated depreciation (a negative shock to the exchange rate) has a positive significant effect, shrinking the growth of private consumption. As noted for Turkey, depreciation increases the cost of imports and decreases consumption demand significantly in Egypt, resulting in a positive correlation between exchange rate shocks and consumption growth over time. In light of asymmetry, statistical significance of the Wald test indicates a reduction in consumption growth with exchange rate variability, on average over time, in Egypt.

---

[23] Consumption of non-durables constitutes 60 per cent of total consumption, and is more-or-less stable for Turkey, i.e., it does not change much with output growth, the exchange rate, or price movements. However, consumption of durable goods is fluctuating and contributes to asymmetry in the behavior of total consumption with respect to unexpected exchange rate fluctuations.

B4. Fluctuations in Investment Growth

Table 3 indicates fluctuations in real investment growth with policy variables and fluctuations in the exchange rate in Turkey and Egypt.

Table 3. Models of Consumption and Investment for Turkey and Egypt

	Turkey		Egypt	
Variables	Dc_t	Di_t	Dc_t	Di_t
Constant	0.09* (2.58)	0.45* (3.49)	0.14* (4.48)	0.08 (0.36)
Dg_t	0.74* (3.75)	2.81* (3.17)	-0.25* (-2.71)	0.07 (0.13)
Dg_{t-1}	-0.12 (-0.71)	-0.07 (-0.12)	-0.21* (-2.93)	-0.33 (-0.85)
Dm_t	-0.19* (-2.80)	-0.65* (-2.87)	-0.07 (-0.38)	-0.91 (-1.05)
Dm_{t-1}	0.15* (2.05)	0.15 (0.61)	0.38* (2.04)	1.10 (1.16)
Do_t	0.78* (3.39)	3.30* (4.75)	0.10 (0.64)	-0.61 (-0.77)
Do_{t-1}	-0.15 (-0.79)	-1.03 (-0.81)	-0.14 (-0.77)	-0.53 (-0.77)
$E_{t-1}Drs_t$	-0.25 (-1.88)	-0.99* (-2.29)	0.02 (0.31)	0.49 (1.07)
$E_{t-2}Drs_{t-1}$	-0.05 (-0.56)	-1.20* (-2.75)	0.07 (1.08)	-0.11 (-0.32)
pos_t	-0.42 (-1.20)	-0.84 (-0.65)	0.20 (0.70)	-3.17 (-1.33)
pos_{t-1}	-0.23 (-0.51)	-1.40 (-1.12)	-0.18 (-0.72)	1.00 (0.47)
neg_t	0.13 (0.56)	-0.16 (-0.19)	1.00* (4.43)	0.22 (0.16)
neg_{t-1}	0.51* (2.67)	2.46* (2.13)	0.18 (0.83)	-0.16 (-0.14)
d1			-0.05 (-1.19)	-0.42* (-2.43)
d2		0.17* (2.34)		
d3				

Table 3. (Continued)

	Turkey		Egypt	
Variables	Dc_t	Di_t	Dc_t	Di_t
d4	-0.13*	-0.55*		
	(-3.62)	(-4.48)		
R^2	0.90	0.89	0.93	0.58
Asym	2.96*	3.57*	3.14*	0.24

* indicates significance at the 5% level, Asym is the result of the Wald test where the null hypothesis is no asymmetry.

The explanatory variables of the model are the growth rates of gt for government spending, mt for the money supply, ot for energy prices, $E_{t-1}Drs_t$ for expected change in the real exchange rate, post for unanticipated exchange rate appreciation, negt for unanticipated exchange rate depreciation, and dummy variables for structural breaks, d1 for the economic crisis in 1988 , d2 for the Gulf crisis in 1992, d3 for integration in the Customs Union in 1996, and d4 for the earthquake in 1999. For Egypt, d1 is for the Gulf crisis in 1991 and d2 is for 1997 for the Luxor attack, the recession of the Arab countries and the Asian Crisis.

Dc is growth of real consumption, and Di is growth of real investment.

Consistent with the effects of government spending in stimulating real output growth in Turkey, investment demand increases significantly. In contrast, monetary growth increases to stimulate investment demand during downturns. Nonetheless, the negative and significant effect on investment demand indicates failure of the monetary stimulus to revive investment demand in the current period. The positive spillover effect of an increase in the oil price on growth is consistent with a positive significant effect on investment demand in Turkey.

Both current and lagged anticipated appreciation has negative significant effects on investment growth. This confirms the negative effect of anticipated appreciation on the supply side of the Turkish economy. Anticipated appreciation decreases competitiveness and demand for exports, forcing a reduction in private investment. The lagged value of the negative shock to the exchange rate (unanticipated depreciation) has a positive and significant effect on investment demand. Unanticipated depreciation increases the cost of imports and decreases investment demand in Turkey, as was evident in 1994, 2001, and 2002. The Wald test indicates significant asymmetry in the effects of positive and negative exchange rate shocks on investment in Turkey.

Parameters of structural break indicate significant increase in investment demand in Turkey during the Gulf crisis in 1991. This could be a reflection of an increase in capital inflow from neighboring countries. In contrast, there was a significant decrease in investment growth surrounding the earthquake in 1999.

In contrast to the evidence for Turkey, government spending and the money supply do not stimulate private investment growth in Egypt. This evidence rules out the role of stabilization policies in determining private investment in Egypt. Further, there is no evidence of a significant effect of changes in the oil price on investment demand in Egypt.

In contrast to the evidence for Turkey, exchange rate fluctuations, both anticipated and unanticipated, do not determine private investment significantly in Egypt. Despite insignificant time series coefficients, several episodes indicate a negative correlation between exchange rate shocks and real investment growth. Accordingly, unanticipated real depreciation (appreciation) stimulates (curbs) investment growth via improving (deteriorating) competitiveness. The structural break dummy indicates a significant reduction in investment growth in Egypt around the Gulf war in 1991.

B5. Fluctuations in Export Growth

Table 4 indicates fluctuations in real export growth with policy variables and fluctuations in the exchange rate in Turkey and Egypt.

The increase in government spending has a negative and significant effect on export demand in Turkey. Higher government spending increases the deficit and raises the interest rate (see above). As Turkey moved to liberalize the capital account, the inflow of capital led to currency appreciation, depressing competitiveness and export demand.

Monetary growth increases during downturns to stimulate export growth. Nonetheless, the negative and significant coefficient indicates ineffective monetary stimulus in the current period. The increase in energy price decreases export growth with a lag. Higher energy price increases cost, resulting in a higher price inflation (with a lag). Loss of competitiveness, through this channel, has a negative significant effect on export growth.

Table 4. Models of Exports and Imports for Turkey and Egypt

	Turkey		Egypt	
Variables	Dx_t	Dim_t	Dx_t	Dim_t
Constant	0.09 (1.70)	0.22 (1.22)	-0.35* (-2.04)	0.10 (0.62)
Dg_t	-1.09* (-4.30)	0.63 (0.77)	0.15 (0.44)	0.17 (0.32)
Dg_{t-1}	0.12 (0.43)	-0.50 (-0.84)	0.47 (0.82)	-0.53 (-1.63)
Dm_t	-0.20* (-2.78)	-0.49 (-1.66)	0.36 (0.38)	-1.04 (-1.53)
Dm_{t-1}	0.18 (1.81)	0.34 (0.73)	0.27 (0.36)	1.10 (1.06)
Do_t	0.28 (1.26)	0.64 (0.60)	2.01* (3.08)	-0.19 (-0.24)
Do_{t-1}	-0.69* (-2.51)	-0.54 (-0.74)	-1.32* (-2.34)	-0.82 (-0.96)
$E_{t-1}Drs_t$	-0.40* (-3.24)	-0.06 (-0.09)	0.08 (0.29)	-0.01 (-0.02)
$E_{t-2}Drs_{t-1}$	0.17 (1.57)	-0.07 (-0.11)	-0.65* (-2.21)	-0.12 (-0.45)
pos_t	0.14 (0.32)	0.10 (0.04)	-0.56 (-0.38)	-0.62 (-0.30)

Table 4. (Continued)

	Turkey		Egypt	
Variables	Dx_t	Dim_t	Dx_t	Dim_t
pos_{t-1}	0.34 (0.67)	-2.05 (-1.31)	3.09* (3.27)	-0.26 (-0.24)
neg_t	-0.22 (-0.59)	0.07 (0.10)	-2.49* (-1.98)	-0.33 (-0.19)
neg_{t-1}	-0.80* (-2.54)	0.45 (0.72)	-3.12* (-2.37)	1.37 (0.88)
d1				-0.96* (-5.28)
d2			0.41* (4.57)	
d3	0.10* (3.86)	0.27* (3.32)	0.78 5.62*	0.78 0.42
d4				
R^2	0.90	0.85		
Asym	8.08*	0.49		

* indicates significance at the 5% level, Asym is the result of the Wald test where the null hypothesis is no asymmetry.

The explanatory variables of the model are the growth rates of gt for government spending, mt for the money supply, ot for energy prices, $E_{t-1}Drs_t$ for expected change in the real exchange rate, post for unanticipated exchange rate appreciation, negt for unanticipated exchange rate depreciation, and dummy variables for structural breaks, d1 for the economic crisis in 1988 , d2 for the Gulf crisis in 1992, d3 for integration in the Customs Union in 1996, and d4 for the earthquake in 1999. For Egypt, d1 is for the Gulf crisis in 1991 and d2 is for 1997 for the Luxor attack, the recession of the Arab countries and the Asian Crisis.

Dx is growth of real exports and Dm is growth of real imports.

Anticipated appreciation of the exchange rate has a negative and statistically significant effect on export growth in Turkey. Anticipated appreciation decreases competitiveness, shrinking demand and switching production in favor of non-tradables. Lagged unanticipated depreciation has a negative and significant effect on export growth. Unanticipated depreciation stimulates export growth, although with a lag, as was evident in 1984, 1988, 1990, 1992, 1994, 2001, and 2002.

In light of asymmetry, exchange rate variability is likely to produce a net positive effect (via the more dominant depreciation channel) on export growth in Turkey. Wald test statistic is significant regarding asymmetry in the effects of exchange rate shocks on export growth.[24]

[24] This result would be interpreted as the macroeconomic consequence of microeconomic theories. Among the micro-based studies, there are a few studies discussing the asymmetric effects of exchange rate shocks. Most

The structural dummy is significant regarding the increase in export growth following integration into the Customs Union in 1996.

The effect of a change in the oil price on export growth in Egypt varies over time. Higher oil price increases export growth significantly in the current period in Egypt. This is the result of an increase in oil exports. Nonetheless, higher energy price increases the cost of fuel and, in turn, the cost of production. This channel has a depressing effect on export growth in the next period.

Similar to the evidence for Turkey, anticipated currency appreciation discourages plans to produce tradables, decreasing real export growth in Egypt. The evidence indicates that the demand for exports, dominated by tourism, appears inelastic with respect to exchange rate appreciation. Consistent with inelastic demand, export growth increases significantly with respect to lagged unanticipated appreciation of the real effective exchange rate in Egypt. In contrast, unanticipated depreciation increases competitiveness and export growth significantly, both in the current and lagged periods. Given evidence of asymmetry, exchange rate variability has a net positive effect, increasing export growth, on average over time, in Egypt. This is evident by the statistically significant Wald test statistic.

The significance of the dummy variable indicates significant increase in export growth in 1997. Egypt may have benefited from instability in East Asia by gaining more export markets.

B6. Fluctuations in Import Growth

Table 4 indicates fluctuations in real import growth with policy variables and fluctuations in the exchange rate in Turkey and Egypt.

The structural dummy indicates a significant increase in import growth following integration into the Customs Union in 1996. Wald test results do not support significant asymmetry in the effects of unexpected exchange rate shocks on imports in Turkey.

The sign and significance of the first dummy variable indicates significant reduction in real imports in Egypt around the first Gulf crisis in 1991.

Lack of statistical significance indicates that imports in Turkey and Egypt follow a structural process that does not vary in the short-run with determinants of cyclicality. This reflects high dependency on imports in both countries.

B7. Fluctuations in Trade Balance

Having analyzed the effects of exchange rate fluctuations on export and import growth, In Turkey, an appreciation of the exchange rate correlates with deterioration in the trade balance in 1988, 1994, 1999, and 2001. In Egypt, a depreciation of the exchange rate correlates with an improvement in the trade balance in 1993, 1995, 2000 and 2004.

---

of them discuss these asymmetric effects within a micro-economic modeling framework. Froot and Klemperer (1989) and Knetter (1989) point out that the asymmetric response of stock prices to currency movements may occur due to asymmetric pricing-to-market (PTM) behavior. When the domestic currency appreciates, exporting firms with a market share objective do not permit local currency prices to increase because of the risk of losing their share, so they decrease their profit margins. Hence, exports do not decrease. On the other hand, under currency depreciations, exporting firms with a market share objective maintain, rather than increase, their profit margins as a result of their focus on sales volume. Therefore, exports increase with the increase in the market share. Other studies supporting the same arguments are Marston (1990) and Goldberg (1995).

CONCLUSION

The analysis has focused on the effects of exchange rate fluctuations using annual data for Egypt and Turkey between 1980 and 2005. To that end, a theoretical rational-expectations model that decomposes movements in the exchange rate into anticipated and unanticipated components is used.

Let the exchange rate be the real price of the domestic currency in terms of a weighted average of the currencies of major trading partners. A positive shock to the exchange rate, an unanticipated appreciation of the domestic currency, decreases net exports and money demand and increases the output supplied. Based on the strength of each channel, the combined effects of demand and supply channels may determine the direction of output and price adjustments in the face of currency fluctuations.

In addition to fluctuations in the exchange rate, the empirical model accounts for the growth of government spending, the growth of the money supply, the change in the energy price, and a number of dummy variables for structural break. The dependent variables under investigation are real output growth, price inflation, and the growth in components underlying aggregate demand: real consumption, real investment, real exports, and real imports. Major highlights of the results are as follows.

Overall, the analysis provides interesting insights into determinants of cyclicality in economic activity in Egypt and Turkey. In Turkey, anticipated depreciation may be stimulating of real growth, albeit it may prove inflationary. In Egypt, anticipated depreciation may stimulate export growth. Moreover, variability of unanticipated exchange rate shocks could be detrimental, given asymmetry in the effects of the exchange rate. Higher variability of the real effective exchange rate around its anticipated value has a net negative effect on the trends of real growth of output, private consumption, and investment in Turkey. Similarly, higher variability of the real effective exchange rate around its anticipated value has a net negative effect on output and consumption growth in Egypt. Consistent with export-oriented strategy, the variability of the exchange rate has a net positive effect on export growth in Turkey and Egypt.

While adhering to a flexible exchange rate policy to boost competitiveness, managing fundamentals to reduce excessive volatility impinging on the economic system over time should top the policy agenda. Excessive volatility in the real effective exchange rate could be detrimental to real growth, over time, as the evidence for Turkey and Egypt illustrates in this chapter.

APPENDIX A: DATA DESCRIPTION AND SOURCES

The analysis is based on an annual data set which covers the 1980-2005 periods.

Data Sources: Turkey

Real exchange rate is the trade weighted real exchange rate from Central Bank of Republic of Turkey (CBRT).

Price inflation is the official consumer price index of CBRT.

Money is represented by M2Y.

Real output is GDP in 1987 prices which is announced by the State Institute of Statistics of Turkey.

Real private consumption, real government consumption, and real investment are from the State Institute of Statistics in 1987 prices.

Exports and imports are taken from the balance of payments statistics of the CBRT. The figures are deflated by the price index and real figures are used in the analysis for consistency purposes.

Trade balance is the difference between exports and imports, and openness is the ratio of the sum of exports and imports to GDP.

Data Sources: Egypt

All variables are provided by the Desk Economist for Egypt, International Monetary Fund. Figures are compiled in consultation with the Egyptian authorities or based on IMF staff estimates.

Energy Prices

Prices are taken from the International Energy Agency Yearbook.

REFERENCES

Agenor, Pierre-Richard, 1991, "Output, Devaluation and the Real Exchange Rate in Developing Countries," *Weltwirtschaftliches Archive*, Band 127.

Bahmani, Mohsen, 1991, "Are Devaluation Contractionary in LDCs?" *Journal of Economic Development*, (June).

Barbone, Luca, and Francisco Rivera-Batiz, 1987, "Foreign Capital and the Contractionary Impact of Currency Devaluation, with an Application to Jamaica," *Journal of Development Economics,* Vol. 26, (June), pp. 1–15.

Bruno, M., 1979, "Stabilization and Stagflation in a Semi-Industrialized Economy," in R. Dornbusch and J. Frankel, eds. *International Economic Policy,* Johns Hopkins University Press, Baltimore, MD.

Buiter, William H., 1990, *International Macroeconomics*, Oxford University Press.

Cooper, Richard N., 1971, "Currency Devaluation in Developing Countries," *Essays in International Finance*, No. 86, International Finance Section, Princeton University.

Diaz-Alejandro, Carlos F., 1963, "Note on the Impact of Devaluation and Redistributive Effect," *Journal of Political Economy,* Vol. 71, (August), pp. 577–80.

Dornbusch, Rudiger, 1988, *Open Economy Macroeconomics*, 2nd edition, New York.

Edwards, S., 1986, "Are Devaluations Contractionary?" *Review of Economics and Statistics*, (August).

Froot, K.A., and P.D. Klemperer, 1989. "Exchange rate pass-through when market share matters" *American Economic Review* 79, pp. 637-54.

Goldberg, P.K., 1995, "Product Differentiation and Oligopoly in International Markets: The Case of the U.S. Automobile Industry," *Econometrica*, 63:891-951.

Guittian, Manuel, 1976, "The Effects of Changes in the Exchange Rate on Output, Prices, and the Balance of Payments," *Journal of International Economics*, Vol. 6, pp. 65–74.

Gylfason, T., and Radetzki, 1991, "Does Devaluation Make Sense in Least Developed Countries?" *Economic Development and Cultural Change*, (October).

Gylfason, Thorvaldur, and Michael Schmid, 1983, ``Does Devaluation Cause Stagflation?" *Canadian Journal of Economics*, Vol. XV1, November.

Hanson, James A., 1983, "Contractionary Devaluation, Substitution in Production and Consumption, and the Role of the Labor Market," *Journal of International Economics*, Vol. 14, pp. 179–89.

Hirschman, Albert O., 1949, "Devaluation and the Trade Balance: A Note," *Review of Economics and Statistics*, Vol. 31, pp. 50–53.

Hoffmaister A., and C. Vegh, 1996, "Disinflation and the Recession Now Versus Recession Later Hypothesis: Evidence from Uruguay," *IMF Staff Papers,* Vol. 43.

Kamin, S.B., and J.H. Rogers, 2000, "Output and the Real Exchange Rate in Developing Countries: An Application to Mexico", *Journal of Development Economics,* 61: 85-109.

Kandil, Magda and Ida Mirzaie, 2002, "Exchange Rate Fluctuations and Disaggregated Economic Activity in the US: Theory and Evidence," *Journal of International Money and Finance*, 21:1-31.

Kandil, Magda, and Ida Mirzaie, 2003, "The Effects of Dollar Appreciation on Sectoral Labor Market Adjustments: Theory and Evidence," *Quarterly Review of Economics and Finance*, Vol. 43, No. 1, pp. 89–117.

Knetter, M.M., 1989, "Price Discrimination by U.S. and German Exporters," *American Economic Review*, 79:198-210.

Krugman, P., and L. Taylor, 1987, "Contractionary Effects of Devaluation," *Journal of International Economics*, No. 8, pp. 445–56.

Lizondo, S., and P. J. Montiel, 1989. "Contractionary Devaluation in Developing Countries: Analytical Overview" *IMF Staff Papers* 36:182-227.

Marston, R.C. 1990. "Pricing to Market in Japanese Manufacturing," *Journal of International Economics*, 29:217-236.

Meade, James E., 1951, *The Theory of International Economic Policy, I: The Balance of Payment*, Oxford University Press, Oxford.

Mendoza, E. G., 1992, "The Effect of Macroeconomic Shocks in a Basic Equilibrium Framework," *IMF Staff Papers*, 39, 4, pp. 855–89.

Rogers, and Wang, 1995, "Output, Inflation, and Stabilization in a Small Open Economy:
Evidence from Mexico," *Journal of Development Economics*, No. 46.

Shone, Ronald, 1989, "Open Economy Macroeconomics," Harvester Wheatsheaf.

Solimano, Andres, 1986, "Contractionary Devaluation in the Southern Cone: The Case of Chile," *Journal of Development Economics*, No. 23, pp. 135–51.

Van Wijnbergen, Sweder Van, 1989, "Exchange Rate Management and Stabilization Policies in Developing Countries," *Journal of Development Economics*, No. 23, pp. 227–47.

In: Exchange Rates: Policies, Effects and Fluctuations
Editor: Natalie B. Perkins, pp. 25-46
ISBN: 978-1-61209-505-9
© 2011 Nova Science Publishers, Inc.

Chapter 2

EXCHANGE RATE POLICY IN CENTRAL AND EASTERN EUROPEAN COUNTRIES

Michael Frömmel*[*] *and Frederick Van Gysegem
Department of Financial Economics, Ghent University, Ghent, Belgium

ABSTRACT

The Central and Eastern European Countries (CEEC) which joined the European Union between 2004 and 2007 show an interesting evolution of their exchange rate regimes. Although they all started from a comparable situation and have the common long-term goal of joining European Monetary Union, they opted for different exchange rate policies. Furthermore, the exchange rate policies were subject to frequent changes and adjustments. We first describe the evolution of exchange rate arrangements in CEEC, and survey in this chapter various aspects of their exchange rate policy.

We start with the discussion of differences between de facto and de jure exchange rate regimes. Second, we analyze the impact of exchange rate policy on exchange rate volatility, focusing on structural breaks or volatility regimes. While the level of volatility shows the external dimension of monetary stability, the break points may help to understand the processes that lead to changes in exchange rate arrangements. Third, we highlight the role of CEEC's exchange rates in monetary policy rules. Finally we review the literature on central bank interventions in CEEC.

JEL: E58, F3

Keywords: European Union, Central and Eastern European Countries, transition economies, exchange rate policy.

[*] Corresponding author: +32-(0)9-264-8979, michael.froemmel@UGent.be

1. INTRODUCTION

The European Union has grown substantially in the 21st century. The first wave of Central and Eastern European Countries (CEEC) joined in 2004, namely the Czech Republic, Estonia, Hungary, Latvia, Lithuania, Poland, Slovenia and Slovakia (plus Cyprus and Malta), while Bulgaria and Romania followed in 2007. All countries have the obligation to join the European Monetary Union. This is, however, conditional on the realization of the Maastricht criteria. Since these criteria include stability of the exchange rate inside the European Exchange Rate Mechanism (ERM II) for two years, the exchange rate policy of the CEEC is of major importance. In this context the question arises which is the 'best' exchange rate arrangement for CEEC.

The CEEC show an interesting evolution of their exchange rate regimes. Although they all started from a comparable situation and have the common long-term goal of joining European Monetary Union, they opted for different exchange rate policies. Furthermore, the exchange rate policies were subject to frequent changes and adjustments. We first describe the evolution of exchange rate arrangements in the CEEC, and survey in this chapter various aspects of their exchange rate policy. Since there has been a plethora of works on exchange rates in CEEC, the survey has to be both subjective and selective. We are aware of the fact that this approach is incomplete and the survey is not intended to be exhaustive.

A natural starting point is the description of the evolution of (official) exchange rate arrangements in the CEEC in section 2. However, it is known that what countries announce to be their exchange rate regime and what they de facto implement often differs. For this reason we also review the literature on differences between de facto and de jure exchange rate regimes.

In section 3 we analyze the relation of exchange rate policy and exchange rate volatility. Since the CEEC frequently modified their exchange rate arrangements, there has been a strong focus on structural breaks or volatility regimes. Since the level of volatility is often understood as the external dimension of monetary stability, one should expect a close relation between monetary policy regimes and exchange rate volatility. At the same time, switches between volatility regimes that deviate from the dates of the respective policy changes may hint at a lack of policy credibility, including the unpeaceful exits from the pegs in the Czech Republic and Slovakia.

The last sections deal with the influence of monetary authorities on the exchange rate. We start in section 4 with the role of the exchange rate in monetary policy rules. In contrast, section 5 reviews the literature on central bank interventions in CEEC, including central bank communication.

2. EVOLUTION OF EXCHANGE RATE REGIMES

The exchange rate regimes in Central and Eastern European countries underwent a remarkable evolution in the past two decades. This evolution is illustrated in Figure 1. We see that most of the CEEC's chose a fixed exchange rate[1] as a tool in their stabilization strategy

[1] A fixed exchange rate is sometimes referred to as a pegged exchange rate.

after the dissolution of the Soviet Union in December 1991. The standard arguments behind the fixed exchange rate are the reduction of transaction costs for external trade and macroeconomic stabilization (Halpern & Wyplosz 1997). Additionally, at least two major reasons can be given for why countries may not let their currency float freely.[2] First, small open economies are highly susceptible to exchange rate movements; therefore, the exchange rate must be considered by monetary authorities even if it is not the primary goal of monetary policy (Ball 1999). Most of the EU accession countries in Central and Eastern Europe belong to this class of countries. Second, in many emerging and transition countries, financial markets are less developed and do not allow domestic firms to borrow in their home currency. This is considered to be the original sin (Eichengreen & Hausmann 1999). Because their debt is nominated in a foreign currency they will have incentives to peg their exchange rates, as (Hausmann *et al.* 2001) argue.

Even after considering the above mentioned arguments, a country may still not find it convenient to commit to an official peg. The political support for the necessary but unpopular measures to defend the peg may be very low in emerging and transition countries (Obstfeld & Rogoff 1995). Furthermore, under an officially floating regime, adjustments of the exchange rate are less visible to the public and less costly politically than devaluations under an official peg (Obstfeld 1997).

We see in Figure 1 that in the late 1990s, many countries moved to more flexible arrangements (Sachs 1996). The Visegrád Group, i.e., the Czech Republic, Hungary, Poland and Slovakia followed entirely this path (Kocenda 2002). The combined strategy of a fixed exchange rate directly after the transition and a more flexible regime later on adds the benefits from pegging to the anchor currency to the ability to cope better with volatile capital movements in the later period (Corker *et al.* 2000).

The Czech Republic and Slovakia opted initially for narrow horizontal bands. Subsequently, these fixed exchange rate regimes became more flexible and, after widening the bands, the Czech Republic (1997) and Slovakia (1998) declared managed floating or freely floating exchange rates.

Poland and Hungary chose narrow crawling bands that served the dual objectives of maintaining competitiveness and moderating inflation (Szapáry & Jakab 1998). In 2000 the Polish zloty was declared freely floating. In Hungary the band was widened in 2001 to 15% and changed from a crawling to a horizontal band to mirror the exchange rate regime envisaged in the Exchange Rate Mechanism (ERM-2). Hungary kept a fixed exchange rate until early 2008. Early in the transition, other countries opted either for completely fixed exchange rates, e.g., the Baltic States and Bulgaria, or rather flexible regimes, e.g., Romania and Slovenia.[3] The Baltic States all stepped in the ERM system. Still, they chose to keep their currencies de facto fixed. The reported bandwidth of 15% remains thus purely theoretical. Estonia joined the Eurozone on the first of January 2011.

---

[2] The literature on optimum currency areas surveyed by (De Grauwe 2003) suggests that the choice of a pegged exchange rate is feasible only for a limited number of countries.

[3] Exchange rate arrangements chosen by transition countries are discussed in (Mussa *et al.* 2000)

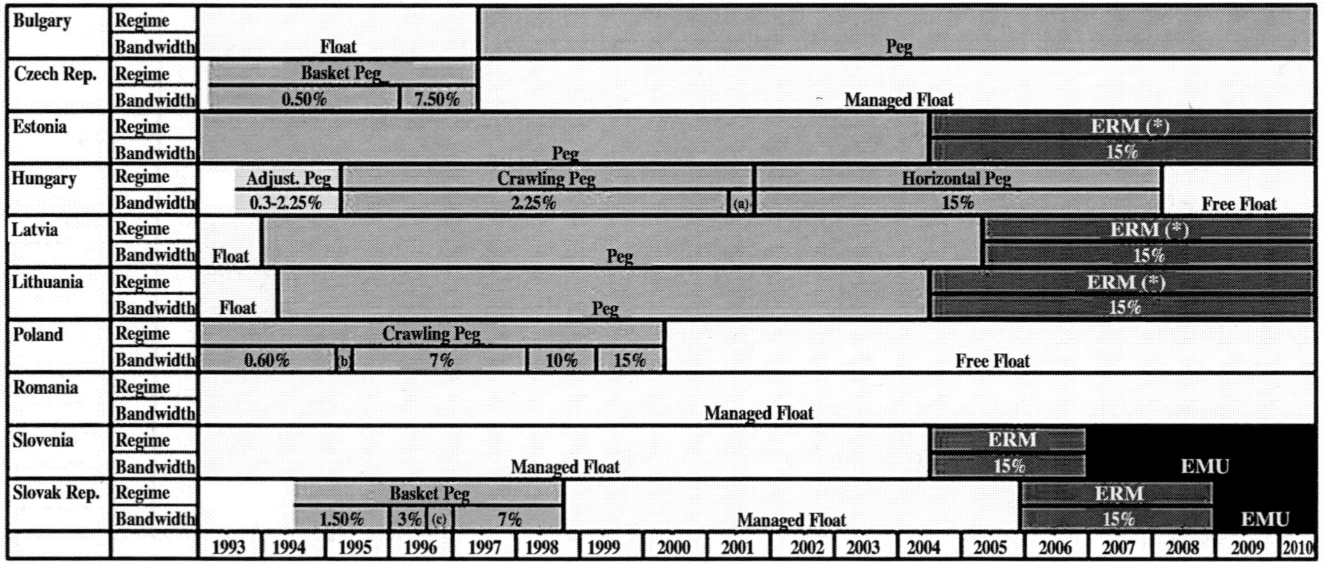

(a) 15%, (b) 2%, (c) 5%
* Note that this is only the official exchange rate regime. After joining the ERM, the Baltic States decided to hold on to their fixed exchange regimes.

Figure 1. Exchange rate regimes in CEEC's.

The development described above follows the so called *bipolar view*.[1] The bipolar view is based on the idea that, in a world of high capital mobility, adjustable pegs may be costly and difficult to defend so that they will be replaced by either hard pegs, i.e. currency boards and currency unions, or absolutely flexible exchange rate systems. The bipolar view is currently a mainstream conclusion in exchange rate policy. Consistent with the bipolar view the official classification by the International Monetary Fund (IMF) reports that the share of intermediate exchange rate regimes has declined during the last decade, as (Fischer 2001) discusses.

3. De Jure versus De Facto Exchange Rate Regimes

In the previous paragraph we gave an overview of the "de jure" exchange rate regimes of the CEEC's, or in other words "what countries say they are doing". Still, this may not be what countries are actually doing. In practice fear of floating and de facto pegging is very common (Calvo & Reinhart 2002).[2] Hence, the IMF acknowledges since 1999 de facto exchange rate regimes. The IMF classification remains a hybrid system: it combines data on actual flexibility with information on the official policy framework (IMF, 2004). According to the hybrid classification, the Slovenian and Romanian exchange rate regimes are crawling pegs, whereas these two countries announced to be managed floats. Relying solely on the official announcements could be misleading, especially for economies in transition. Knowing whether countries follow their officially announced exchange rate is crucial for assessing economic performance in terms of growth, volatility, inflation, and sensitivity to crises, as (Reinhart & Rogoff 2004) discuss. In the literature most studies are based on de jure classifications until the late 1990s. Recent literature, e.g. (Flood & Rose 2005), tries to classify exchange rate arrangements in a more realistic manner.

In general, two main approaches can be followed to identify de facto exchange rate regimes. One approach analyzes the development of exchange rates and policy variables that are indicative of exchange rate management by the central bank. (Popper & Lowell 1994) take this approach for Pacific Basin countries; (Hausmann *et al.* 2001) and (Levy-Yeyati & Sturzenegger 2005) use it on a broad sample of countries. (Schnabl 2004) applies this technique to Central and East European countries (CEEC). The second approach considers the outcomes of implicit exchange rate targeting, i.e., the time series of exchange rates. This can be done by comparing exchange rate developments with those of some possible anchor currencies. Exemplary for this approach is the work of (Haldane & Hall 1991). They analyze the transition of the British Pound from a dollar peg to a Deutsche mark peg. Other examples include (Frankel & Wei 1992), who investigate the influence of the yen on the exchange rate policies of some Asian countries and (Frankel *et al.* 2001), who consider its impact on other emerging market economies. Some CEEC have been included in the work of (Bénassy-Quéré 1996), who investigates de facto pegs during their early period of transition. (Reinhart &

[1] The bipolar view is also named as the hollowing out hypothesis or the two-corner hypothesis

[2] (Fischer 2001), (Reinhart & Rogoff 2004), (Levy-Yeyati & Sturzenegger 2005), and (McKinnon & Schnabl 2004) also support this view. (Rogoff *et al.* 2004) state that, from an ex post perspective, the de facto exchange rate regime differs from the announced one about 50% of time.

Rogoff 2004) stress the importance of market-determined exchange rates and also consider the behavior of parallel exchange rates to construct a natural classification algorithm.

(Frömmel & Schobert 2006) use the approach by (Frankel & Wei 1992) to analyze the de facto exchange rate regimes of six CEEC, namely the Czech Republic, Hungary, Poland, Romania, Slovakia and Slovenia. They use daily data from 1994 to 2004, when most of the countries under consideration joined the European Union and estimate the regression:

$$\Delta s_t = d + \sum_{i=1}^{N} w_i \cdot \Delta s_{i,t} + \varepsilon_t \qquad (3.1)$$

where s_t is the currency under observation expressed in special drawing rights that are used here as a numeraire, d is the rate of crawl, t the time parameter and $s_{i,t}$ are currencies to which s_t is pegged. The currencies $s_{i,t}$ are expressed in the same numeraire as s_t and weighted in the basket with some weights w_i, which are nonnegative real numbers. The specification of equation (1) nests several relevant alternative regimes. A simple peg implies d=0 and N=1, while a crawling peg indicates d>0 and N=1. A basket peg results in d=0 and N>1, while a crawling basket implies d>0 and N>1.

The setting of eq. (3.1) allows testing the de facto exchange rate regime. First one may test whether the rate of crawl (d) or the estimated weights (w_i) are different from zero. Second it is possible to test whether the estimated weights significantly differ from the officially announced ones.

Their findings imply that the Polish zloty and the Hungarian forint have most likely behaved according to their officially announced regime during the periods of higher exchange rate flexibility, while the results for the Czech Republic and Slovakia suggest a somewhat higher importance of the euro (and Deutsche mark) than officially announced. The Slovenian regime before 2004 matches rather the IMF's de facto classification as a crawling peg than its official announcement of a managed float. Although (Frömmel & Schobert 2006) cannot clearly confirm the Romanian regime as a de facto crawling peg, it occasionally seemed like a crawling peg to a basket of euro and US dollar.

4. Exchange Rate Regimes and Volatility

As pointed out above, we observe an increasing degree of exchange rate flexibility for the CEEC between 1994 and 2004.[3] This increased flexibility of the exchange rate, however, may not necessarily lead to higher volatility. In support of this, (Krugman 1991) argues that widening the fluctuation band will make it more credible, because it gets less likely that the fluctuation margins will be reached. Consequently volatility decreases. In contrast, (Flood & Rose 1999) conclude that fixed exchange rate regimes are in general less volatile than floats. This was also found by (Hughes-Hallett & Anthony 1997) and (Frömmel &

[3] This movement towards more flexible exchange rate arrangements stopped in recent years after several of the CEEC joined the exchange rate mechanism (ERM2) of the European Monetary System and pegged their exchange rate to the euro within a band of ±15 percent. This is the case in particular for Slovakia and Slovenia, which had officially announced managed floats prior to their entry to ERM2. Slovenia and Slovakia joined EMU in 2007 and 2009, respectively.

Menkhoff 2001) for the European Monetary System. (Stancík 2007) corroborates this result for the Visegrád countries and Slovenia, but also stresses the importance of trade openness. (Frömmel & Menkhoff 2003) additionally show that changes in monetary policy settings determine volatility switches for exchange rates of major industrial countries.

Some empirical results suggest that the effect on volatility of the type of exchange rate regime is conditional on the appropriateness of the exchange rate regime. The work of (Berger *et al.* 2000) confirms that the type of exchange rate regime affects volatility, but that the "wrong" choice of a peg (that is, the choice of a peg by a country for which a flexible exchange rate would be more appropriate) induces higher exchange rate volatility than a peg which is in line with the macroeconomic conditions. Accordingly, volatility can here be seen as a measure of credibility of an exchange rate arrangement and serves as "a symbolic and visible measure of the government's success in macroeconomic management" (Duttagupta *et al.* 2004). (Fidrmuc & Horváth 2008) apply various GARCH-type models to five new member states of the EU and find an inverse relation between credibility of the exchange rate regime and exchange rate volatility.

There are only few works which investigate structural breaks in the exchange rate volatility of Central and Eastern European transition economies. (Kocenda 1998) compares GARCH estimates for the Czech koruna before and after the exchange rate band was widened in 1996 and finds significantly differing volatility patterns. (Kóbor & Székely 2004) apply a simple Markov switching model to the exchange rates of the so called Visegrád Group (the Czech Republic, Hungary, Poland, and Slovakia) between 2001 and 2003 and find frequent regime switches. Their sample period however does not include any change of the officially announced exchange rate system. (Kocenda 2005) argues that a lack of coincidence between policy changes and structural breaks in exchange rate behavior may hint at policy settings which are not consistent with the opinion of market participants and, accordingly, low credibility of the system. This is in line with the observation that if the costs of changing an exchange rate regime are high, a country may uphold an exchange rate regime even though it is not the optimal choice or even sustainable in the long run (Eichengreen & Masson 1998), (Juhn & Mauro 2002).

(Frömmel 2010) picks up the relation between credibility and volatility and applies a Markov switching GARCH model to exchange rates of the Visegrád countries between 1994 and their entry to the European Union in 2004. Romania joins the sample as a country that never announced an official peg.

The model allows the coefficients in a GARCH volatility equation (see (Bollerslev 1986) to switch between two states:

$$\sigma_{t,s_t}{}^2 = \omega_{s_t} + \alpha_{s_t}\varepsilon_{t-1}{}^2 + \beta_{s_t}\sigma_{t-1}{}^2 \tag{4.1}$$

where σ_{t-1}^2 and ε_{t-1} are the conditional variance and the innovation respectively of the previous period. The state process s_t follows a time-discrete Markov process with two possible states.[4] The process is characterized by the transition matrix P and the probability distribution in t = 1:

[4] The model can be easily generalised to k states, as well as the mean process can be modified. This will, however, not lead to substantial changes in the model, so we rely on the simple model as described in the main text.

$$P = \begin{bmatrix} p_{11} & p_{21} \\ p_{12} & p_{22} \end{bmatrix}, \tag{4.2}$$

with $p_{ij}=P(s_t=j|\ s_{t-1}=i)$, and $\Phi_t = \{r_t, r_{t-1}, .., r_1; \vartheta\}$ is the set of available information at time t, i.e. the set of all realisations of the returns process up to time t and the vector ϑ of parameters, see (Hamilton 1994), p. 237. For details of the model see (Frömmel 2010).

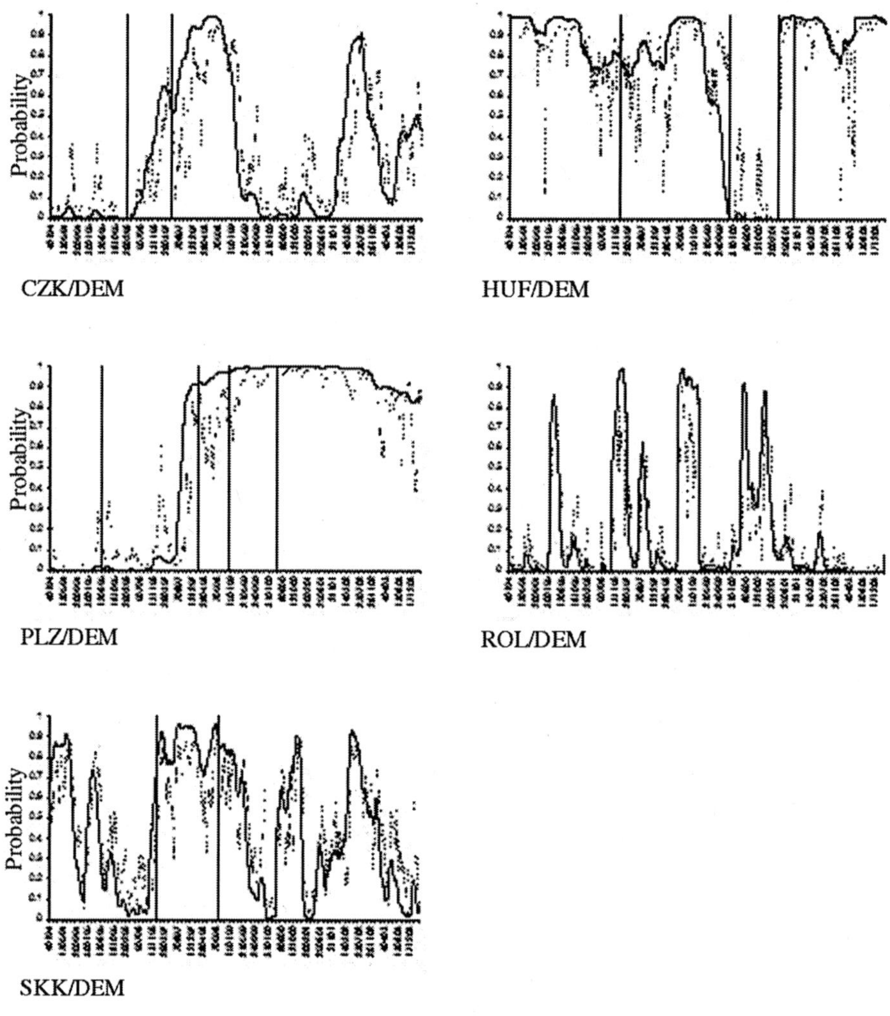

Source: Frommel 2010.

Figure 2. Filter and smoothed probabilities for EU accession countries. The bold lines are the smoothed probabilities $P(s_t=1\ |\ \Phi_T)$ of being in the high volatility regime, the dotted lines are the smoothed probabilities $P(s_t=1\ |\ \Phi_t)$ of being in the high volatility regime 1. The smoothed probabilities correspond with an ex post analysis, whereas the filter probabilities are the probabilities as observed on the respective day. The vertical lines represent changes in the exchange rate system of the respective country.

The model allows then to distinguish a high and a low volatility state, with the switches between high and low volatility being of particular interest. As pointed out by (Kocenda 2005) a coincidence of switches between volatility states and changes of the officially announced regimes hint at high credibility and primacy of the policy. Figure 2 shows the probabilities of being in the high volatility regime for the five countries. Volatility regimes and policy regimes clearly coincide in the cases of Hungary and Poland. The control by policy was comparatively high, providing some evidence for the success of gradually increasing exchange rate flexibility for exiting a peg (Eichengreen 1999). This is in particular the case when countries have liberalized financial markets, as it is typical for the CEEC. They need to manage their exposure to international capital accounts and are more vulnerable to being forced off their currency pegs. This high vulnerability of intermediate exchange rate arrangements is also stressed by the results for the Czech Republic and Slovakia, which had to follow the pressure by markets and leave their pegs during currency crises. Accordingly we can observe a switch to the high volatility regime *before* policy reacted in the course of the crisis. In these cases the markets rather than policy drove the evolution of exchange rate policy.

As a conclusion, the results are strongly in favour of gradually and early widening the bandwidth of currency pegs. Furthermore crawling pegs instead of horizontal ones seem to be advantageous, giving a certain degree of flexibility to react to an evolving environment. The credibility of an exchange rate arrangement is a crucial condition for its success and it is hardly possible to exit smoothly from a peg when markets expect it.

5. Exchange Rate Regimes and Monetary Policy

Exchange rate policy and monetary policy are interdependent. For this reason we will discuss here the monetary policy in the CEEC, which can (again) be looked at from two different perspectives: the "de jure" and the "de facto" policy.

5.1. Overview of the "De Jure" Monetary Policy in the CEEC's since 1994

In the *Czech Republic,* the monetary policy initially followed a strategy of jointly targeting the exchange rate and monetary aggregates. Although this policy worked well in the early 1990s, increasing capital inflows made the system unsustainable. After widening the exchange rate band in March 1996, the Czech National Bank (CNB) switched to a managed float in May 1997. Later on, in 1998, monetary policy changed to a strategy of inflation targeting because the CNB considered the demand for money to be too unstable to use a monetary aggregate as an intermediate target (CNB 1998).[5] However, during the period of inflation targeting, the CNB kept on intervening in the foreign exchange market. (Holub 2004) argues that these interventions in early 1998 and in 1999/2000 are not consistent with inflation targeting. These claims are supported by regular discussions in the central bank's

[5] From 1998 to 2001, the CNB pursued a net inflation target, i.e. headline inflation minus regulated prices and changes in indirect taxes. In 2002 the CNB switched to headline inflation targeting with a continuous and declining target band.

council about the equilibrium exchange rate.[6] An in-depth survey of Czech monetary policy can be found in (Böhm & Zdarsky 2005).

In *Hungary* the monetary policy concentrated until 2001 on managing the nominal exchange rate within a fairly narrow crawling band (Kiss 2005). During 2001, the National Bank of Hungary (NBH) widened the band substantially. The following transition from a crawling band to a horizontal band coincided with the adoption of inflation targeting. The inflation target is surrounded by a one percent tolerance band, which was achieved until 2002. According to (Dibooglu & Kutan 2001) and (Barlow 2005), the Hungarian policy mix was successful in gaining internal and external stability of the economy.

Until 1998, the *National Bank of Poland (NBP)* attempted to combine money and exchange rate targets by pursuing a crawling devaluation of the zloty vis-à-vis a basket of currencies. This strategy did not result in both intermediate targets being met in full, but it did facilitate the reduction of inflation initially. Beginning in 1995, Poland experimented with targeting money growth, the interest rate, and the monetary base. However, the NBP did not wait for a crisis to widen the exchange rate band substantially. Due to increased financial market integration, direct inflation targeting was introduced in the last quarter of 1998, although not announced formally until January 1, 1999. Until 2010 the exchange rate didn't play a major role in monetary policy: The NBP didn't intervene on the foreign exchange market. In April 2010 the NBP did intervene, because the strong zloty was considered to be a threat for the economic growth in Poland. The intervention was preceded by more than a month of efforts of the NBP to talk the zloty down. The central bank declared after this intervention that it "can't exclude intervening again".

Although no official commitment is made to any specific exchange rate or inflation path, statements of officials from the *National Bank of Romania* openly express that monetary policy has aimed at a certain exchange rate path to maintain external competitiveness. The 2001 Annual Report states that the central bank is trying to change this policy: "The support was mainly aimed at enlarging the monetary policy's room for maneuvers through abolishing intensive reliance on the exchange rate as an instrument providing an underpinning to external competitiveness" (NBR 2001). In discussions with the IMF, Romanian authorities have mentioned that they pursue twin objectives of gradual disinflation and maintaining a sustainable external position by using the exchange rate as an implicit nominal anchor (IMF 2003). The Romanian authorities also mentioned the use of an informal euro/dollar basket, which should be replaced gradually by only the euro as the reference exchange rate on the path to EU accession.

Slovakia focused from the beginning on exchange rate stability, combined with tracking a broad money aggregate, namely M2. Following policies in the Czech Republic, the National Bank of Slovakia (NBS) widened its exchange rate band in January 1997 and changed to a managed float in October 1998. The NBS has used inflation bands as an informal guide for monetary policy since 1999, but the authorities do not consider this strategy to be formal

[6] The minutes of the CNB board meeting of December 21, 1999 report that a considerable amount of time was spent discussing exchange rate developments. Board members agreed on the importance of guarding against inadequate appreciation of the koruna's nominal exchange rate. From the minutes of October 26, 2000 meeting: "A large-volume transaction... was responsible for the koruna's strengthening against the euro during the past few days. However, attention was drawn to the fact that, in the present phase of completing state share privatization, this distinct type of divergence could occur again, and even possibly lead to new exchange rate levels. The CNB would carefully monitor and analyze any developments in this direction."

inflation targeting. According to (Beblavy 2002), current monetary policy in Slovakia can be characterized as implicit inflation targeting with a significant amount of discretion. Furthermore, the exchange rate still plays an important role, even though it is officially floating. For example, the monetary program for 2000 reports: "NBS expects appreciation pressures. It is ready to intervene ..., the intent of NBS will be to stabilize the foreign exchange rate approximately at the current level" (NBS 1999).

Slovenia's official policy was monetary targeting until switching to a two-pillar strategy similar to that of the European Central Bank in 2001. Within this official framework, the Bank of Slovenia states that it "pursues the core aim of monetary policy, namely price stability, by simultaneously modifying the quantity of money in circulation and the exchange rate. In order to maintain control over the money supply in the face of the free flow of capital, the Bank must adjust interest rates and the exchange rate interdependently" (BOS 2002). However, if the Bank pursues only price stability as its primary objective in a managed floating exchange rate regime, it would not need to adjust exchange rate developments in reaction to capital flows. Rather, the statement reveals implicit dual objectives, namely internal price stability and an exchange rate target.

The *Bulgarian* policy was over the whole period characterized by a firm focus on a fixed exchange rate. There was one break in the monetary policy in mid-1997, together with the launch of the currency board. The stabilization of inflation and inflation expectations then became also important objectives of the Bulgarian National Bank. Some authors argue that after the introduction of these objectives Bulgaria reached the lowest and most stable inflation rates combined with the highest and most stable output growth since the beginning of the transition process (Hristov & Zaimov 2003). One should however not neglect that Bulgaria was in a period of hyperinflation before the introduction of the above mentioned objectives, which makes a comparison difficult.

In the *Baltic States* the monetary policy was, because of the currency board arrangements in these countries, characterized by exchange rate targeting. For Estonia there was a strong focus on the exchange rate since the early nineties (Hartsenko 2002). Latvia and Lithuania were in exactly the same situation (Repse 1999; BOL 2007).

The "de jure" exchange rate policies are summarized in Figure 3. Based on these brief histories, we conclude that, despite the fact that countries announce fairly flexible exchange rate regimes officially, central banks in transition economies pay considerable attention to the exchange rate in monetary policy, which is often embedded in broader macroeconomic programs. In the next section we focus on the research on de facto monetary policy.

5.2. Research on the De Facto Monetary Policy in the CEEC's

An important tool to analyze the de facto exchange rate regime is the Taylor rule, which was first proposed in 1993. The Taylor rule suggests that interest rates would be changed according to the deviation of inflation from a target and an output gap (Taylor 1993). Other studies often focus on the comparison of the actual setting of policy rates by central banks

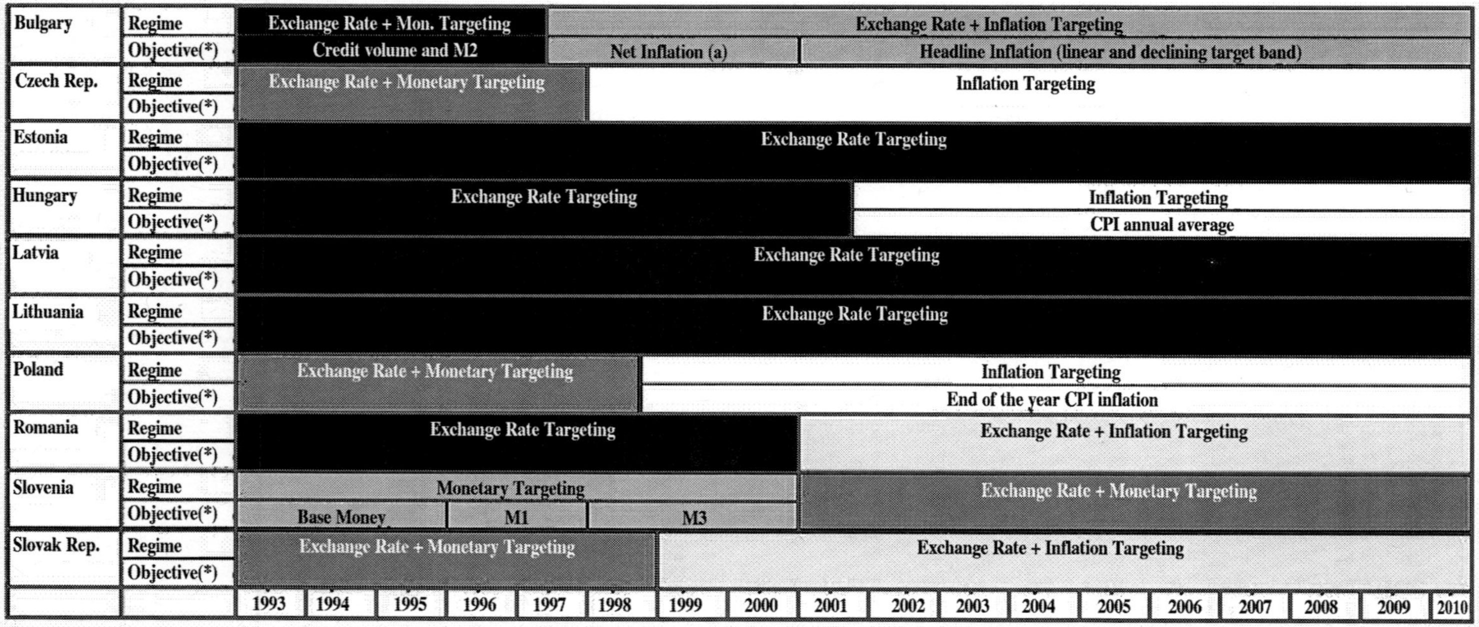

(*) If available we included the inflation or monetary target variable

(a) Net inflation = Headline Inflation minus regulated prices and changes in indirect taxes

Figure 3. “De Jure” Monetary Policy Regimes in CEEC’s

with what would have been predicted by the Taylor rule as a benchmark. However, as (Peersman & Smets 1999) among others emphasize, the Taylor rule should be perceived as a descriptive instrument to understand the interest rate setting behavior of central banks rather than as a normative guide for monetary authorities. The empirical literature on such interest rate rules for industrial countries has grown significantly during the past decades and has proven the ability of interest rate rules to describe the interest rate setting behaviour of central banks.[7]

In contrast, research in the context of emerging market economies and particularly transition economies is of more recent origin and relatively scarce. An important finding is that central banks in emerging market economies tend to look beyond inflation and focus on other objectives as well, most prominently on exchange rate changes. (Mohanty & Klau 2004) find that many central banks in their sample of emerging market economies change interest rates systematically in response to exchange rate changes. For some countries the response is even found to be stronger than that to the inflation rate or the output gap.

There are few papers on monetary policy rules in CEEC. This is due to several reasons. First, the time series available are comparatively short. They usually start in the middle of the 1990s. Second, most CEEC have not followed one single strategy of monetary policy and also gradually made their exchange rates more flexible (See Figure 1 and Figure 3). Third, it is not quite clear which target values for inflation the CEEC followed, as most countries introduced inflation targeting and explicit inflation goals only between 1997 and 2001. The unstable and dynamic economic situation in the CEEC makes this task even more demanding.

However, there have been recently some attempts to describe the monetary policy in selected CEEC using interest rate rules: (Maria-Dolores 2005) estimates Taylor rules for the Visegrad countries (The Czech Republic, Hungary, Poland and Slovakia) between 1998 and 2003 and comes to the conclusion that the Taylor rule describes the interest rates well for all countries but Slovakia. Similarly to the original Taylor rule, the rules used by (Maria-Dolores 2005) do not consider exchange rate movements. The lagged interest rate, however, is included. The same set of countries is considered by (Paez-Farell 2007), whereas the sample periods differ from country to country. He compares different versions of interest rate rules and finds that there is a reaction to exchange rate movements. (Angeloni *et al.* 2007) estimate interest rate rules for the Czech Republic, Hungary and Poland from 1995-2004. They introduce the US dollar interest rate as a proxy for inflationary pressures of global origin and dummies for the years preceding the adoption of inflation targeting. (Yilmazkuday 2008) applies Taylor rules to the Czech Republic, Hungary and Poland for the period 1994-2007. He includes the exchange rate in the interest rate rule, but also considers structural breaks. (Moons & Van Poeck 2008) focus on the period 1999-2003 and find that the accession countries do not differ substantially from the current EMU members with respect to the interest rate setting behavior. Furthermore it seems that the potential new entrants have witnessed a notable tendency for increased convergence during the last years. Finally, (Horváth 2009) analyzes the policy neutral rate in the Czech Republic from 2001 to 2006 using a time-varying parameter model with endogenous regressors. The results indicate that the policy neutral rate decreases gradually over the course of the sample period showing a substantial interest rate convergence to levels comparable to the euro area.

[7] For monetary policy rules in the context of inflation targeting see Neumann and von Hagen (2002) and the references therein.

All of these studies conclude that a Taylor-like rule is helpful in understanding monetary policy of the CEEC. However, in most cases inflation coefficients are found to be far below unity, thus violating the so-called Taylor principle. If the Taylor principle holds, the policy rate should move more than one-for-one with increases in the inflation rate and thereby raise the real interest rate. If the monetary policy rule violates the Taylor principle, it will mean that the central bank does not react adequately on bringing down inflation.[8] This result is counterintuitive as the CEEC have experienced a remarkable degree of disinflation during the last 15 years. The literature suggests mainly two explanations: (Angeloni *et al.* 2007) argue that part of the reaction on inflation is captured by the coefficient on the US interest rate included in their equation. An increase in global inflation would then lead to a composed reaction, which is partly due to domestic inflation via the conventional inflation coefficient and partly due to foreign inflation via the coefficient on the foreign interest rate. One might similarly argue that the exchange rate included in the interest rate rule partially takes the reaction on inflation, as it anchors expectations on future monetary policy. Another argument, proposed by (Golinelli & Rovelli 2005) is that the reaction to an increase in inflation may be modest, if the initial interest rate compared to inflation was set high enough. Thus a smaller coefficient means that in the course of the disinflation process monetary policy is getting even more aggressive. The scenario seems to be well applicable to the CEEC. However, one would at least expect the inflation coefficient to be close to unity during periods of autonomous monetary policy.

Besides the above mentioned empirical research, the treatment of exchange rate changes in monetary policy rules is also discussed in the theoretical literature. (Svensson 2000) compares strict inflation targeting (when stabilizing inflation around the inflation target is the only objective for monetary policy) with flexible inflation targeting (when there are additional objectives for monetary policy). His results also indicate that strict inflation targeting implies a vigorous use of the direct exchange rate channel for stabilizing (CPI-) inflation at a short horizon. In contrast, flexible inflation targeting ends up stabilizing inflation at a longer horizon, and thereby also stabilizes real exchange rates and other variables to a significant extent. In comparison with the Taylor rule, the reaction function under inflation targeting in an open economy respond to more information, in particular to foreign disturbances. The particular importance of the exchange rate for monetary policy rules in the case of emerging economies is also stressed by (Amato & Gerlach 2002).

(Taylor 2001) argues that a monetary policy rule that reacts directly to the exchange rate, as well as to inflation and output, sometimes works worse than policy rules that do not react directly to the exchange rate and thereby avoid more erratic fluctuations in the interest rate. In (Taylor 2002), however, he points out that monetary policy in open economies is different from that in closed economies. Open-economy policymakers seem reluctant to considerable variability in exchange rate. In his view they should target a measure of inflation that filters out the transitory effects of exchange rate fluctuations and they should also include the exchange rate in their policy reaction functions. He leaves open to further research, whether the exchange rate should appear on the left- or the right-hand side of the rule – that is, whether the policy instrument should be an interest rate or rather a monetary condition index.

(Frömmel *et al.* 2009) extend the existing work on monetary policy rules in CEEC by splitting up the exchange rate into two components, one of them (b_t) capturing the “technical”

[8] For a more detailed discussion of the Taylor principle see Woodford (2001).

reaction to deviations from the central parity in a peg, and the other one (Δs_t) measuring trends in the exchange rate:

$$i_t = r^* + \pi_t + \alpha\pi_t^* + \beta y_t^* + \delta\Delta s_t + \gamma b_t \quad (5.1)$$

Here r* is a long run real exchange rate, π_t the in inflation rate, π_t* the inflation gap, and y_t* the output gap. The "band distance" b_t is a nonlinear function of the exchange rate's distance to the edges of the band of a currency peg (if there is one at that time), as shown in Figure 4. The band distance reflects pressure on the exchange rate, as every time the market rate tends to or actually does exceed one of the borders, the central bank is obliged to react by interventions and/or interest rate changes. This implies that there should be a strong influence of the band distance on the interest rate stance of the monetary policy. The closer the exchange rate comes to the intervention margins the stronger the central bank should react, and the values of b_t increase dramatically during times of crises, when boundaries are reached or exceeded.

Figure 5 and Figure 6 show the evolution of the band distance element as an example for Hungary (crawling peg) and the Czech Republic (horizontal peg) respectively. Obviously the band distance takes in general higher values if the exchange rate pegs are narrow (i.e., during the first parts of the respective sample periods). Furthermore the violation of the band during the Czech exchange rate crisis 1997 substantially increased the pressure on the Czech interest rate policy.

(Frömmel *et al.* 2009) estimate equation (5.1) in a cointegration approach and let the coefficients vary depending on whether the exchange rate regime is classified as "fixed" or "floating" regime. They find that, during the "fixed exchange rate regime" the Taylor principle is violated, but the band distance explains most of the interest rate variation. This is in line with the argument by (Angeloni *et al.* 2007), see above. In contrast, in the "flexible exchange rate regime" for all countries but Slovakia the Taylor principle is fulfilled. Their approach therefore leads to a substantial improvement of empirical results.

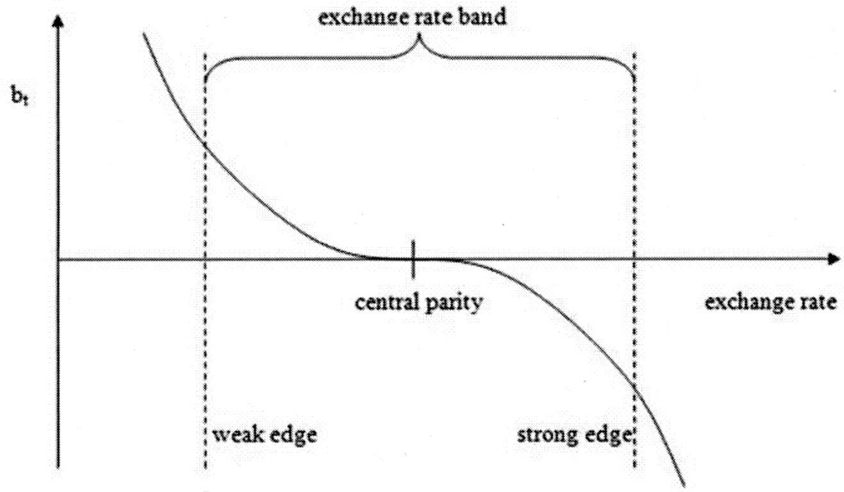

Figure 4. The band distance.

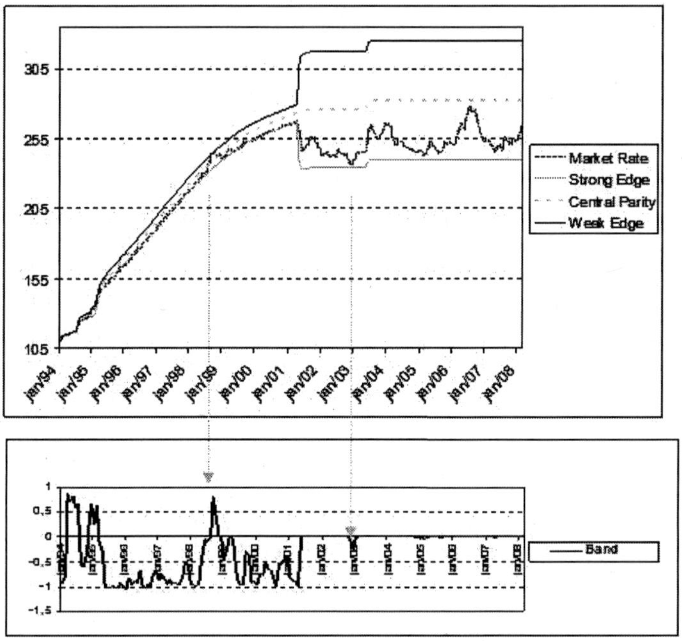

Source: Frommel, et al. 2009.

Figure 5. The Derivation of the band distance element from the historical exchange rate peg values for Hungarian Forint/ Deutsche Mark.

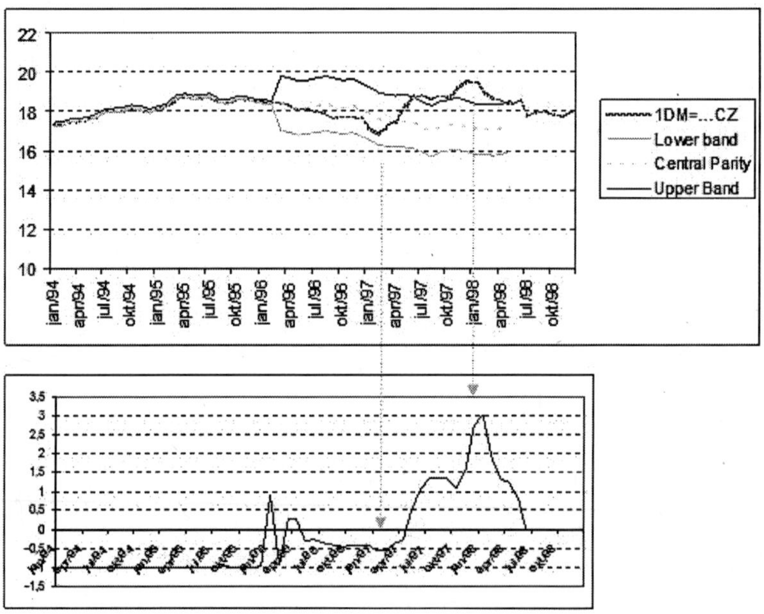

Source: Frommel, et al. 2009.

Figure 6. The Derivation of the band distance element from the historical exchange rate peg values for the Czech Republic (Czech Koruna/ Deutsche Mark).

Two interesting features stand out. First, the exchange rates of Central and Eastern European countries often had appreciating pressure during fixed regimes and therefore, were close to the strong edge of the narrow bands (see Figure 5 and Figure 6). Second, the values increase dramatically during times of crises, when boundaries are reached or exceeded (see Figure 6).

6. Exchange Rate Regimes and Interventions

Monetary policy influences the exchange rate. In this section we review how central bank interventions and central bank communication can influence the exchange rate. A basic insight of the research on central bank interventions (for surveys see e.g. (Sarno & Taylor 2001; Vitale 2007)) is that interventions are able to move the exchange rate. They affect the first two moments of the exchange rate (Scalia 2008) and the impact is usually stronger in emerging than in developed countries (Canales-Kriljenko 2003). This may be due to less sterilization, the market's size and organization.

Besides direct interventions central bank communication may also be seen as a form of intervention, that is – although less obvious at first sight – able to affect the exchange rate as well (Ehrmann & Fratzscher 2007). There is a huge amount of research providing some ambiguous empirical evidence on an exchange rate impact of central bank communication (see the survey in (Blinder et al. 2008)). The impact of verbal interventions or communication stems from their role in anchoring expectations on future monetary policy, i.e. the signaling or expectation channel of monetary policy (Sarno & Taylor 2001), but also by functioning as a coordination advice for market participants (Reitz & Taylor 2008). Thus, communication may complement intervention or substitute it (Fratzscher 2008).

Due to the more dynamic economic environment in a transition economy verbal interventions may be more effective than in developed markets. However, again most of the work deals with developed markets, mostly for the Fed, the ECB, the Bank of England and the Bank of Japan, and there are only few papers that focus on transition economies: (Rozkrut et al. 2007) find for the Czech Republic, Hungary and Poland, that speeches about monetary policy affect the exchange rate. (Égert 2007) finds influence of central bank communication for Hungary, but not for other CEEC. He also concludes that the Hungarian National Bank (MNB) used actual interventions very rarely, but mainly relies on verbal interventions. The latter is also analyzed by (Frömmel *et al.* 2010) who estimate the impact of communication by central bankers and politicians on high-frequency exchange rates. They find that central bank communication mainly affects the exchange rate indirectly via order flow, i.e., signed transaction volume.

Conclusion

The exchange rates of CEEC have been subject of numerous studies. In this selective survey we have described the evolution of exchange rate arrangements of CEEC and reviewed four aspects of their exchange rate policy: the deviation of de facto from de jure exchange rate regimes, the relation between exchange rate volatility and exchange rate arrangements, the inclusion of exchange rates in monetary policy rules and the intervention policy of CEEC.

Acknowledgments

We would like to thank Franziska Schobert and Nora Srzentic for helpful suggestions.

Reviewed By

Franziska Schobert (Deutsche Bundesbank).

References

Amato, J.A., Gerlach, S., 2002. Inflation Targeting in Emerging Market and Transition Economies: Lessons after a Decade. *European Economic Review*, 46, 781-790.

Angeloni, I., Flad, M., Mongelli, F.P., 2007. Monetary Integration of the New EU Member States: What Sets the Pace of Euro Adoption? *Journal of Common Market Studies*, 45, 367-409.

Ball, L., 1999. Policy Rules for Open Economies. University of Chicago Press, Chicago.

Barlow, D., 2005. The Hungarian Exchange Rate and Inflation over the Transition. *Economic Systems*, 87-97.

Beblavy, M., 2002. Exchange Rate and Exchange Rate Regime in Slovakia: Recent Developments. European Center Working Paper on Macroeconomic Studies.

Bénassy-Quéré, A., 1996. Potentialities and Opportunities of the Euro as an International Currency. CEPII Report for the European Commission.

Berger, H., Sturm, J.-E., De Haan, J., 2000. An Empirical Investigation into Exchange Rate Regime Choice and Exchange Rate Volatility. CESifo Working Paper Series.

Blinder, A.S., Ehrmann, M., de Haan, J., Frzatzscher, M., Jansen, D.-J., 2008. Central Bank Communication and Monetary Policy: A Survey of Theory and Evidence. *ECB Working Paper Series*.

Böhm, J., Zdarsky, V., 2005. Conducting Monetary Policy in a Small Open Economy under Globalized Capital Markets: The Experience of the Czech Republic. *BIS Papers*, 141-149.

BOL, 2007. Annual Report 2007 of the BOL (Bank of Lithuania). *Annual Reports*, 25-29.

Bollerslev, T., 1986. Generalized Autoregressive Conditional Heteroskedasticity. *Journal of Econometrics*, 31, 302-327.

BOS, 2002. BOS (Bank of Slovenia) *Annual Report*, 2002.

Calvo, G.A., Reinhart, C.M., 2002. Fear of Floating. *Quarterly Journal of Economics*, 117, 379-408.

Canales-Kriljenko, J.I., 2003. Foreign Exchange Intervention in Developing and Transition Economies: Results of a Survey. IMF Working Paper Series.

CNB, 1998. CNB (Czech National Bank) Annual Report.

Corker, R., Beaumont, C., van Elkan, R., Iakova, D.M., 2000. Exchange Rate Regimes in Selected Advanced Transition Economies - Coping with Transition, Capital Inflows and EU Accession. . *IMF Policy Discussion Papers*, PDP/00/03.

De Grauwe, P., 2003. The Economics of Monetary Union. Oxford University Press, Oxford.

Dibooglu, S., Kutan, A., 2001. Sources of Real Exchange Rate Fluctuations in Transition Economies: The Case of Hungary and Poland. *Journal of Comparative Economics*, 257-275.

Duttagupta, R., Fernandez, G., Karacadag, C., 2004. From Fixed to Float: Operational Aspects of Moving Towards Exchange Rate Flexibility. IMF Working Paper Series.

Égert, B., 2007. Central Bank Interventions, Communication and Interest Rate Policy in Emerging European Economies. *Journal of Comparative Economics*, 35, 387-413.

Ehrmann, M., Fratzscher, M., 2007. Communication by Central Bank Committee Members: Different Strategies, Same Effectiveness? *Journal of Money, Credit and Banking*, 39, 509-541.

Eichengreen, B., 1999. Kicking the Habit: Moving from Pegged Rates to Greater Exchange Rate Flexibility. *Economic Journal*, C1-C14.

Eichengreen, B., Hausmann, R., 1999. Exchange Rates and Financial Fragility. *NBER Working Papers*, 7418.

Eichengreen, B., Masson, P., 1998. Exit Strategies: Policy Options for Countries Seeking Greater Exchange Rate Flexibility. *IMF Occasional Papers*, 168.

Fidrmuc, J., Horváth, R., 2008. Volatility of Exchange Rates in Selected New EU Members: Evidence from Daily Data. *Economic Systems*, 32, 103-118.

Fischer, S., 2001. Exchange Rate Regimes: Is the Bipolar View Correct? *Journal of Economic Perspectives*, 15, 3-24.

Flood, R.P., Rose, A.K., 1999. Understanding Exchange Rate Volatility without the Contrivance of Macroeconomics. *Economic Journal*, 109, 660-672.

Flood, R.P., Rose, A.K., 2005. A New Approach to Asset Integration: Methodology and Mystery. *Pacific Economic Review*.

Frankel, J.A., Fajnzylber, E., Schmukler, S.L., Servén, L., 2001. Verifying Exchange Rate Regimes. *Journal of Development Economics*, 66, 351-386

Frankel, J.A., Wei, S.-J., 1992. Yen Bloc or Dollar Bloc? Exchange Rate Policies in the East Asian Economies. In: Takatoshi I & Krueger A (eds.) Macroeconomic linkages: Savings, Exchange Rates and Capital Flows. University Press of Chicago, Chicago.

Fratzscher, M., 2008. Oral Interventions versus Actual Interventions in FX Markets - An Event Study Approach. *Economic Journal*, 118, 1079-1106.

Frömmel, M., 2010. Volatility Regimes in Central and Eastern European Countries' Exchange Rates. *Czech Journal of Economics and Finance*.

Frömmel, M., Garabedian, G., Schobert, F., 2009. Monetary Policy Rules in Central and Eastern European Countries: Does the Exchange Rate Matter? Ghent University Working Paper Series.

Frömmel, M., Kiss, M., Pintér, K., 2010. Central Bank Communication, Macroeconomic Announcements, and Order Flow: An Analysis of the Hungarian Foreign Exchange Market. *International Journal of Finance & Economics*.

Frömmel, M., Menkhoff, L., 2001. Risk Reduction in the EMS: Evidence from Exchange Rate Properties. *Journal of Common Market Studies*, 39, 285-306.

Frömmel, M., Menkhoff, L., 2003. Increasing Exchange Rate Volatility during the Recent Float? *Applied Financial Economics*, 13.

Frömmel, M., Schobert, F., 2006. Exchange Rate Regimes in Central and East European Countries: Deeds vs. Words. *Journal of Comparative Economics*, 34, 467-483

Golinelli, R., Rovelli, R., 2005. Monetary Policy Transmission, Interest Rate Rules and Inflation Targeting in Three Transition Countries. *Journal of Banking and Finance*, 183-201

Haldane, A.G., Hall, S.G., 1991. Sterling's Relationship with the Dollar and the Deutschemark: 1976-89. *Economic Journal*, 101, 436-443

Halpern, L., Wyplosz, C., 1997. Equilibrium exchange rates in transition economies. *IMF Staff Papers*, 430-461.

Hamilton, J., 1994. Time Series Analysis. Princeton University Press, Princeton.

Hartsenko, J., 2002. Estonian Monetary System and Banking Development on Way to the Euro Zone. Effect of Accession to the European Union on the Economic Policy of Estonian. In: Scientific and Educational Conference, pp. 65-71. Berlin Verlag Arno Spitz GmbH, Berlin.

Hausmann, R., Panizza, U., Stein, E., 2001. Why do Countries Float the Way they Float. *Journal of Development Economics*, 66, 387-414.

Holub, T., 2004. Foreign Exchange Interventions under Inflation Targeting: The Czech Experiences. CNB (Czech National Bank) Internal Research and Policy Note.

Horváth, R., 2009. The Time-varying Policy Neutral Rate in Real-time: A Predictor for Future Inflation? *Economic Modelling*, 26.

Hristov, K., Zaimov, M., 2003. Shadowing the Euro: Bulgaria's Monetary Policy Five Years on.

Hughes-Hallett, A., Anthony, M.L., 1997. Exchange Rate Behaviour under the EMS Regime: Was there any Systematic Change? *Journal of International Money and Finance*, 16, 537-560

IMF, 2003. IMF Country Report.

Juhn, G., Mauro, P., 2002. Long-run Determinants of Exchange Rate Regimes: A Simple Sensitivity Analysis. IMF Working Paper Series 02/104

Kiss, G., 2005. Monetary Policy Issues in Hungary on the Eve of EU Membership.

Kóbor, Á., Székely, I., 2004. Foreign Exchange Market Volatility in EU Accession Countries in the Run-up to Euro Adoption: Weathering Uncharted Waters. *Economic Systems*, 28, 337-352.

Kocenda, E., 1998. Altered Band and Exchange Volatility. *Economics of Transition*, 6, 173-181.

Kocenda, E., 2002. Exchange Rate Movements in European Transition Economies. Nova Science, New York.

Kocenda, E., 2005. Beware of Breaks in Exchange Rates: Evidence from European Transition Countries. *Economic Systems*, 29, 307-324.

Krugman, P.R., 1991. Target Zones and Exchange Rate Dynamics. *Quarterly Journal of Economics*, 106, 669-682.

Levy-Yeyati, E., Sturzenegger, F., 2005. Classifying Exchange Rate Regimes: Deeds vs. words. *European Economic Review*, 1603-1635.

Maria-Dolores, R., 2005. Monetary Policy Rules in Accession Countries to EU: Is the Taylor Rule a Pattern? *Economic Bulletin*, 5, 1-16.

McKinnon, R., Schnabl, G., 2004. The East Asian Dollar Standard, Fear of Floating and Original Sin. *Review of Development Economics*, 331-360.

Mohanty, M.S., Klau, M., 2004. Monetary Policy Rules in Emerging Market Economies: Issues and Evidence. BIS Working Papers.

Moons, C., Van Poeck, A., 2008. Does One Size Fit All? A Taylor-rule Based Analysis of Monetary Policy for Current and Future EMU Members. *Applied Economics*, 40, 193-199.

Mussa, M., Masson, P., Swoboda, A., Jadresic, E., Mauro, P., Berg, A., 2000. Exchange Rate Regimes in an Increasingly Integrated World Economy. IMF Occasional Papers.

NBR, 2001. NBR (National Bank of Romania) Annual Report, 2001. 63

NBS, 1999. NBS (National Bank of Slovakia) Menovy Program na Rok 2000 (Exchange Rate Program for the Year 2000).

Obstfeld, M., 1997. Destabilizing Effects of Exchange-rate Escape Clauses. *Journal of International Economics*, 43, 61-77.

Obstfeld, M., Rogoff, K., 1995. The Mirage of Fixed Exchange Rates. *Journal of Economic Perspectives*, 73-96.

Paez-Farell, J., 2007. Understanding Monetary Policy in Central European Countries using Taylor-type Rules: The Case of the Visegrad Four. *Economics Bulletin*, 5, 1-11.

Peersman, G., Smets, F., 1999. The Taylor Rule: A Useful Monetary Policy Benchmark fo the Euro Area. *International Finance*, 2, 85-116.

Popper, H., Lowell, J., 1994. Officially Floating, Implicitly Targeted Exchange Rates: Examples from the Pacific Basin. In: Glick R & Hutchison M (eds.) Exchange Rate Policy and Interdependence: Perspectives from the Pacific Basin. Cambridge University Press, Cambridge.

Reinhart, C.M., Rogoff, K., 2004. The Modern History of Exchange Rate Arrangements: A Reinterpretation. *Quarterly Journal of Economics*, 1-48.

Reitz, S., Taylor, M.P., 2008. The Coordination Channel of Foreign Exchange Intervention: A Nonlinear Microstructural Analysis. *European Economic Review*, 52, 55-76.

Repse, E., 1999. Speech on Monetary Policy in Latvia and Exchange Rate Strategies. In: Central Bank Articles and Speeches. BIS, Basel

Rogoff, K., Husain, A.M., Mody, A., Brooks, R., Oomes, N., 2004. Evolution and Performance of Exchange Rate Regimes. IMF Occasional Papers.

Rozkrut, M., Rybinski, K., Sztaba, L., Szwaja, R., 2007. Quest for Central Bank Communication: Does it Pay to be Talkative? *European Journal of Political Economy*, 23, 176-206.

Sachs, J.D., 1996. Economic Transition and the Exchange Rate Regime. *American Economic Review*, 86, 147-152.

Sarno, L., Taylor, M.P., 2001. Official Intervention in the Foreign Exchange Market: Is It Effective, and if so, How Does It Work? *Journal of Economic Literature*, 839-868.

Scalia, A., 2008. Is Foreign Exchange Intervention Effective? Some Microanalytical Evidence from the Czech Republic. *Journal of International Money and Finance*, 529-546.

Schnabl, G., 2004. De Jure vs. de Facto Exchange Rate Stabilization in Central and Eastern Europe. *Aussenwirtschaft*, 59, 171-190.

Stancík, J., 2007. Determinants of Exchange Rate Volatility: The Case of the New EU Members. *Czech Journal of Economics and Finance*, 57, 414-432.

Svensson, L.E.O., 2000. Open-economy Inflation Targeting. *Journal of International Economics*, 50, 155-183.

Szapáry, G., Jakab, Z., 1998. Exchange Rate Policy in Transition Economies: The case of Hungary. *Journal of Comparative Economics*, 26, 691-717

Taylor, J.B., 1993. Discretion versus Policy Rules in Practice. *Carnegie-Rochester Conference Series on Public Politic*s, 195-214

Taylor, J.B., 2001. The Role of the Exchange Rate in Monetary Policy Rules. *The American Economic Review*, 91, 263-267

Taylor, J.B., 2002. The Monetary Transmission Mechanism and the Evaluation of Monetary Policy Rules In: Loayza N & Schmidt-Hebbel K (eds.) Monetary Policy: Rules and Transmission Mechanisms. *Central Bank of Chile*, pp. 21-46.

Vitale, P., 2007. A Guided Tour of the Market Microstructure Approach to Exchange Rate Dermination. *Journal of Economic Surveys*, 903-934.

Yilmazkuday, H., 2008. Structural Breaks in Monetary Policy Rules: Evidence from Transition Countries. *Emerging Markets Finance and Trade*, 44, 87-97.

In: Exchange Rates: Policies, Effects and Fluctuations
Editor: Natalie B. Perkins, pp. 47-73
ISBN: 978-1-61209-505-9
© 2011 Nova Science Publishers, Inc.

Chapter 3

EXCHANGE RATE FLUCTUATIONS AND ECONOMIC ACTIVITY: COMPETITIVENESS AND CAPACITY BUILDING IN MENA COUNTRIES

***Magda Kandil*[1] *and Ida Aghdas Mirzaie*[2]**
[1] International Monetary Fund, Washington, B.C.
[2] Department of Economics, The Ohio State University, Columbus, OH, USA

NOTE

The views in this chapter are those of the authors and should not be interpreted as those of the International Monetary Fund.

1. INTRODUCTION

Many Middle Eastern countries are resource-constrained, i.e., they are running a current account deficit. The deficit in the current account indicates that aggregate demand exceeds aggregate supply. Alternatively, domestic investment cannot be financed using national savings, necessitating continued reliance on foreign resources to fill in the resource gap.

Given the resource deficit, many countries have taken a closer look into ways to revive the current account balance and supplement domestic resources. There are two policy tracks. First, domestic policies may aim at constraining aggregate demand, particularly domestic consumption, to provide more domestic resources to finance domestic investment. Under this agenda, constraining the budget deficit usually takes top priority. The second priority is to pursue reforms to expand productive capacity and increase aggregate supply. The former track (demand management) may be difficult to implement given priorities for fiscal spending and in light of constraints on government revenues. The second track (supply management) is even more difficult given resource constraints and the time necessary to stimulate output supply and implement structural reforms.

In addition to domestic policies, countries may pursue an exchange rate management policy in order to stimulate exports and constrain imports. Nonetheless, exchange rate policy may not yield the desired results. Export competitiveness may not be stimulated, despite exchange rate depreciation, absent measures to revive quality, improve productivity, and guarantee access to new external markets. Moreover, many Middle Eastern countries have suffered from the J-curve effect whereby depreciation, in the short-run, may increase the value of imports, absent domestic alternatives to substitute for necessary imports.

The purpose of this chapter is to study the significance of the exchange rate in a sample of countries in the Middle East. We estimate empirical models that explain real output growth, price inflation, and the growth in real components of aggregate demand. The empirical models account for major policy variables: government spending, the money supply, and the exchange rate. In addition, we account for FDI flows in the empirical models.

2. Background

A depreciation (or devaluation) of the domestic currency may stimulate economic activity through the initial increase in the price of foreign goods relative to home goods. By increasing the international competitiveness of domestic industries, exchange rate depreciation diverts spending from foreign goods to domestic goods. As illustrated in Guittian (1976) and Dornbusch (1988), the success of currency depreciation in promoting trade balance largely depends on switching demand in proper direction and amount, as well as on the capacity of the home economy to meet the additional demand by supplying more goods[1].

While the traditional view indicates that currency depreciation is expansionary, new structuralism school stresses some contractionary effects. Meade (1951) discusses this theoretical possibility. If the Marshall-Lerner condition is not satisfied, currency depreciation could produce contraction.[2] Hirschman (1949) points out that currency depreciation from an initial trade deficit reduces real national income and may lead to a fall in aggregate demand. Currency depreciation gives with one hand, by lowering export prices, while taking away with the other hand, by raising import prices. If trade is in balance and terms of trade are not changed these price changes offset each other. But if imports exceed exports, the net result is a reduction in real income within the country. Cooper (1971) confirms this point in a general equilibrium model.

Diaz-Alejandro (1963) introduced another argument for contraction following devaluation. Depreciation may raise the windfall profits in export and import-competing industries. If money wages lag the price increase and if the marginal propensity to save from profits is higher than from wages, national savings will go up and real output will decrease. Krugman and Taylor (1978) and Barbone and Rivera-Batiz (1987) have formalized the same views.

Supply-side channels further complicate the effects of currency depreciation on economic performance. Bruno (1979) and Wijnbergen (1989) postulate that in a typical semi-

---

[1] Empirical support of this proposition for Group 7 countries over the 1960-89 period is provided in Mendoza (1992).

[2] The Marshall-Lerner condition states that devaluation will improve the trade balance if the devaluing nation's demand elasticity for imports plus the foreign demand elasticity for the nation's exports exceed 1.

industrialized country where inputs for manufacturing are largely imported and cannot be easily produced domestically, firms' input cost will increase following a devaluation. As a result, the negative impact from the higher cost of imported inputs may dominate the production stimulus from lower relative prices for domestically traded goods. Gylfson and Schmid (1983) provide evidence that the final effect depends on the magnitude by which demand and supply curves shift because of devaluation.[3]

To summarize, currency depreciation increases net exports and increases the cost of production. Similarly, currency appreciation decreases net exports and the cost of production. The combined effects of demand and supply channels determine the net results of exchange rate fluctuations on real output and price.[4]

The complexity of demand and supply channels may determine the results of exchange rate fluctuations as follows:

1) In the goods market, a positive shock to the exchange rate of the domestic currency will make exports more expensive and imports less expensive. As a result, the competition from foreign markets will decrease the demand for domestic products, decreasing domestic output and price.
2) In the money market, a positive shock to the domestic currency relative to anticipated value, prompts agents to hold less domestic currency and decreases the interest rate. This channel moderates the contraction of aggregate demand and, therefore, the reduction in output and price in the face of a positive exchange rate shock.
3) On the supply side, a positive shock to the exchange rate decreases the cost of imported intermediate goods, increasing domestic output and decreasing the cost of production and, hence, the aggregate price level.

Table 1 presents summary statistics for variables under investigation. Based on average time-series, the highest real growth is 5% for Libya and Pakistan, the highest inflation rate is 19% for Iran, the highest real consumption growth is 7% for Libya, the highest real investment growth is 6% for Pakistan, the highest real export growth is %5 for Pakistan, and the highest real import growth is 6% for Libya.

3. Empirical Model

The empirical investigation analyzes annual time-series data of real GDP growth in eight countries in the Middle East: Egypt, Iran, Jordan, Libya, Oman, Pakistan, Qatar, Syria, and Tunisia. Data, for the majority of tests, range from 1975-2003.

---

[3] Hanson (1983) provides theoretical evidence that the effect of currency depreciation on output depends on the assumptions regarding the labor market. Solimano (1986) studies the effect of devaluation by focusing on the structure of the trade sector. Agenor (1991) introduces a theoretical model for a small open economy and distinguishes between anticipated and unanticipated movement in the exchange rate. Examples of empirical investigations include Edwards (1986), Gylfason and Radetzki (1991), Roger and Wang (1995), Hoffmaister and Vegh (1996), Bahmani (1998), Kamin and Rogers (2000), and Kandil and Mirzaie (2002, and 2003).

[4] For an analytical overview, see Lizondo and Montiel (1989).

Table 1. Summary Statistics

a) Shares of FDI inflow to GDP (Numbers are in percentages)

	1990	1995	2000	2003	Average 1975-2003
Egypt	0.8	0.99	1.25	0.29	1.48
Iran	-0.44	0.02	0.04	0.09	0.09
Jordan	0.94	0.2	9.3	3.8	1.44
Libya	0.55	-0.27	-0.41	3	-0.6
Oman	1.22	0.21	0.08	0.64	1.33
Pakistan	0.61	1.14	0.5	1.91	0.57
Qatar	0.07	1.15	1.42	1.69	0.87
Syria	0.58	0.6	1.42	0.7	0.43
Tunisia	0.73	1.79	4	0.24	2.23

b) Means and Standard Deviations of dependent variables

	GDP		Price		Consumption	
	Growth	Inflation	Growth			
	Means	STD	Means	STD	Means	STD
Egypt	0.04	0.03	0.11	0.08	0.04	0.05
Iran	0.02	0.09	0.19	0.1	0.01	0.08
Jordan	0.04	0.05	0.06	0.06	0.04	0.11
Oman	0.03	0.07	0.06	0.13	0.02	0.16
Libya	0.05	0.05	0.04	0.13	0.07	0.12
Pakistan	0.05	0.02	0.08	0.03	0.05	0.03
Qatar	0.03	0.09	0.05	0.17		
Syria	0.04	0.06	0.1	0.08	0.02	0.11
Tunisia	0.04	0.02	0.06	0.06	0.05	0.03

	Investment		Export		Import	
	Growth		Growth		Growth	
	Means	STD	Means	STD	Means	STD
Egypt	0.03	0.2	0.01	0.09	0.01	0.18
Iran	0.04	0.35	0.02	0.17	0.04	0.31
Jordan	0.03	0.2	0.03	0.05	0.04	0.12
Oman	-0.04	0.41	0.01	0.14	0.02	0.04
Libya	0.04	0.24	0.03	0.09	0.06	0.13
Pakistan	0.06	0.04	0.05	0.08	0.04	0.05
Qatar			-0.004	0.12		
Syria	0.01	0.36	-0.05	0.39	0.02	0.15
Tunisia	0.03	0.22	-0.1	0.65	0.03	0.22

In the first step, we estimate an empirical model in which real GDP growth varies with real government spending, the money supply, the nominal exchange rate, the energy price, and foreign direct investment.

To formalize the investigation, we test real output growth for non-stationarity[5]. Given evidence of non-stationarity, the empirical model is specified in first-difference form as follows:

$$Dy_t = A_0 + A_1\, Dm_t + A_2 Dg_t + A_3 Dneer_t + A_4\, Dinflow_t + A_5 Do_t + A_6 DC_{t-1} + v_{yi} \quad (1)$$

Here, y_t is the log value of real output, where $D(.)$ is the first-difference operator. We denote the log values of the money supply, government spending, the nominal effective exchange rate, inflows of FDI, and the oil price by m_t, g_t, $neer_t$, *inflow*, and o_t. Since the model is estimated in first-difference form, we should test if the non-stationary dependent variable (y_t) is jointly cointegrated with all non-stationary right-hand side variables (in level form)[6]. Given evidence of cointegration (see Table A2), the error correction term is included in the empirical model.[7] The unexplained residual of the model is denoted by v_{yi}.

In the first model, real output varies with the growth in the money supply, real government spending, the nominal effective exchange rate, inflows and the energy price. If stabilization policies are effective real output varies positively with an increase in the money supply and/or government spending. An increase in the nominal exchange rate indicates currency appreciation. There are supply and demand channels that determine the response of real output to currency appreciation. On the supply side, currency appreciation decreases the cost of imported inputs and increases the output supply. On the demand side, currency appreciation decreases competitiveness and net exports. Also, on the demand side, currency appreciation may stimulate a reduction in money demand and an increase in velocity.[8] The final effect will depend on the dominant channel.

Channels determining the effect of inflows on real growth vary with the type of inflows. Initially, remittance inflows increase national savings. Their effect on real growth will depend, however, on their effects on demand composition. In one scenario, additional inflows maybe used to finance consumption spending. The initial increase in savings will be absorbed in consumption demand. If capacity constraints are binding, the increase in consumption will be inflationary with no effect on real growth. Moreover, the increase in consumption may stimulate an increase in imports. In another scenario, the increase in saving will finance an increase in investment, which contributes to real growth. The effects of FDI flows are

---

5 For details, see Kwiatkowski et al. (1992), which tests the null-hypothesis of stationarity. To select lags for the KPSS test, we follow the suggestions of Newey and West (1994). Non-stationarity indicates that the series follows a random walk process. Upon first-differencing, the resulting series is stationary. Table Al in the appendix summarizes the results of non-stationarity. The results are robust with respect to alternative tests for the null-hypothesis of non-stationarity.

6 In theory, real output is endogenous with respect to domestic and external variables that appear on the right-hand side. It is possible, therefore, that they have a common stochastic trend in the long-run.

7 As long as there exists at least one cointegrating vector, it is necessary to control for this long-run relationship in the empirical model using stationary data. The error correction term captures deviation around the long-run trend, i.e., the lagged value of the residual from regressing the non-stationary dependent variable on the non-stationary variables in the model. For details, see Pesaran, Shin, and Smith (2001).

8 For details, see Kandil and Mirzaie (2002).

expected, however, to aim more directly at relaxing capacity constraints and expanding real growth. Moreover, there may be a positive spillover effect of growth on the external sector, increasing exports and maybe imports. Nonetheless, structural constraints may prevent immediate results of FDI flows on real growth.

An increase in the oil price is likely to decrease consumption demand and increase the cost of production, shrinking the output supply. Many of the countries under investigation are oil-producing or neighboring countries. Hence, there may be a positive, direct or indirect, effect of an increase in the oil price on real growth.

To verify channels of interaction between inflows and the macroeconomy, it is necessary to test the effects of these inflows on price inflation and the growth in real components of aggregate spending. To that end, we substitute price inflation or the real values of components of demand for the dependent variable in equation (1). An increase in consumption in response to inflows may be inflationary, without a positive effect on real growth. In contrast, an increase in real investment and real exports are likely to stimulate real growth. Imports may increase with the increase in consumption and/or investment.

4. Empirical Results

Following our previous work (see Kandil and Mirzaie (2002, 2003, 2005)), the estimation methodology is described in Appendix A. The model equation is estimated using instrumental variables. In addition, the errors are assumed to be AR(1) and estimated accordingly.

The empirical investigation analyzes time-series data of real output growth, price inflation, the growth of real private consumption, real private investment, real exports and real imports in a sample of MENA countries. We summarize the results in Tables 2:7.

4.1. Results Explaining Real GDP Growth

The first empirical model, in Table 2, explains real GDP growth using domestic policy variables: the money supply and real government spending, the nominal effective exchange rate, FDI flows and the energy price.

Monetary policy appears to be ineffective to stimulate real output growth across countries. Two factors may explain the results. Many countries under investigation have been following a fixed exchange rate policy. Under such a policy, the priority of the central bank is devoted to defending the peg, eliminating any role for monetary policy to stabilize domestic conditions. Moreover, there may not be a scope for an independent monetary policy as the priorities of the Central Bank are devoted to providing domestic financing to the budget deficit.

The growth of government spending has a positive and significant effect that contributes to output growth in Oman and Pakistan. While the results for other countries are statistically insignificant, there is no evidence of a negative significant effect, ruling out the possibility of a dominant crowding out effect of government spending.

Table 2. 2SLS Parameter Estimates

Real GDP as a function of Money Supply, Real Government Spending, Nominal Effective Exchange Rate, Foreign Direct Investment, and Energy Prices								
	A0	A1	A2	A3	A4	A5	A6	RH0
Egypt								
	0.03	0.07	0.01	0.04	-0.01	-0.02		0.56**
	-1.1	-0.98	-0.54	-1.1	(-1.11)	(-1.31)		-3.1
	R-square: 0.41							
Iran								
	0.1	-0.11	0.09	0.06	0.0001	0.07	-C.4	0.55**
	-0.84	(-0.46)	-1.14	-0.84	-0.06	-1	(-1.69)	-2.57
	R-square: 0.51							
Jordan								
	0.03**	0.12	0.01	0.39**	0.003*	-0.001	-0.45**	-0.28
	-3.24	-0.92	-0.18	-2.99	-1.94	(-0.02)	(-2.58)	(-1.49)
	R-square: 0.67							
Libya								
	0.005	-0.02	0.13	-0.06	0.004	0.04	-0 71	-0.01
	-0.26	(-0.09)	-1.33	(-0.56)	-0.62	-0.65	(-1.10)	(-0.02)
	R-square: 0.37							
Oman								
	0.04**	0.08	0.21**	0.19*	-0.001	-0.04		0.16
	-3.84	-1.02	-2.79	-1.92	(-0.10)	(-1.36)		-0.96
	R-square: 0.68							

Table 2. (Continued)

Real GDP as a function of Money Supply, Real Government Spending, Nominal Effective Exchange Rate, Foreign Direct Investment, and Energy Prices								
	A0	**A1**	**A2**	**A3**	**A4**	**A5**	**A6**	**RH0**
Pakistan								
	0.03**	0.04	0.14**	0.03	0.001	0.004	-.026**	0.47**
	-2.53	-1.19	-2.61	-0.73	-0.02	-0.58	(-2.19)	-2.9
	R-square: 0.74							
Qatar								
	0.01	0.04	0.3	-0.09	-0.002	0.002	-0.31	0.42
	-0.28	-0.3	-1.33	(-0.23)	(-0.31)	-0.02	(-0.97)	-1.16
	R-square: 0.10							
Syria								
	0.05*	-0.1	0.12	-0.02	-0.0201	-0.34*	-0.1	
	-1.85	(-0.47)	-1.58	(-0.42)	(-1.16)	(-0.50)	(-1.83)	(-0.37)
	R-square: 0.34							
Tunisia								
	0.05**	0.03	-0.13	0.14	0.005	0.05**	0.04	-0.27
	-5.62	-0.41	(-1.28)	-1.23	-0.56	-2.24	-0.36	(-1.20)
	R-square: 0.49							

A0 Intercept
A1 Change in Money Supply
A2 Change in Real Government Spending
A3 Change in Nominal Effective Exchange Rate
A4 Change in Foreign Direct Investment
A5 Change in Energy Prices
A6 Error Correction
RH0 Serial correlation
** Significant at 5%.
* Significant at 10%.
t-ratios are in parenthesis

Appreciation of the exchange rate has a positive and significant effect that stimulates output growth in Jordan and Oman. Given high dependency on imports, exchange rate appreciation decreases the cost of imported inputs and increases the output supply. There is no evidence of a dominant contractionary effect of currency appreciation on real growth in any country.

With the exception of Jordan, there is no evidence of an increase in output growth with FDI flows. In the case of Jordan, the surge in FDI flows over time (see Table 1) has contributed to the growth of real output, attesting to the country's success to maximize the benefits of FDI flows. For other countries, failure to institute speedy reforms has hindered the success of FDI flows to stimulate real growth.

The change in energy price appears insignificant on output growth across countries. In the case of Tunisia, higher oil price stimulates real output growth. Higher oil price may carry a positive spill over effect on output growth in Tunisia, a non-oil producing country.

In three cases, Jordan, Pakistan, and Syria, the sign and significance of the error correction term indicates a tendency for the cointegrated variables in the model to converge towards full-equilibrium in the short-run.

4.2. Results Explaining Price Inflation

The first empirical model, in Table 3, explains the rate of inflation in the GDP deflator using domestic policy variables; the nominal effective exchange rate, FDI flows, and the energy price.

The inflationary effect of monetary policy is evident and significant in Iran and Tunisia. It is interesting to note the negative and significant effects of an increase in real government spending on price inflation in Egypt, Jordan, Pakistan, and Syria. This indicates that an increase in real government spending contributes to capacity building and moderates price inflation. In contrast, an increase in government spending stimulates price inflation in Iran. Higher government spending increases demand, which proved to be inflationary given capacity limitations in Iran.

An appreciation of the nominal effective exchange rate increases price inflation significantly in Libya. This may be the result of the effect of appreciation on money demand. Appreciation decreases money demand, increasing velocity and, therefore, price inflation. In contrast, price inflation decreases significantly with exchange rate appreciation in Iran, Oman and Syria. Currency appreciation decreases the cost of imports and price inflation.

In general, FDI flows do not increase price inflation. Nonetheless, all coefficients are not statistically significant, ruling out significant effects of FDI flows on the demand or supply sides. In Tunisia, however, there is a significant positive effect of FDI flows on price inflation, indicating a significant increase in demand.

Table 3. 2SLS Parameter Estimates

Price deflator as a function of Money Supply, Real Government Spending, Nominal Effective Exchange Rate, Foreign Direct Investment, and Energy Prices								
	A0	**A1**	**A2**	**A3**	**A4**	**A5**	**A6**	**RH0**
Egypt								
	0.13**	-0.002	-0.14**	0.06	-0.02	-0.04	-0.17**	0.7**
	-2.12	(-0.02)	(-4.14)	-1.2	(-1.35)	(-1.26)	(-2.19)	-3.91
	R-square: 0.80							
Iran								
	0.05*	0.55**	0.23	-0.09**	0.001	0.02	-1.06**	0.06
	-1.84	-3.29	-6.89	(-2.68)	-1.17	-0.53	(-5.28)	-0.46
	R-square: 0.92							
Jordan								
	0.04*	0.07	-0.15** -0.10	-0.022		0.50**		
	-1.75	-0.64	(-2.18)	(-0.99)	(-1.18)	(-0.53)		-3.48
	R-square: 0.65							
Libya								
	0.04*	0.23	0.43**	0.31**	-0.01	-0.18	-0.64**	0.02
	-1.73	-1.03	-3.57	-2.49	(-0.82)	(-1.58)	(-3.31)	-0.19
	R-square: 0.66							
Oman								
	0.01	0.03	0.16	-0.51**	-0.01	0.43**	-0.32	0.29**
	-0.19	-0.19	-1.11	(-2.63)	(-1.11)	-7.31	(-1.55)	-2.19
	R-square: 0.84							
Pakistan								
	0.07**	0.1	-0.27*	-0.02	0.1	-0.01		0.35
	-2.85	-1.05	(-2.02)	(-0.21)	-0.92	(-0.49)		-1.69
	R-square: 0.36							
Qatar								
	0.03	0.02	0.09	-0.17	0.01	0.55**		0.26*
	-1.12	-0.16	-0.5	(-0.52)	-1.23	-5.9		-1.81
	R-square: 0.76							

Table 3. (Continued)

Price deflator as a function of Money Supply, Real Government Spending, Nominal Effective Exchange Rate, Foreign Direct Investment, and Energy Prices								
	A0	A1	A2	A3	A4	A5	A6	RH0
Syria								
	0.10**	-0.03	-0.16**	-0.12*	0.0001	0.02	-0.70**	0.35
	-2.12	(-0.14)	(-2.29)	(-2.25)	-0.06	(0.36)(-3.15)	-1.63	
	R-square: 0.74							
Tunisia								
	0.01	0.44*	0.08	-0.2	0.05**	-0.01	-0.58*	0.01
	-0.21	-1.96	-0.31	(-0.82)	-2.47	(-0.24)	(-1.83)	-0.05

A0 Intercept
A1 Change in Money Supply
A2 Change in Real Government Spending
A3 Change in Nominal Effective Exchange Rate
A4 Change in Foreign Direct Investment
A5 Change in Energy Prices
A6 Error Correction
RH0 Serial correlation
** Significant at 5%.
* Significant at 10%.
t-ratios are in parenthesis

An increase in the energy price has a positive and significant effect on price inflation in Oman and Qatar. Higher energy price is consistent with an increase in foreign reserves, a higher standard of living, and, therefore, higher price inflation in oil-producing countries.

The negative and significant coefficient on the error correction term for Egypt, Iran, Syria, and Tunisia indicates fast convergence towards full-equilibrium following a shock in the short-run.

4.3. Results Explaining Consumption

Table 4 presents the results of the model explaining real private consumption, using domestic policy variables, the nominal effective exchange rate, FDI flows, and the energy price. Monetary growth increases liquidity to finance the increase in private consumption in Jordan only. In general, monetary policy is not an important policy tool to determine liquidity and private consumption in many MEN A countries.

The growth in government spending provides resources to finance private consumption in Iran, Libya, Oman, Pakistan, and Syria. Clearly, the increase in government spending (a dominant sector in production and employment) provides important resources to finance private consumption in several countries.

An increase in the nominal effective exchange rate increases consumption growth in Jordan. As many imported goods are used for consumption, the appreciation of the exchange rate decreases the cost of imports and increases private consumption significantly.

The change in FDI flows does not stimulate consumption spending in any country. FDI does not provide direct incentives to increase consumption demand.

There is an evidence of a significant effect of the change in energy price on consumption demand. Higher energy price increases final consumption, indicating inelastic demand.

The negative and significant coefficients on the error correction term for Iran, Jordan, Libya, Pakistan, and Syria indicates convergence towards full-equilibrium in the short-run for cointegrated variables in the model.

4.4. Results Explaining Investment

Table 5 presents the results of the model explaining real private investment, using domestic policy variables, the nominal effective exchange rate, FDI flows and the energy price. Consistent with the evidence for consumption, monetary growth does not determine variation in investment demand significantly. The change in government spending has a significant positive effect on private investment in Libya. Higher government spending may entail direct spending on investment or may entail an increase in income that finances private investment spending.

There is no evidence of a significant effect of the change in nominal effective exchange rate on private investment. The effect of the change in exchange rate on supply and demand does not determine investment growth significantly.

Table 4. 2SLS Parameter Estimates

Real Consumption as a function of Money Supply, Real Government Spending, Nominal Effective Exchange Rate, Foreign Direct Investment, and Energy Prices								
	A0	**A1**	**A2**	**A3**	**A4**	**A5**	**A6**	**RH0**
Egypt								
	0.03*	0.03	0.02	0.09	0.02	0.08**	-0.02	-0.27
	-1.86	-0.24	-0.63	-1.37	-1.39	-2.15	(-0.14)	(-1.28)
	R-square: 0.52							
Iran								
	0.08	-0.15	0.18**	0.1	0.001	0.05	-0.58**	0.33**
	-1.04	(-0.70)	-2.56	-1.64	-0.39	-0.86	(-2.94)	-1.77
	R-square: 0.58							
Jordan								
	0.02*	0.39**	0.09	1.23**	0.001	0.04	-0.71**	-0.62**
	-1.92	-2.69	-1.02	-6.17	-0.71	-0.88	(-3.42)	(-3.52)
	R-square: 0.87							
Libya								
	0.02	0.39	0.35**	0.13	0.01	-0.12	-1.12**	0.52*
	-0.35	-1.6	-2.6	-0.97	-1.2	(-1.02)	(-3.02)	-1.84
	R-square: 0.74							
Oman								
	0.04*	0.04	0.76**	0.05	-0.02	0.01	-0.69**	-0.14
	-2.02	-0.17	-4.22	-0.24	(-1.58)	-0.14	-2.64	(-0.05)
	R-square: 0.73							
Pakistan								
	0.02	-0.01	0.26**	-0.14	-0.01	0.02	-0.65**	0.36
	-1.35	(-0.15)	-2.16	(-1.54)	(-1.21)	-1.02	(-2.66)	-1.37
	R-square: 0.58							
Qatar								

Table 4. (Continued)

Real Consumption as a function of Money Supply, Real Government Spending, Nominal Effective Exchange Rate, Foreign Direct Investment, and Energy Prices								
	A0	**A1**	**A2**	**A3**	**A4**	**A5**	**A6**	**RH0**
Syria								
	0.05	-0.27	0.37**	-0.01	0	0.12	-0.42**	0.31
	-1.16	(-0.71)	-2.33	(-0.12)	(-1.24)	-1.57	(-1.80)	(-1.16)
	R-square: 0.46							
Tunisia								
	0.03	0.12	-0.06	0.07	0.01	0.06	-0.51	0.28
	-1.13	-0.77	(-0.40)	-0.46	-0.82	-1.4	(-1.37)	-0.91
	R-square: 0.31							

A0 Intercept
A1 Change in Money Supply
A2 Change in Real Government Spending
A3 Change in Nominal Effective Exchange Rate
A4 Change in Foreign Direct Investment
A5 Change in Energy Prices
A6 Error Correction
RH0 Serial correlation
** Significant at 5%.
* Significant at 10%.
t-ratios are in parenthesis

Table 5. 2SLS Parameter Estimates

Real Investment as a function of Money Supply, Real Government Spending, Nominal Effective Exchange Rate, Foreign Direct Investment, and Energy Prices								
	A0	**A1**	**A2**	**A3**	**A4**	**A5**	**A6**	**RH0**
Egypt								
	0.01	0.06	0.04	-0.27	-0.06	0.37**	-0.58	0.14
	-0.14	-0.1	-0.28	(-1.04)	(-0.93)	-2.2	(-1.04)	-0.27
	R-square: 0.34							
Iran								
	0.33	-0.82	0.55	-0.01	-0.003	0.44		0.43
	-0.56	(-0.72)	-1.56	(-0.04)	(-0.41)	-1.39		-0.87
	R-square: 0.40							
Jordan								
	0.004	0.58	-0.08	-0.12	0.002	0.16		-0.24
	-0.07	-0.97	(-0.19)	(-0.18)	-0.25	-0.81		(-0.95)
	R-square: 0.18							
Libya								
	-0.05	0.06	0.85*	0.33	0.001	0.54		-0.11
	(-0.55)	-0.06	-1.71	-0.67	-0.04	-1.23		(-0.51)
	R-square: 0.34							
Oman								
	0.03	0.12	0.54	0.83	-0.04	-0.07	-0.56	-0.11
	-0.5	-0.21	-1.08	-1.34	(-1.12)	(-0.43)	(-1.36)	(-0.22)
	R-square: 0.48							
Pakistan								
	0.04	0.17	-0.11	0.1	0.0002	0.03	-0.65**	0.36
	-1.21	-1.33	(-0.64)	-0.65	-0.01	-0.96	(-2.24)	-1.06
	R-square: 0.53							
Qatar								

Table 5. (Continued)

Real Investment as a function of Money Supply, Real Government Spending, Nominal Effective Exchange Rate, Foreign Direct Investment, and Energy Prices								
	A0	**A1**	**A2**	**A3**	**A4**	**A5**	**A6**	**RH0**
Syria								
	0.06	-0.08	0.59	0.27	-0.0004	-0.38	-0.81*	0.01
	-2.32	(-0.07)	-1.36	-0.77	(-0.89)	(-1.58)	(-2.03)	-0.01
	R-square: 0.46							
Tunisia								
	0.06	-0.14	-0.39	0.92	0.15**	0.28	-0.97*	0.14
	-0.61	(-0.18)	(-0.43)	-1.02	-2.05	-1.5	(-1.82)	-0.34
	R-square: 0.58							

A0 Intercept
A1 Change in Money Supply
A2 Change in Real Government Spending
A3 Change in Nominal Effective Exchange Rate
A4 Change in Foreign Direct Investment
A5 Change in Energy Prices
A6 Error Correction
RH0 Serial correlation
** Significant at 5%.
* Significant at 10%.
t-ratios are in parenthesis

An increase in FDI has a direct positive effect increasing private investment significantly in Tunisia. For other countries, FDI flows do not contribute significantly to private investment growth.

An increase in the energy price stimulates private investment demand significantly in Egypt. Higher energy price may stimulate additional investment in the oil sector in Egypt.

The negative and significant coefficient on the error correction indicates fast convergence towards full equilibrium in Pakistan and Tunisia.

4.6. RESULTS EXPLAINING EXPORTS

Table 6 presents the results of the model explaining real exports, using domestic policy variables, the nominal effective exchange rate, FDI flows, and the energy price. An increase in the money supply has a negative and significant effect on export growth in Syria. Monetary growth may be consistent with an increase in domestic demand that results in a switch in production towards non-tradables.

An increase in government spending provides the necessary support to the export sector in many countries. Indeed, higher government spending stimulates real export growth in Iran, Libya, Pakistan and Syria. In contrast, there is a negative and significant effect of an increase in government spending on export growth in Tunisia. Higher government spending raises the interest rate and the price level, crowding out private resources in the export sector.

Exchange rate appreciation decreases competitiveness and, therefore, export growth. This is evident by the negative and statistically significant coefficient in Egypt, and Syria.

There is no evidence that FDI flows have determined export growth significantly in any country. Clearly, FDI flows are not targeting the export sector.

An increase in the energy price stimulates export growth significantly in a number of countries: Egypt, Iran, Jordan, Oman, Qatar, Syria, and Tunisia. A number of these countries are oil-producing. Other countries may benefit indirectly from a boom in neighboring oil-producing countries, by boosting export growth. One exception is the case of Libya. An increase in the oil price has a negative statistically significant effect on export growth. Higher oil price may have an adverse effect, shrinking the non-oil export sector (the Dutch disease). The coefficient on the error correction term is negative and statistically significant in Libya, Syria, and Tunisia, indicating fast convergence towards full-equilibrium.

4.7. RESULTS EXPLAINING IMPORTS

Table 7 presents the results of the model explaining real imports, using domestic policy variables, the nominal effective exchange rate, FDI flows and the energy price.

Monetary growth does not determine import growth significantly. In contrast, the growth of government spending contributes to an increase in real imports in Egypt, Iran, Oman, and Pakistan. Higher government spending increases consumption and investment, increasing pressure on limited domestic resources.

Table 6.

Real Export as a function of Money Supply, Real Government Spending, Nominal Effective Exchange Rate, Foreign Direct Investment, and Energy Prices								
	A0	**A1**	**A2**	**A3**	**A4**	**A5**	**A6**	**RH0**
Egypt								
	-0.01	-0.17	0.2	-0.42*	0.05	0.48**		0.46**
	(-0.10)	(-0.31)	-1.47	(-1.78)	-0.9	-4.13		-2.37
	R-square: 0.62							
Iran								
	0.19	-0.7	1.19**	0.01	0.002	0.77**	-0.53	0.27
	-0.62	(-0.71)	-3.94	-0.03	-0.35	-2.76	(-1.38)	-0.97
	R-square: 0.65							
Jordan								
	0.02	0.27	0.25	-0.26	-0.002	0.19**		0.15
	-0.6	-0.95	-1.34	(-0.88)	(-0.42)	-2.21		-0.77
	R-square: 0.46							
Libya								
	-0.03	0.55	1.33**	0.31	-0.01	-0.47**	-0.61**	-0.05
	(-0.72)	-1.19	-5.08	-1.17	(-0.78)	(-2.11)	(-2.11)	(-2.11)
	R-square: 0.75							
Oman								
	0.01	0.34	0.41	0.11	0.01	0.49**		-0.12
	-0.27	-1.23	-1.64	-0.35	-0.91	-5.42		(-0.93)
	R-square: 0.82							
Pakistan								
	0.001	0.18	0.51**	-0.12	0.01	-0.01	-0.26	0.18
	-0.06	-1.34	-2.67	(-0.88)	-0.44	(-0.44)	(-1.25)	-0.89
	R-square: 0.57							
Qatar								
	0.01	-0.09	0.32	0.73	0.01	0.49**		0.004
	-0.29	(-0.41)	-0.99	-1.03	-1.34	-3.88		-0.02
	R-square: 0.63							

Real Export as a function of Money Supply, Real Government Spending, Nominal Effective Exchange Rate, Foreign Direct Investment, and Energy Prices

	A0	A1	A2	A3	A4	A5	A6	RH0
Syria								
	0.14	-0.83*	0.52**	-0.50**	-0.00001	0.36**	-0.70**	0.14
	-1.69	(-1.93)	-3.01	(-5.33)	(-0.09)	-4.74	(-2.92)	-0.92
	R-square: 0.79							
Tunisia								
	0.04	0.39	-1.03**	0.29	0.01	0.33**	-0.82**	0.37**
	-0.9	-1.46	(-2.96)	-0.88	-0.4	-3.78	(-3.13)	-2.45
	R-square: 0.56							

A0 Intercept
A1 Change in Money Supply
A2 Change in Real Government Spending
A3 Change in Nominal Effective Exchange Rate
A4 Change in Foreign Direct Investment
A5 Change in Energy Prices
A6 Error Correction
RH0 Serial correlation
** Significant at 5%.
* Significant at 10%.
t-ratios are in parenthesis

Table 7. 2SLS Parameter Estimates

Real Import as a function of Money Supply, Real Government Spending, Nominal Effective Exchange Rate, Foreign Direct Investment, and Energy Prices							
	A0	**A1**	**A2**	**A3**	**A4**	**A5**	**A6**	**RH0**
Egypt								
	-0.11	0.42	0.24**	0.03	0.10**	0.29**	-0.88**	0.36*
	(-1.45)	-1.04	-2.62	-0.15	-2.49	-3.26	(-5.15)	-1.82
	R-square: 0.75							
Iran								
	0.23	-0.65	1.27**	0.22	0.004	0.36*	-0.52	0.29
	-1.01	(-1.00)	-6.35	-1.34	-0.99	-1.88	(-1.57)	-1.37
	R-square: 0.74							
Jordan								
	0.06*	-0.08	0.23	0.43	-0.0001	0.24	0.25**	-0.004
	-2.77	(-0.28)	-1.28	-1.44	-0.01	-3.04	(-2.74)	(-0.01)
	R-square: 0.67							
Libya								
	0.01	-0.14	0.38	-0.12	-0.05**	0.16	-0.48	0.95
	-0.01	(-0.32)	-1.12	(-0.47)	(-2.94)	-0.7	(-1.19)	-1.6
	R-square: 0.74							
Oman								
	0.04	-0.11	0.70**	0.58*	-0.01	-0.06	-0.22	-0.003
	-1.3	(-0.40)	-3.01	-2.02	(-0.30)	(-1.01)	(-1.01)	(-0.01)
	R-square: 0.59							
Pakistan								
	0.001	-0.01	0.45*	-0.13	-0.02	0.05	-0.81*	0.45
	-0.03	(-0.06)	-1.94	(-0.72)	(-1.26)	-1.37	(-2.03)	-1.36
	R-square: 0.54							
Qatar								

Real Import as a function of Money Supply, Real Government Spending, Nominal Effective Exchange Rate, Foreign Direct Investment, and Energy Prices

	A0	A1	A2	A3	A4	A5	A6	RH0
Syria								
	0.07	-0.31	0.08	-0.12	-0.0003	0.28**	-0.56**	0.2
	-0.75	(-0.65)	-0.36	(-1.12)	(-1.35)	-3.14	(-2.19)	-0.66
	R-square: 0.56							
Tunisia								
	0.08	-0.06	-0.5	0.73*	0.05	0.37**	-1.22**	0.38**
	-1.22	(-0.18)	(-1.35)	-1.9	-1.64	-3.73	(-4.45)	-2.52
	R-square: 0.45							

A0 Intercept
A1 Change in Money Supply
A2 Change in Real Government Spending
A3 Change in Nominal Effective Exchange Rate
A4 Change in Foreign Direct Investment
A5 Change in Energy Prices
A6 Error Correction
RH0 Serial correlation

** Significant at 5%.
* Significant at 10%.
t-ratios are in parenthesis

The appreciation of the nominal effective exchange rate decreases the cost of imports. Indeed, appreciation has a positive and statistically significant effect on imports in Oman and Tunisia.

An increase in FDI flows has a positive and statistically significant effect on imports in Egypt. In Libya, where FDI flows have been negative (on average), imports have been increasing despite the reduction in FDI flows.

There is a strong positive effect of the increase in energy price on imports. This is evident by the positive and statistically significant effect in Egypt, Iran, Jordan, Syria and Tunisia. In oil-exporting countries, a higher oil price increases capacity for imports. In oil-importing countries, imports increase with the energy price.

There is a strong evidence of fast convergence towards full-equilibrium, as evident by the negative and statistically significant coefficients in Egypt, Jordan, Pakistan, Syria, and Tunisia.

5. Summary and Conclusion

We estimate empirical models that explain real output growth using domestic policies, the energy price, the exchange rate, and inflow of FDI. In general, the role of monetary growth appears rather limited. Monetary growth stimulates real output growth in Egypt and accelerates price inflation in Iran. Monetary growth does not stimulate, however, growth in specific components of aggregate demand.

The growth of real government spending appears more relevant to economic activity across MENA countries. Higher growth of government spending stimulates real output growth significantly in Jordan, Oman, and Pakistan. Real government spending contributes to productive capacity, moderating price inflation significantly in Egypt, Jordan, Libya, and Syria. Real government spending stimulates the growth of real private consumption significantly in Iran, Jordan, Libya, Oman, Pakistan, and Syria. The effect of real government spending appears less pronounced on private investment, increasing significantly in Libya only. Nonetheless, government spending contributes positively to export growth in Egypt, Iran, Jordan, Libya, Pakistan, and Syria. Imports also increase significantly with real government spending in Egypt, Iran, Jordan, Oman, and Pakistan.

Exchange rate appreciation decreases the cost of imports, increasing real output growth significantly in Jordan and Oman. Appreciation may increase or decrease price inflation. The former channel, as evident in Libya and Egypt, indicates a reduction in money demand and an increase in velocity. The reduction in price inflation, as evident in Iran, Oman, and Syria, indicates a reduction in the cost of imported inputs and an increase in output supply. Exchange rate appreciation, by decreasing the cost of imports, increases consumption significantly in Jordan and Tunisia. The impact of exchange rate fluctuations is less pronounced on investment growth. One exception is Tunisia where appreciation, by decreasing the cost of imported inputs increases investment demand. Appreciation has a negative and significant effect on export growth in Egypt, Jordan, and Syria. In contrast, appreciation increases import growth significantly in Oman and Tunisia.

FDI flows stimulate real output growth in Jordan and increase price inflation in Tunisia. FDI flows do not stimulate an increase in real consumption in any country; they increase investment significantly only in Tunisia. There is no evidence of a significant increase in export growth with FDI flows in any country. Imports increase significantly with FDI flows in one country, Egypt.

While the share of FDI flows remains very moderate, the evidence points to the potential positive effects of these flows on output growth. Moreover, sustaining FDI inflows may provide an incentive to improve domestic policies and strengthen macroeconomic fundamentals. As countries continue to search for means to supplement domestic resources, maximizing FDI flows should top the policy priority towards expanding productive capacity via long-term investment that provides its own financing.

The result indicates that exchange rate appreciation decreases competitiveness and, therefore, export growth. This is evident by the negative and statistically significant coefficient in Egypt, and Syria.

In Jordan, there is further support for the adverse effect of currency appreciation on real export growth. Higher appreciation decreases competitiveness and, therefore, export growth, as evident by the negative and statistically significant coefficient. In Tunisia, however, the positive and significant coefficient provides a sharp contrast. Exports appear inelastic, increasing (decreasing) with appreciation (depreciation). Other factors related to quality and market access may have dominated.

Exchange rate appreciation decreases the cost of imports, increasing real output growth significantly in Jordan and Oman. Appreciation may increase or decrease price inflation. The former channel, as evident in Libya and Egypt, indicates a reduction in money demand and an increase in velocity. The reduction in price inflation, as evident in Iran, Oman, and Syria, indicates a reduction in the cost of imported inputs and an increase in output supply. Exchange rate appreciation, by decreasing the cost of imports, increases consumption significantly in Jordan and Tunisia. The impact of exchange rate fluctuations is less pronounced on investment growth. One exception is Tunisia where appreciation, by decreasing the cost of imported inputs increases investment demand. Appreciation has a negative and significant effect on export growth in Egypt, Jordan, and Syria. In contrast, appreciation increases import growth significantly in Oman and Tunisia. In addition, the appreciation of the exchange rate reduces the cost of imported inputs and stimulates an increase in private investment in Tunisia.

The contrast in the evidence of the impact of exchange rate fluctuations on economic activity and the underlying channels highlight the pros and cons. Where the adverse effect on competitiveness prevails, targeted policies should be geared to preserve competitiveness and offset appreciation in the real exchange rate on account of high inflation. In contrast, where countries have benefited from exchange rate depreciation to increase capacity to export, a thorough evaluation of the export strategy still remains necessary to establish a forward looking approach for sustainable growth.

APPENDIX A: ECONOMETRIC METHODOLOGY

To account for endogenous variables in the empirical model (1), instrumental variables are used in estimation. The instrument list includes three lags of the growth rate of real government spending, the money supply, energy prices, the nominal exchange rate, FDI, nominal GDP and CPI. In a few cases, the number of lags has been modified until the estimation did converge. The chapter's evidence remains robust with respect to modifications that alter variables or the lag length in the instruments list.

Table A1. The KPSS Statistics for Null of Level Stationary (the 10% critical value is 0.347)

	LM Statistic (Bandwidth)+					
Countries	**GDP**	**Consumption**	**Investment**	**Export**	**Import**	**Price**
Egypt	0.68* (4)	0.45*(0)	0.44*(0)	0.45*(3)	0.40*(0)	0.66*(4)
Iran	0.59* (4)	0.28 (4)	0.71*(0)	0.54*(4)	0.46*(4)	0.57*(4)
Jordan	0.69*(4)	0.66*(4)	0.50*(4)	0.68*(4)	0.66*(4)	0.68*(4)
Libya	0.21 (3)	0.61*(3)	0.49* (0)	0.31 (4)	0.32 (4)	0.64*(4)
Oman	0.68* (4)	0.13 (2)	0.64*(4)	0.62*(4)	0.66*(4)	0.62*(4)
Pakistan	0.69* (4)	0.69*(4)	0.68*(4)	0.69*(4)	0.69*(4)	0.64*(4)
Qatar	0.69* (4)			0.16 (4)		0.71*(4)
Syria	0.66* (4)	0.41*(4)	0.29 (0)	0.60*(4)	0.41*(4)	0.64*(4)
Tunisia	0.68* (4)	0.69*(4)	0.59*(4)	0.66*(4)	0.65*(4)	0.67*(4)

Test description:

The KPSS (Kwiatowski, Phillips, Schmidt, and Shin) stationarity test procedure examines the null hypothesis of stationarity of a univariate time series. The KPSS test assumes that a time series variable X_t could be decomposed into the sum of a deterministic trend, a random walk, and a stationary error. Then the random walk term is assumed to have two components: an anticipated component and an error term. The stationarity of the error term is established by testing if the variance of the error is zero.

If the calculated lag truncation variable is greater than 0.463, we reject the null hypothesis of stationarity.

+ Bandwidth is specified using Newey-West using Bartlett Kernel. For detail see Newey-West (1994).

* The variable has a unit root.

Following the suggestions of Engle (1982), the results of the test for serial correlation in simultaneous equation models are consistent with the presence of first-order autoregressive errors. To maintain comparability, it is assumed in all models that the error term follows an AR(1) process. The estimated models are transformed, therefore, to eliminate any possibility of serial correlation. The estimated residuals from the transformed models have zero means and are serially independent. Moreover, the residuals are orthogonal to variables in the instruments list and right hand-side variables in the final empirical model.

APPENDIX B: DATA SOURCES

The sample period for the majority of tests ranges from 1975-2003.

1. Data Base: WEO

- Gross Domestic Product in Constant Prices.
- Gross Domestic Product in Current Prices.
- GDP Deflator.
- Private Consumption Expenditure.

- Gross Private Capital Formation.
- Export of Goods and Services.
- Import of Goods and Services.
- Consumer Price Index.
- Government Expenditures.
- Foreign Direct Investment, Inflow.

2. Data Base: IFTS

- Moncy.
- Nominal Exchange Rate.

3. Data Base: WDI2K5

- Energy Price: Crude Oil Dubai Prices.

Table A2: Cointegration Test Results (Continued)
ADF test statistics for the null hypothesis of non-stationary residuals.
Critical value at 10% = -2.61

Cointegration regression includes: Real value of the dependent variable, Money Supply, Real Government Spending, Nominal Effective Exchange Rate, Energy Price, and Inflow of Foreign Direct Investment

			t-Statistic (# of Lags)$^+$			
Countries	**GDP**	**Consumption**	**Investment**	**Export**	**Import**	**Price**
Egypt	-2.12 (0)	-6.87*(0)	-5.15*(0)	-2.50(3)	-6.99*(0)	-2.81*(0)
Iran	-4.67*(2)	-3.59*(2)	-5.06*(1)	-3.94*(0)	-3.19*(0	-3.76*(0)
Jordan	-2.86*(0)	-5.55*(0)	-2.11 (0)	-2.05(0)	-3.25*(0)	-1.44(0)
Libya	-4.44*(0)	-5.45*(1)	-2.37(8)	-4.46*(0)	-4.91*(0)	-3.76*(0)
Oman	-2.31(0)	-2.86*(0)	-3.83*(0)	-1.99(4)	-3.71*(0)	-3.28*(0)
Pakistan	-3.94*(7)	-4.62*(8)	-3.18*(3)	-3.70*(8)	-3.72*(0)	-2.17(0)
Qatar	-4.53*(7)			-2.26 (0)		-2.53(0)
Syria	-4.88*(7)	-4.00*(0)	-3.70*(0)	-3.70*(6)	-3.15*(0)	-3.06*(5)
Tunisia	-2.68* (0)	-4.30*(1)	-5.15*(0)	-3.31*(0)	-4.15*(0)	-3.51*(0)

Test Description:

If we have n endogenous variables, each of which is first-order integrated (that is, each has a unit root or stochastic trend or random walk element), there can be from zero to n-1 linearly independent cointegrating vectors. If there is one cointegrating equation, the regression models of the text include a lag of error correction term.

To check for cointegration, we apply the ADF unit root test to the residual from the cointegration regression in which the non-stationary levels of real and nominal consumption are regressed on the level of variables that enter the model.

* The results reject the null hypothesis of non-stationarity at the 10% level.

\+ The numbers in parentheses represent the lag lengths. The lag length is selected based on Schwartz Information Criteria (SCI) out of max lag of 12).

REFERENCES

Adams, Richard Jr., "Remittances and Poverty in Guatemala," *World Bank Policy Research Working Paper,* No. 3418.

Agarwal, Reene and Andrew W. Horowitz, "Are International Remittances Altruism or Insurance? Evidence from Guyana Using Multiple'-Migrant Households," *World Development* 30:2033'-2044.

Chami, Ralph, Thomas F. Cosimano, and Michael T. Gapen, "Beware of Emigrants Bearing Gifts: Optimal Fiscal and Monetary Policy in the Presence of Remittances," *IMF Working Paper,* (2006).

Chami, Ralph, Connell Fullenkamp, and Samir Jahjah, "Are Immigrant Remittance Flows a source of Capital for Development?" *IMF Staff Papers,* 52:55'-81, 2005.

Dixit, Avinash K., and Joseph E. Stigliz, "Monopolistic Competition and Optimum Product Diversity," *American Economic Review, Vol.* 67 (June), No. 3, 1977, pp. 297'-308.

Engle, R. R. "A General Approach to Lagrange Multiplier Model Diagnostics," *Journal of Econometrics,* (1982) 20, 83'-104.

Fujita, Masahisa, Paul Krugman, and Anthony J. Venables, *The Spatial Economy,* 1999, (Cambridge, Massachusetts: MIT Press). Gupta, Poonam, "Macroeconomic Determinants of Remittances: Evidence from India," *IMF Working Paper,* 05/224.

Hanson, Gordon H., "Should Countries Promote Foreign Direct Investment?" *G'-24 Discussion Paper Series,* (February) No. 9, (2001).

International Monetary Fund, *World Economic Outlook, April 2005: Globalization and External Imbalances,* World Economic and Financial Surveys, Washington D.C.: International Monetary Fund, (2005).

Kandil, Magda and Ida Aghdas Mirzaie, "The Effects of Exchange Rate Fluctuations on Output and Prices: Evidence from Developing Countries," *Journal of Developing Areas,* Vol. 38, no. 2, Spring 2005, pp. 189'-219.

Kandil, Magda and Ida Aghdas Mirzaie, "The Effects of Dollar Appreciation on Sectoral Labor Market Adjustments: Theory and Evidence," *The Quarterly Review of Economics and Finance,* Vol. 43, no. 1, (2003), pp. 89'-117.

Kandil, Magda and Ida Aghdas Mirzaie, "Exchange Rate Fluctuations and Disaggregate Economic Activity in the U.S.: Theory and Evidence," *Journal of International Money and Finance,* Vol. 21, no. 1, February 2002, pp. 1'-31.

Krugman, Paul, "Increasing Returns and Economic Geography," *Journal of Political Economy,* Vol. 99 (June), 1991, pp. 483'-99.

Lucas, Robert E. Jr., "Why Doesn't Capital Flow from Rich to Poor Countries?" *American Economic Review,* Vol. 80, No. 2, 1990, pp. 92'-96.

Lucas, Robert E. and Odel Stark, "Motivations to Remit: Evidence from Botswana," *Journal of Political Economy,* 93:901'-918, 1990.

McKenzie, David J., "Beyond Remittances: The Effects of Migration on Mexican Households," In *International Migration, Remittances and the Brain Drain,* edited by Caglar Ozden and Maurice Schiff. Washington D.C. and New York: The World Bank and Pal'-grave Macmillan, 2005.

Newey, Whitney and Kenneth West, "Automatic Lag Selection in Covariance Matrix Estimation," *Review of Economic Studies,* 61, pp. 631'-653.

Pesaran, M. H., Y. Shin, and R. J. Smith, "Bounds Testing Approaches to the Analysis of the Level Relationships," *Journal of Applied Econometrics,* Special Issue in Honour of J. D. Sargan on the theme "Studies in Empirical Macroeconomics," (eds) D. F. Hendry and M. H. Pesaran, 16, 289'-326.

Rodrick, Dani, "Policy Uncertainty and Private Investment in Developing Countries," *Journal of Development Economics,* Vol. 36, November, 1991.

Rodriguez'-Clare, Andres, "Multinationals Linkages and Economic Development," *American Economic Review,* Vol. 86, (September), 1996, No. 4, pp. 852'-73.

Taylor, J. Edward, "The New Economics of Labor Migration and the Role of Remittances in the Development Process," *International Migration,* (1999), 37: 63'-88.

UNCTAD (United Nations Conference on Trade and Development), *World Investment Report: The Shift Towards Services* (United Nations: New York and Geneva), 2004.

World Bank, *Global Economic Prospects: Economic Implications and Migration,* Washington, D.C.: The World Bank.

Yehoue, Etienee, "Clusters as a Driving Engine for FDI," IMF Working Paper, WP/05/193.

In: Exchange Rates: Policies, Effects and Fluctuations
Editor: Natalie B. Perkins, pp.75-97
ISBN: 978-1-61209-505-9
© 2011 Nova Science Publishers, Inc.

Chapter 4

MONETARY SHOCKS AND EXCHANGE RATES IN A WORLDWIDE ECONOMY DIVIDED IN NORTH-SOUTH AREAS: THE ROLE OF THE RAW MATERIALS TRADE FROM THE SOUTH TO THE NORTH

Juan Antonio Garcia-Cebro
and Ramón Varela-Santamaria
University of A Coruña, Spain

ABSTRACT

Within the framework of the classical North-South linkages, in this chapter, we analyze the role of imported raw materials from the South in the transmission of a Northern relative monetary shock to exchange rates changes and welfare. In this context, we find that a low substitutability between Northern inputs (labor) and imported raw materials from the South is a source of exchange rate volatility as well as differential welfare effects.

JEL Classification: F3; F4

Keywords: Exchange rates; Monetary shocks; Raw materials; North-South trade.

INTRODUCTION

The economic linkages North-South has been an issue studied since long because of its importance for the development of both North (developed countries) and the South (developing countries). According to the standard North-South model, developed among others by Findlay (1980), the cyclical fluctuations and growth in the South are determined primarily by the development in the North.

Over the past two decades, trade and financial linkages between the North and the South have become even much stronger. Understanding the implications of that worldwide economic structure is important for the design of macroeconomic policies and theoretical models. Deeper trade and financial integration between the North and the South can prompt faster cross-border transmission of the effects of economic policy changes. In this chapter, we are going to tackle those implications from the point of view of its impact on exchange rate changes and welfare.

Specifically, the objective of the chapter is to address the implications of a structure of trade North-South characterized by classical trade, according to which the South produces and exports to the North raw materials, where they are combined with Northern inputs to produce final or manufacturing goods to be exported to the world markets. In this traditional framework, the growth in the South is driven by the Northern demand for the Southern exports which are used as inputs in the Northern manufacturing sector. The growth spillovers across these regions are transmitted primarily through terms of trade fluctuations.

There are several more modern papers, for instance Kouparitsas (2001), attributing to that trade structure the strong contemporaneous correlations between the Northern industrial activity and the overall Southern economy activity. In a more recent paper, the results of Arora and Vamvakidis (2006) suggest that one percentage point increase in the U.S. growth is associated with an average of one percentage point increase in other industrial and developing countries. In the last few years, others authors have documented a certain change in the nature of North-South linkages, driven by the process of globalization (the phenomenon of rising international trade and financial flows). Thus, Akin and Kose (2007), instead of a unique North-South relation, consider the South composed by two groups of countries, the Emerging South (China, India, etc) and the Developing South. They find that the impact of the Northern economic activity on the Emerging South has declined during the globalization period (1986-2005). In contrast, the growth linkages between the North and Developing South have been rather stable over time.

That said, many raw materials continue to be important inputs for the efficient functioning of the Northern economy. Besides the importance of oil and gas, it is also necessary take into account the essential role of non-energy materials. Many of industrial minerals are essential for a wide range of Northern downstream industries. A few examples are: feldspar is used in the production of television and computer screens, car headlamps, and soda bottles; silica is used in products such as tableware, ornaments and wall and floor tiles; while talc can be used to improve the performance of biological wastewater treatment plants. In fact, metals are indispensable to Northern modern industrial activity as well as to the infrastructure and products used in daily-life. For instance, copper and aluminum are materials in cables that transport electrical power over great distances to the most remote locations, and zinc protects the steel infrastructure under all weather conditions. In addition, there are other metals which are necessary inputs for the development of a strategic industry in the North such as the high tech industry. In this way, we can mention products such as modern cars, flat-screen televisions, mobile phones in which production are used as inputs antimony, cobalt, lithium, tantalum, tungsten and molybdenum. In the same line, there are other high-tech metals also indispensable for producing other high-tech products: electric cars require lithium and neodymium, car catalysts platinum, solar panels use indium, gallium, and selenium, and new fuel-efficient aircraft rhenium alloys.

Other examples of high-tech raw materials and its applications are: gallium (thin layer photovoltaics, IC, and WLED), neodymium (permanent magnets, laser technology), indium (displays, thin layer photovoltaics), germanium (optical fiber cable, optical technologies), platinum (fuel cells, catalysts), tantalum (micro capacitors, medical technology), silver (RFID, lead-free soft solder), cobalt (lithium-ion batteries, synthetic fuels), palladium (catalysts, seawater desalination), titanium (seawater desalination, implants), copper (efficient electric motors, RFID), antimony (ATO, micro capacitors), chromium (seawater desalination, marine technologies), coltan (mobile phones batteries), etc.

The earlier list asserts the economic importance of imported raw materials from the South in the Northern economic future because they are basic inputs in many new products and services. In many cases, their rapid diffusion can drastically increase the demand for certain raw materials. The activity of Northern industrial sectors depends on an extraordinary variety of raw materials applications in industrial sectors, the technologies used there and the products they manufacture. Systemic advances are also possible when known technologies are used for new applications. Coping with and marketing new technologies is particularly important for industry and its global competitiveness.

The Northern economy is therefore highly dependent on imports from the South of many of those raw materials. The European Commission is aware of that in the latest raw materials report (June 2010), entitled Raw Materials Initiative. It highlights that the European Union depends to a very large extent on imports of all principal raw materials. The import dependency rate the raw materials ranges from 74 per cent for copper ore, 80 per cent for zinc ore and bauxite, 86 percent for nickel and 100 percent for minerals such as cobalt, platinum and chromium. In this same line, it is the report for the U.S Congress by Humphries (2010) referred to the rare earth elements (REEs). Some of the major end uses for REEs include, among others, use in automotive catalytic converters, phosphors in color television and flat panel (cell phones, portable DVDs, and laptops), permanent magnets and rechargeable batteries for hybrid and electric vehicles, and generator for wind turbines, and numerous medical devices. The United States was once self-reliant in domestically produced REEs, but over the past 15 years has become 100% reliant on imports, primarily from China because of lower-cost operations.

In general, many high-tech raw materials are found in countries of the South. Specifically, in China, besides REEs, there are high share of worldwide production in other elements (antimony, fluorspar, gallium, germanium, graphite, indium, and magnesium), Zambia is known for its copper mines, The Democratic Republic of Congo is particularly resource-rich (copper, cobalt, tin ore, and coltan), Brazil (niobium and tantalum), etc.

The objective of the chapter is to use the New Open Economy Macroeconomics Models methodology to assess the importance of the international trade pattern described above in the transmission mechanism of the monetary shocks to exchange rate changes and welfare. In order to reach that objective, in the chapter we develop a model that has two main backgrounds: firstly, the seminal paper by Obstfeld and Rogoff (1995), which is commonly recognized as the contribution that launched a new wave of research in an open economy characterized by imperfect competition, nominal rigidities and intertemporal framework with microfoundations. Secondly, the Garcia-Cebro and Varela-Santamaria's (2004) and (2007) models; in the later, it is studied the impact of a rise in the world price of imported raw materials (oil) on the small open economy exchange rate. So, it is different from the chapter model because the small open economy framework implies that, among other things, the raw materials price is exogenous and not endogenous as in this chapter model. In the former, the authors develop a model structured around that of Obstfeld and Rogoff but incorporating the idea of vertical specialization, studied empirically by Hummels et al. (2001). In order to take into account a relevant empirical feature, they assume that the North exports intermediate goods to the South, where they are assembled for producing final goods and re-exported them to world markets. This implies to locate steps of the production chain of the same product in the different countries in a specific direction. Hence the model of this chapter differs from the Garcia-Cebro and Varela-Santamaria's (2004) model in two main aspects: first, in the model of this chapter we treat to capture the influence of the classical North-South trade (the South exports to the North raw materials where they are used as inputs in the production process to produce final goods), focusing on the fact of that many of those raw materials are essential inputs to develop the Northern high tech industry. In contrast, in Garcia-Cebro and Varela-Santamaria (2004) it is introduced other relevant empirical feature of the recent international trade which implies intra-industry trade flows: a vertical integration where the South assembles components exported from the North and re-exported to world markets. Moreover, in the model of this chapter, we assume in the North a flexible production technology by considering CES production functions instead of Leontief production functions. This allows us to explore, in an explicit way, the role of the degree of substitutability between the Northern inputs (labor) and imported raw materials from the South in the impact of monetary shocks on exchange rate volatility and welfare. In this way, a relevant result of the model we develop in the chapter is that whether that substitutability is low (this is the empirically relevant case), a permanent Northern relative monetary expansion generates a magnified depreciation in its currency. This leads, in turn, to a greater differentiation in the welfare effect, benefiting in a larger degree to the South.

The chapter is structured as follows. In section 2 we develop the model through equations which describe the behavior of agents. In section 3 we define the steady state conditions whereas in section 4, in order to make easier a formal solution, we log-linearize the main equations. In sections 5 and 6 we solve the model finding the short and long term solutions for exchange rate and welfare after a relative permanent monetary shock. Finally, in section 7 we show a quantitative illustration of the model and section 8 concludes.

2. The Model

We consider a worldwide economy structured around of two countries of identical size: the North or domestic country and the South or foreign country. We assume that the world is populated by a continuum of agents (households and firms) on the interval [0,1] in such a way that agents belonging to the South are on the interval [0,1/2] and those of the North are located on the interval (1/2,1]. Each area or country is inhabited by a continuum of differentiated consumers and producers or firms. The pattern of international trade is characterized as follows. The Southern firms produce only differentiated raw materials z^*, $z^* \in [0,1/2]$, which are imported by Northern firms to produce, combined with domestic inputs (labor), differentiated final goods z, $z \in (1/2,1]$, being consumed by both Northern and Southern households.

2.1. Households

Households supply labor inputs to firms and the behavior of both is monopolistically competitive. Households everywhere in the world have the same preferences, which are defined over a final goods consumption index, real money balances, and effort expended in production. Let $C(z)$ be a Northern household's consumption of final good *z*. Then the consumption index, on which Northern utility depends, is given by

$$C = \frac{1}{(1/2)^{1/(\theta-1)}}\left[\int_{1/2}^{1} C(z)^{(\theta-1)/\theta}\, dz\right]^{\theta/(\theta-1)} \tag{1}$$

where the parameter θ is the price elasticity of demand faced by each monopolistic. It is required $\theta > 1$ to ensure an interior equilibrium with a positive level of output. Also, θ can be interpreted as the elasticity of substitution between two different final goods.

The Southern consumption index C^* is defined analogously (throughout, asterisks denote Southern variables). The Northern final goods price index, corresponding to equation (1), is

$$P = \frac{1}{(1/2)^{1/(1-\vartheta)}}\left[\int_{1/2}^{1} P(z)^{1-\theta}\, dz\right]^{1/(1-\theta)} \tag{2}$$

where $P(z)$ is Northern-currency price of final good *z*. (The expression for the Southern price index P^* is analogous).

Denoting by $P^*(z)$ the price of the same good in Southern currency, then the law of one price for every good leads to

$$P(z) = EP^*(z) \tag{3}$$

where E is the nominal exchange rate, defined as the Northern-currency price of the Southern currency.

Since we assume that both Northern and Southern' households have the same preferences, equation (3) implies that the final goods price indices are linked in the following way:

$$P = EP^* \tag{4}$$

In the model, there is no capital or investment, but we stress that these are not an endowment economies because the labor supplies are elastic. In fact, households maximize a utility function that depends positively on consumption (C) and real money balances (*M/P*), and negatively on work effort (labor supply), *L*. Thus the representative Northern household *i* has preferences given by the following utility function (Southern households have the same utility function):

$$U(i)_t = \sum_{s=t}^{\infty} \upsilon^{s-t} \left[\log C_s + \chi \lg\left(\frac{M_s}{P_s}\right) - \frac{k}{2} L(i)_s^2 \right] \tag{5}$$

where β, $0 < \beta < 1$, is the discount rate, and χ, k are positive parameters.

The Northern household's demand for final good *z* resulting from cost minimization is given by

$$C(z) = \left[\frac{P(z)}{P}\right]^{-\theta} 2C \tag{6}$$

So each Northern firm faces the constant-elasticity world demand curve:

$$Y_T^d(z) = \left(\frac{P(z)}{P}\right)^{-\theta} \left(\int_0^{1/2} 2C^* dz^* + \int_{1/2}^{1} 2C dz\right) = \left(\frac{P(z)}{P^*}\right)^{-\theta} 2C^W \tag{7}$$

being C^W world final goods consumption demand, which Northern firms take as given.

In the model we consider an integrated world capital market in which both North and South can borrow and lend. We suppose that the only traded asset is a riskless real bond, denominated in the composite consumption final good, denoting by *r* the real interest rate on bonds between periods *t* and *t+1*. Under these assumptions, the period budget constraint for a representative Northern household can be written in nominal terms as

$$P_t C_t + M_t + P_t B_t + P_t T_t = W_t L(i)_t + \pi_t + M_{t-1} + P_t (1 + r_{t-1}) B_{t-1} \tag{8}$$

The right-hand side of equation (8) indicates the sources of income of households: labor income (*WL*) with *W* denoting the nominal wage for each unit supplied of labor *L*, ownership of firms (π), holdings of nominal money balances entering period *t* (M_{t-1}), and income coming from the stock of bonds ($P_t(1 + r_{t-1})B_{t-1}$).

The left-hand side of equation (8) shows the allocation of the previous income: to finance consumption (*PC*), to hold money balances and bonds in period *t* (*M* and *PB*), and to pay lump-sum taxes (*PT*).

The representative Southern household has a similar budget constraint.

The first order conditions for the maximization problem (maximization of (5) subject to (8)), of Northern and Southern households are

$$C_{t+1} = \upsilon C_t (1 + r_t);\ C_{t+1}^* = \upsilon C_t^* (1 + r_t) \tag{9}$$

$$\frac{M_t}{P_t} = \chi C_t \frac{(1 + r_t)P_{t+1}}{(1 + r_t)P_{t+1} - P_t};\ \frac{M_t^*}{P_t^*} = \chi C_t^* \frac{(1 + r_t)P_{t+1}^*}{(1 + r_t)P_{t+1}^* - P_t^*} \tag{10}$$

$$\frac{W_t}{C_t P_t} = kL(i)_t; \quad \frac{W_t^*}{C_t^* P_t^*} = kL_t(i^*) \qquad (11)$$

Equations (9) are the standard first-order consumption Euler equations, which optimize the intertemporal consumption. Equations (10) denote the optimal money real balances held by households. Finally, equations (11) reflect the optimal labor supply; that is, the labor supply that ensures that the marginal disutility of effort equals the marginal utility from consuming coming from the revenue of an extra unit of work.

2.2. Firms

In the firm side, we consider two types of firms monopolistically competitive: the Northern firms produce final goods using Northern inputs (labor) and imported raw materials from the South, where they are produced using labor as the only production input. So the production function for Southern firms is

$$Y_I^*(z^*) = \alpha_I L^*(z^*) \qquad (12)$$

where α_I is a productivity parameter and L^* is the Southern labor employed in the production of raw materials z^* given by

$$L^*(z^*) = \frac{1}{(1/2)^{1/(\vartheta-1)}} \left[\int_0^{1/2} L(i^*, z^*)^{(\vartheta-1)/\vartheta} di^* \right]^{\vartheta/(\vartheta-1)} \qquad (13)$$

On the other hand, the production function of Northern firms (that produce final goods z) is

$$Y_T(z) = \alpha_T \left[\delta L(z)^{\frac{\sigma-1}{\sigma}} + (1-\delta) I(z)^{\frac{\sigma-1}{\sigma}} \right]^{\frac{\sigma}{\sigma-1}} \qquad (14)$$

where α_T is a productivity parameter, $1-\delta$ is the share of imported raw materials in the final goods production, and σ is the elasticity of substitution between Northern labor L and imported raw materials I, which are given by

$$L(z) = \frac{1}{(1/2)^{1/(\theta-1)}} \left[\int_{1/2}^{1} L(i, z)^{(\theta-1)/\theta} di \right]^{\theta/(\theta-1)} \qquad (15)$$

and

$$I(z)=\frac{1}{(1/2)^{1/(\theta-1)}}\left[\int_0^{1/2} Y_I^*(z^*,z)^{(\theta-1)/\theta}\,dz^*\right]^{\theta/(\theta-1)} \tag{16}$$

In this setup, the profit function of the Southern firms is

$$\pi_I^*(z^*)=P_I^*(z^*)Y_I^*(z^*)-W^*L^*(z^*) \tag{17}$$

The first-order condition gives us the optimal price set for raw materials z^*

$$P_I^*(z^*)=\frac{\theta}{\theta-1}\frac{W^*}{\alpha_I} \tag{18}$$

For the Northern firms, we have the following profit function:

$$\pi(z)=P(z)Y(z)-(WL(z)+P_I I(z)) \tag{19}$$

The optimal production techniques and prices lead to

$$\frac{W}{P_I}=\frac{\delta L^{-\frac{1}{\sigma}}}{(1-\delta)I^{-\frac{1}{\sigma}}} \tag{20}$$

and

$$P(z)=\frac{\theta}{\theta-1}\frac{1}{\alpha_T}\left[\delta^{\sigma}W^{1-\sigma}+(1-\delta)^{\sigma}P_I^{1-\sigma}\right]^{\frac{1}{1-\sigma}} \tag{21}$$

where $\theta(\theta-1)^{-1}$ represents the markup set by firms derived from their market power.

3. The Steady State

We shall denote the steady state's variables by an upper bar. As is usual, we assume in the steady state that all exogenous variables (including the money supply) are constant and wages and prices fully flexible. This implies that consumption is constant in both countries. Then, each country's intertemporal budget constraint requires that real consumption spending be equal to net real interest payments from abroad ($\bar{r}\bar{B}$ for the North, and $\bar{r}\bar{B}^*$ for the South) plus real added value in the each country's output $((\bar{P}(z)\bar{Y}_T-\bar{P}_I\bar{I})/\bar{P}$ for the North, and $(\bar{P}_I^*(z^*)\bar{Y}_I^*)/\bar{P}^*$ for the South):

$$\overline{C} = \frac{\overline{P}(z)\overline{Y}_T - \overline{P}_I \overline{I}}{\overline{P}} + \overline{r}\overline{B} = \frac{\overline{P}(z)}{\overline{P}}\overline{Y}_T - \overline{R}\overline{I} + \overline{r}\overline{B} \tag{22}$$

$$\overline{C}^* = \frac{\overline{P}_I^*(z^*)}{\overline{P}^*}\overline{Y}_I^* + \overline{r}\overline{B}^* \tag{23}$$

where R denote the terms of trade, given by

$$R \equiv \frac{P_I}{P} = \frac{P_I^*}{P^*} \tag{24}$$

The models of this type do not yield simple closed-form solutions for general paths of the exogenous shocks, because of monopoly distortions and endogenous output. For this reason, in order to show the intuition of its results, it is useful to study a linearized version around a well-defined steady state to which to approximate the changes of the endogenous variables. Thus we first need to find the aforementioned steady state that may be sufficient for illustrating the main points of the model. In this line, in order to simplify the derivation of a closed-form solution for the initial steady state, which we shall denote by subscript "0", we consider

$$\overline{B}_0 = \overline{B}_0^* = 0 \quad \text{and} \quad \overline{L}_0 = \overline{I}_0 = \overline{Y}_{I0}^* = \left(\frac{\overline{Y}_{T0}}{\alpha_T}\right) \tag{25}$$

Accordingly, from (18), (20), and (25), we can write:

$$\overline{P}_{I0}^* = \frac{\theta}{\theta - 1}\frac{\overline{W}_0^*}{\alpha_I} \tag{26}$$

and

$$\frac{\overline{W}_0}{\overline{P}_{T0}} = \frac{\delta}{(1-\delta)} \tag{27}$$

In turn, using equation (27) and the expression for optimal prices of final goods produced in the North, equation (21), we write that

$$\overline{P}_0 = \frac{\theta}{\theta - 1}\frac{\overline{W}_0}{\delta \alpha_T} \tag{28}$$

Also, by substituting equations (25) and (27) in equation (24), we obtain the terms of trade in the initial steady state:

$$\overline{R}_0 = \frac{(\theta - 1)(1 - \delta)}{\theta}\alpha_T \tag{29}$$

From the above equations, we can derive the expressions of steady state consumption. Namely, by making use of the initial steady state conditions, equation (25), and the cost minimization condition, equation (29), and by substituting the expressions of those equations in equations (22) and (23), one arrives at

$$\overline{C}_0^* = \frac{(\theta - 1)(1 - \delta)}{\theta}\overline{Y}_{T0} \tag{30}$$

and

$$\overline{C}_0 = \left(1 - \frac{(\theta - 1)(1 - \delta)}{\theta}\right)\overline{Y}_{T0} \tag{31}$$

So, in the initial steady state, world consumption is given by

$$\int_0^{1/2}\overline{C}_0^* dz^* + \int_{1/2}^{1}\overline{C}_0 dz = \frac{\overline{Y}_{T0}}{2} = \overline{C}_0^W \tag{32}$$

Finally, on the one hand, taking the Southern optimal labor supply, given by equation (11), in the particular initial steady state defined by (25), and taking into account (12) and (26), we have

$$\overline{L}_0^* = \left(\frac{\theta - 1}{k\theta}\right)^{1/2} \tag{33}$$

On the other hand, in the special initial steady state characterized by (25), the labor-leisure trade-off condition (11), which represents the optimal labor supply in the North, and introducing in it equations (28) and (31), yields the following closed-form solution

$$\overline{L}_0 = \left(\frac{(\theta - 1)\delta}{k(1 + (\theta - 1)\delta)}\right)^{1/2} \tag{34}$$

Equations (33) and (34) show that labor supply (and output) is lower than its competitive level (which is approached as $\theta \to \infty$) in both countries due to monopoly distortions. In addition, equation (34) also shows that the higher the share of imported raw materials from the South (the lower δ), the lesser Northern labor required to produce a given quantity of final goods output.

4. Log-Linearized Equations

We now log-linearize the model around the initial steady state to obtain the deviations from that situation brought about by a small permanent monetary shock. Those deviations, expressed as percentage changes from the baseline steady-state path, shall be denoted by hats. Thus, for any variable X, the deviation at the time *t* from the initial steady state is denoted by $\hat{X}_t, \hat{X}_t = dX_t / \overline{X}_0$, being $\overline{X}_0$ the initial steady-state value.

In the same way, for any variable X, the percentage change between the initial steady state and the new steady state (where all variables are adjusted) will be denoted by $\hat{\overline{X}}$, $\hat{\overline{X}} = d\overline{X} / \overline{X}_0$

In this section we won't check exhaustively the linearizations (which is done in Appendix).[1] It is only will be useful to do it with some of them.

One ease linearization is the one of the purchasing power parity. Because the law of one price holds for both final goods and raw materials, we have that changes in the final goods prices index, produced in the North, in the South are given by

$$\hat{\overline{P}}^* = \hat{\overline{P}} - \hat{\overline{E}} \tag{35}$$

On the other hand, Northern price index changes of the raw materials imported from the South can be expressed by

$$\hat{\overline{P}}_I = \hat{\overline{P}}_I^* + \hat{\overline{E}} \tag{36}$$

As regards the Euler equations [equation (9) for the North and its Southern counterpart] take the following log-linear form

$$\hat{\overline{C}} = \hat{C} + \frac{\overline{r}}{1+\overline{r}} \hat{r} \tag{37}$$

$$\hat{\overline{C}}^* = \hat{C}^* + \frac{\overline{r}}{1+\overline{r}} \hat{r}, \tag{38}$$

while log-linear versions of the labor-leisure trade-off [equation (11) for the North and its Southern counterpart] are

$$\hat{\overline{W}} - \hat{\overline{C}} - \hat{\overline{P}} = \hat{\overline{L}} \tag{39}$$

$$\hat{\overline{W}}^* - \hat{\overline{C}}^* - \hat{\overline{P}}^* = \hat{\overline{L}}^* \tag{40}$$

[1] Hereinafter, equation numbers containing an "A" are referred to Appendix.

Equations (10), which describe the optimal money demand, are approximated by

$$\hat{\bar{M}} - \hat{P} = \hat{C} - \frac{1}{\bar{r}}\left(\hat{\bar{P}} - \hat{P}\right) - \frac{1}{1+\bar{r}}\hat{r} \qquad (41)$$

$$\hat{\bar{M}}^* - \hat{P}^* = \hat{C}^* - \frac{1}{\bar{r}}\left(\hat{\bar{P}}^* - \hat{P}^*\right) - \frac{1}{1+\bar{r}}\hat{r} \qquad (42)$$

Note that if one subtracts equation (42) from eq. (41) and applies the purchasing power parity equation (35), the results is

$$\hat{\bar{M}} - \hat{\bar{M}}^* - \hat{E} = \hat{C} - \hat{C}^* - \frac{1}{\bar{r}}(\hat{\bar{E}} - \hat{E}) \qquad (43)$$

From the above equations, several points deserve to be noted: firstly, subtracting equation (38) from eq. (37), we have an important feature of the model:

$$\hat{\bar{C}} - \hat{\bar{C}}^* = \hat{C} - \hat{C}^* \qquad (44)$$

(44) says us that the relative consumption changes between countries are permanent; that is, the changes occurred in the time t they are maintained in the new steady state.

On the other hand, taking into account equation (37), we may write eq. (41) as[2]

$$\hat{C} = \hat{\bar{M}} - \hat{P} \qquad (45)$$

Likewise, doing the same for the counterpart Southern, equation (42) is written as

$$\hat{C}^* = \hat{\bar{M}}^* - \hat{P}^* \qquad (46)$$

Using equations (41) and (42) and taking into account eqs. (45) and (46), we derive a second important feature of the model:

$$\hat{E} = \hat{\bar{E}} \qquad (47)$$

Eq. (47) means that the behaviour of the exchange rate is the same in the moment of the shock that in the new steady state.

---

[2] From (41), we also can derive that $\hat{\bar{M}} - \hat{\bar{P}} = \hat{\bar{C}}$.

5. Monetary Shocks in the Long-Run and in the Short-Run

In the chapter we focus in the analysis of relative monetary shocks between the North and the South. In this framework, we consider that the Northern economy is affected at time *t* by an unanticipated permanent relative monetary shock in a such a way that $\hat{M} - \hat{M}^* > 0$. Specifically, we assume that $\hat{M} > 0$ and $\hat{M}^* = 0$. As in models of this type, we study the effects of those shocks in two temporal scenarios: starting from the initial steady state, once occurred the shock in a moment of period t, the short-run is the framework where the economies are subject to nominal rigidities. Following the notation used in the previous section, the effects of the shock on the variables extended on the short-run are denoted by hats, "^". In particular, following, for instance, Hau (2000), one first feature in the short-run is that wages are set for period t, so that

$$\hat{W} = \hat{W}^* = 0 \tag{48}$$

However, from period *t+1* on, wages can be adjusted and the economies come into a new steady state. The impact brought about by the shock between steady states (between the initial steady state and the new steady state) is marked by both hats and overbar; thus, for any variable X, $\hat{\bar{X}}$ denotes the change of X between the initial steady state and the new steady state.

After defining the short-run and the long-run, we can derive the implications of the short-run. Firstly, from (44), it is clear that in our model any shock has permanent effects on the difference between Northern and Southern per capita consumption; that is, that difference is the same in the short-run and in the long-run. Secondly, if consumption differential and money differential are both expected to be constant in the short-run and in the long-run, then agents must expect a constant exchange rate change as well. This is what is said in equation (47).

We next focus on the behavior of others key variables in the short-run. From (11A) and (48), we can write that $\hat{P}_I^*\left(z^*\right) = 0$, and taking into account (6A) we derive that

$$\hat{P}_I\left(z^*\right) = \hat{E} \tag{49}$$

Equation (49) says that, in the North, the price changes in the imported raw materials from the South depend only on the exchange rate movement. Therefore, in this scenario the exchange rate movements also determine the Northern production costs and, thereby the final goods price changes. Indeed, this can be seen from (12A), (48) and (49), by obtaining

$$\hat{P}(z) = (1-\delta)\hat{E} \tag{50}$$

and

$$\hat{P} - \hat{E} - \hat{P}_I^* = -\delta\hat{E} \tag{51}$$

Equation (50) shows that the final goods price changes come from exchange rate movements weighted by the share of imported raw materials from the South in the Northern production technology, $(1-\delta)$. On the other hand, equation (51) states that the depreciation of the Northern currency worsens its terms of trade, being the worsening more and more intense, the larger both that depreciation and the parameter δ.

One interesting question to be analyzed in the framework of the North-South integration assumed in this chapter is for what extent the movements in the exchange rate lead to international correlations of outputs. In our model, this can be seen taking equations (2A), (3A), (15A), (48) and (49) to derive that

$$\hat{Y}(z) - \hat{Y}_I^*(z^*) = \delta\sigma\hat{E} \tag{52}$$

In equation (52) we see that the impact of exchange rate movements on the international correlation of outputs is weighted by both the degree of substitutability by Northern inputs (σ) and the share of the imported raw materials in the production technology in the North, ($1-\delta$). Thus for a Leontief production technology ($\sigma = 0$), either exchange rate movement leads to a perfect international output correlation. In the other cases, in which the Northern production technology is more flexible, $\sigma > 0$, the exchange rate movement decreases the correlation the more and more the substitutability increases. In the same way, for some degree of technology flexibility, as the share of imported raw materials increases, it also increases the outputs correlation. In the extreme case where that share tends to be maximum, when δ tends to 0, the correlation also tends to be perfect. Therefore, the exchange-rate effect on international outputs correlation is larger, the smaller the substitutability and the larger the share are the imported raw materials from the South in the Northern production technology.

One further difference between the short-run and long-run is that in the period when a shock takes place, a country income need not equal expenditure, contrary to the long-run. Thus, while in the long-run the current accounts must be balanced, in the short-run however, the economies can run current-account imbalances, translating into changes in net foreign assets. One can ask what type of link there is between an exchange rate change, the international relative consumptions and the net foreign assets.

Making use of equations (4A), (18A), (19A), (49), (50) and (52), we obtain that relationship:

$$\hat{B} = -\frac{2(\theta-1)(1-\delta)}{\theta}\left(\left(1-\frac{(\theta-1)(1-\delta)}{\theta}\right)\left(\hat{C}-\hat{C}^*\right)+(1-\sigma)\delta\hat{E}\right) \tag{53}$$

Equation (53) shows the interplay between the change in the net foreign assets and the dynamics of both relative consumption and exchange rate. In turn, the relationship (53) can be simplified using equations which explain the behavior of home and foreign consumption in the long-run (equations (16A) and (17A)), as well as the fact that, according to equations (44) and (47), changes in both relative consumption and exchange rate are permanent. By doing so, we arrive at

$$\hat{C} - \hat{C}^* = \frac{\delta(\sigma - 1)(1 + \sigma)\theta\bar{r}}{(1 + \sigma)(\delta\vartheta + 2(1 - \delta)) + 2\sigma\vartheta\delta}\hat{E} \tag{54}$$

Equation (54) relates relative consumption changes to exchange rate changes. This relationship, which is so-called GG schedule, was derived using the short-run equilibrium conditions as well as the net asset positions changes, providing a crucial link between the short-run and long-run systems. The slope of the GG locus depends on whether the value of the elasticity of substitution of imported raw materials from the South exceeds or is below the unity. In eq. (54) the denominator is unambiguously positive. Instead, the numerator is positive only if σ is greater than one, thus indicating that a depreciation of the Northern currency would increase its relative consumption respect to the South. In that case, a Northern currency depreciation, which makes the imported raw materials from the South more expensive in terms of Northern currency, leads to a very intense use of the Northern labor in the production technology of final goods, and to a surplus in the Northern current account. This would mean that the substitution effect outweighs the negative income effect, and the rise in Northern price of imported raw materials would create a demand for Northern labor high enough to be able of increasing the Northern relative consumption. However, if σ were less than one, the negative income effect would dominate, the Northern economy would run a current account deficit, and the increase in the demand for Northern labor would not be high enough to offset the higher cost of imported raw materials, and thereby the Northern relative consumption would fall. Therefore, in the former case, where $\sigma > 1$, the GG locus would have a positive slope. In the later, with $\sigma < 1$, the slope would be negative.

In the money market side, we have already log-linearized the money demand equations to arrive to equation (43). Finally, taking the result (47) we can write eq. (43), which works as the money market equilibrium condition, in the following way:

$$\hat{E} = (\hat{\bar{M}} - \hat{\bar{M}}^*) - (\hat{C} - \hat{C}^*) \tag{55}$$

According to equation (55), a reduction in the relative Northern consumption leads also to a decline in its relative money demand. Therefore, for a relative money-supply given, the Northern relative price level must go up, implying a depreciation of the exchange rate. This negative relationship between the exchange rate changes and the relative consumption changes, for every relative money-supply given, is the so-called MM schedule, being its slope negative. It shifts up for every increase in the relative money-supply.

Since the schedules GG and MM give both two relationships between $\hat{E}$ and $\hat{C} - \hat{C}^*$, by combining them, we can obtain solutions jointly for $\hat{E}$ and $\hat{C} - \hat{C}^*$. The diagrammatic analysis can be seen in the diagram below

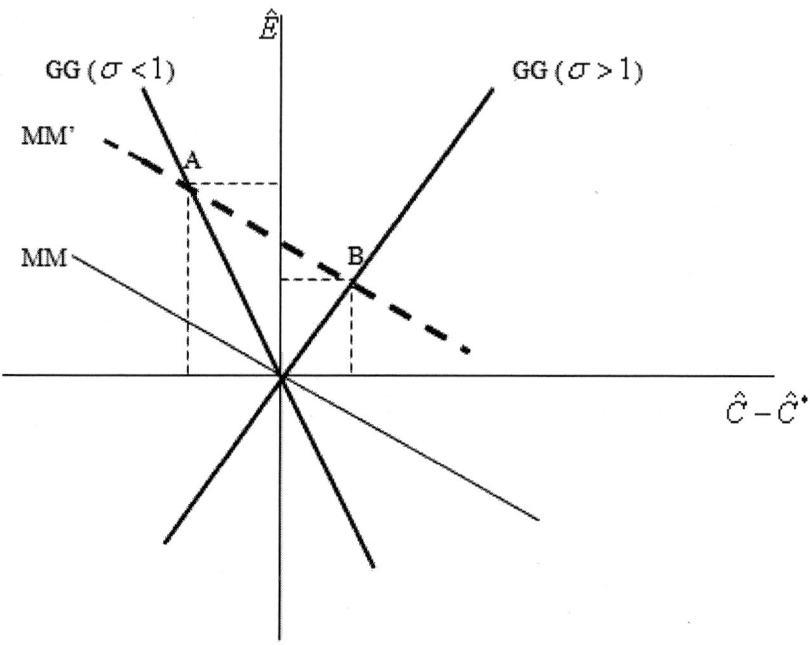

Figure 1. A Northern permanent relative monetary expansion.

In figure 1, the equilibrium exchange rate changes and consumption differential changes lie at the intersection of the MM and GG curves. The pre-shock equilibrium, where $\hat{\overline{M}}-\hat{\overline{M}}^*=0$, is in the coordinates origin, that is, where the MM curve intersects the GG curve. However, the post-shock equilibrium is given by the intersection of the MM' and GG curves. In this case, as one can see from that figure, the equilibrium lies at two possible points: points A and B. Of what does it depend that and what are the implications? That depends on the slope of the GG curve, which depends in turn (as was explained earlier) on whether the elasticity of substitution between imported raw materials from the South and Northern inputs is higher or lower than one. If, it is higher than one, as we saw before, the GG curve has positive slope, and an unanticipated permanent relative Northern money supply increase, which is graphically seen as a shift of the initial MM schedule to MM', leads the equilibrium to point B. This means that the Northern currency depreciates, but by an amount proportionally smaller than the increase in the relative Northern money supply. This is because, as was noted earlier and figure also shows, the Northern relative consumption must rise. However, if the slope of the GG curve is negative, which occurs when the elasticity of substitution between imported raw material from the South and Northern inputs (labor) is lower than one, the post-shock equilibrium is at point A. In that case, the Northern currency also depreciates, but by amount proportionally greater than the increase in the Northern relative money supply because, as we have also previously explained, in this case the Northern depreciation must lead to a decline in the Northern relative consumption.

Finally, in the case of $\sigma=1$ the GG schedule becomes a vertical curve and the exchange rate volatility reflects exactly the magnitude of the increase in the Northern relative money supply; that is, the Northern currency depreciates by an amount proportionally equal to the increase in the Northern relative money supply, without altering the current account and the Northern consumption.

Therefore, a low substitutability of imported raw materials from the South by Northern inputs introduces a source of greater volatility of the exchange rates, magnifying the impact of the relative monetary shocks.

In algebraic terms, we find those solutions for $\hat{E}$ and $\hat{C}-\hat{C}^*$ solving the equations system (54) and (55) to obtain:

$$\hat{E} = \Lambda\left(\hat{\bar{M}} - \hat{\bar{M}}^*\right) \tag{56}$$

and

$$\hat{C} - \hat{C}^* = (1-\Lambda)(\hat{\bar{M}} - \hat{\bar{M}}^*) \tag{57}$$

where

$$\Lambda = \frac{(1+\sigma)[1-\delta+(\delta\theta+1-\delta)\bar{r}]+2\sigma\theta\delta}{(1+\sigma)[1-\delta+(\sigma\delta\theta+1-\delta)\bar{r}]+2\sigma\theta\delta}$$

It is obvious to see in Λ that when $\sigma \geq 1$ then $\Lambda \leq 1$ and thereby, in (56) and (57), it verifies that $\dfrac{\hat{E}}{(\hat{\bar{M}} - \hat{\bar{M}}^*)} \leq 1$ and $\dfrac{\hat{C} - \hat{C}^*}{(\hat{\bar{M}} - \hat{\bar{M}}^*)} \geq 0$.

In contrast, if $\sigma < 1$ we see that $\Lambda > 1$, which leads in (56) and (57) to

$$\frac{\hat{E}}{(\hat{\bar{M}} - \hat{\bar{M}}^*)} > 1 \text{ and } \frac{\hat{C} - \hat{C}^*}{(\hat{\bar{M}} - \hat{\bar{M}}^*)} < 0$$

6. WELFARE

The asymmetric money shocks between the North and the South engender effects not only on the exchange rate but also, through the exchange rate effects, on welfare. The exchange rate changes have effects on outputs, current account balance, and the terms of trade. This affects consumption and agents' work effort and thereby utility. To assess these effects formally and see how overall utility changes, we log-linearize the intertemporal utility function (5), focusing on the "real" components because the term which depends on real money balances seems to have effects on utility empirically small. In addition, although the permanent monetary shock has intertemporal effects on consumption and outputs, we take into account the fact that the new steady state is reached after just one period. Therefore, the change in both Northern and Southern residents' lifetime welfare due to consumption and output changes is given by

$$dU = \hat{C} - k\overline{L}_0^2\hat{L} + \frac{1}{\overline{r}}\left(\hat{\overline{C}} - k\overline{L}_0^2\hat{\overline{L}}\right) \tag{58}$$

$$dU^* = \hat{C}^* - k\overline{L}_0^{*2}\hat{L}^* + \frac{1}{\overline{r}}\left(\hat{\overline{C}}^* - k\overline{L}_0^{*2}\hat{\overline{L}}^*\right) \tag{59}$$

From (33) and (34), and using the expressions of $\hat{\overline{C}}, \hat{\overline{C}}^*, \hat{\overline{L}}, \hat{\overline{L}}^*$, which were obtained from equations system, we can write the difference $dU - dU^*$ as a function of the exchange rates movement in the following way:

$$dU - dU^* = -\Pi\hat{E} \tag{60}$$

where

$$\Pi = \frac{(1+\sigma)(1+r)(2\theta-1)\left(\frac{\sigma(\theta-1)}{(2\theta-1)} + \frac{\delta\theta^2}{(2\theta-1)} - \delta\sigma\right)}{\theta(\sigma+1)\left[(\delta\theta+1-\delta)r+1-\delta\right]+2\delta\theta^2\sigma}$$

In the expression of Π, we can see that the denominator is unambiguously positive. So the sign of Π depends only on the sign of its numerator: Only for (counterfactually) high enough values of σ and δ, that numerator would be negative which would imply that a depreciation of the Northern currency ($\hat{E} > 0$) would lead to a relative increase of the Northern welfare respect to that one of the South ($dU - dU^* > 0$). However, in the other (more factual) cases, that is, when the value of the elasticity of substitution of the imported raw materials from the South is not very high, and/or the share of those raw materials in the Northern production technology is not very small, the numerator of the expression Π is positive. This means that the depreciation in the Northern currency has a more positive impact on the Southern welfare than on the Northern welfare, $dU - dU^* < 0$. This is because in this later case, there is a worsening in the Northern terms of trade.

On the other hand, equation (60) states that the exchange rate changes have a proportional impact on utility differentials. Thus exchange rate changes induced by relative money supply changes have first-order effect on welfare differentials. Therefore, those factors that magnify or amplify the exchange rate changes, they also do it with welfare differentials. In particular, given a permanent relative monetary expansion in the North, the lower the substitutability in the North of imported raw materials from the South, the higher the relative (respect to the North) welfare beneficial effect in the South. We already have seen earlier that when that elasticity of substitution is less than one, the depreciation in the Northern currency leads to a decrease in the relative Northern consumption in both the short-run and the long-run.

7. A QUANTITATIVE ILLUSTRATION

The objective of this section is to assess the sensitivity of the main results to the values of the parameters. To this end, following the literature we next choose values for the parameters. The steady state interest rate is determined by the parameter β , for which, following Betts and Devereux (2000), we choose $\beta = 0.94$ to produce a steady-state real interest rate of six percent. As regards the parameter θ, following Rotemberg and Woodford (1992) we set $\theta = 6$, which corresponds to an average markup of 1.2. On the other hand, according to Betts and Devereux we assume a unitary value for the elasticity of labor supply. In the framework of that base case, we assume a Northern relative monetary shock consisting, as in Tille (2001), in a unitary monetary expansion in the North, and we want to report the sensitivity of results for a range of values of the substitutability of imported raw materials from the South. Figures 2 and 3 illustrate the sensitivity of exchange rate changes and welfare differentials for a range of substitutability in the North of Southern inputs (raw materials).

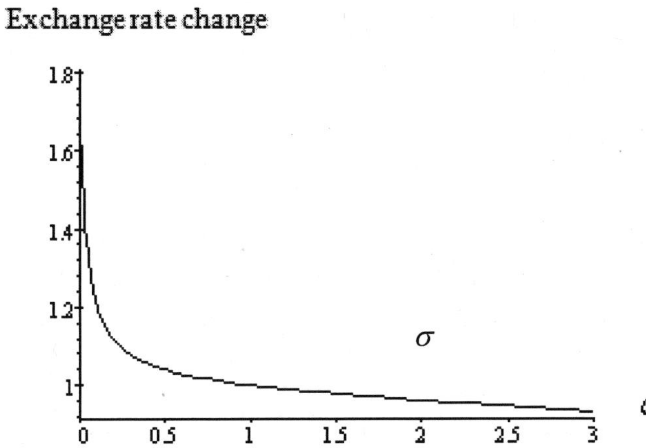

Figure 2. Exchange rate changes and the degree of substitutability of row materials.

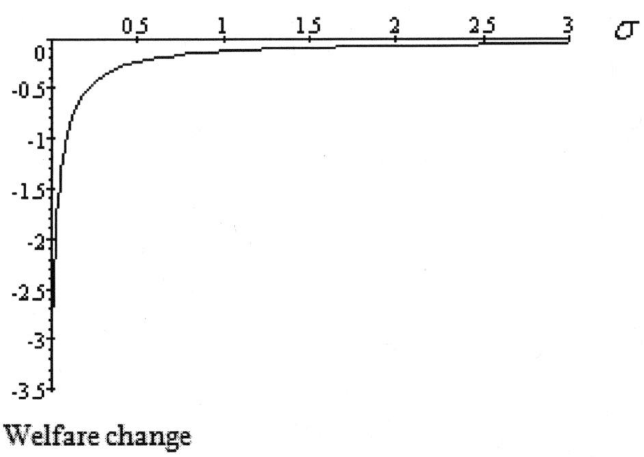

Figure 3. Differential welfare changes and the degree of substitutability of row materials.

In figure 2, we show the response of the exchange rates after a Northern permanent unitary relative monetary expansion. To put the role of the substitutability of the Southern raw materials into perspective, figure 2 plots the exchange rate changes as a function of σ. In generating the plot, δ is set to 0,7, following Campa and Golbert (2006). As can be seen from that figure, as σ rises from 0 the depreciation of the Northern currency becomes smaller, but its magnitude will stay above the magnitude of the monetary shock until σ reaches 1, where the percentage depreciation equals exactly the percentage increase of the Northern relative monetary expansion. In fact, taking, following Campa and Golberg (2006), $\sigma = 0.3$, a percentage increase of a 1 percent in σ would reduce the depreciation in 0.07 percent. Under the same parameter combination, in figure 3 we derive that the welfare differential would increase a 0.70 percent. So, as long as the values of σ lie between 0 and 1, an increase in the Northern relative monetary expansion leads to a magnified depreciation of the Northern currency as well as to become greater the beneficial effect for the South. However, when σ overcomes 1 figure 2 shows that the exchange rate depreciation is slightly smaller than the Northern relative money supply change, and at the same time that the beneficial effect for the South it is reduced (figure 3).

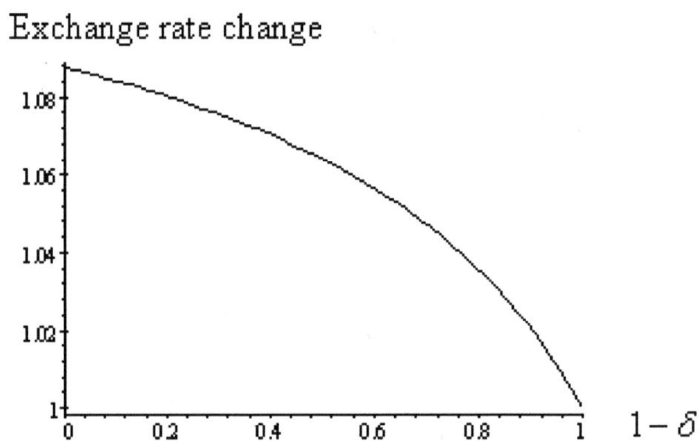

Figure 4. Exchange rate changes and the share of row materials.

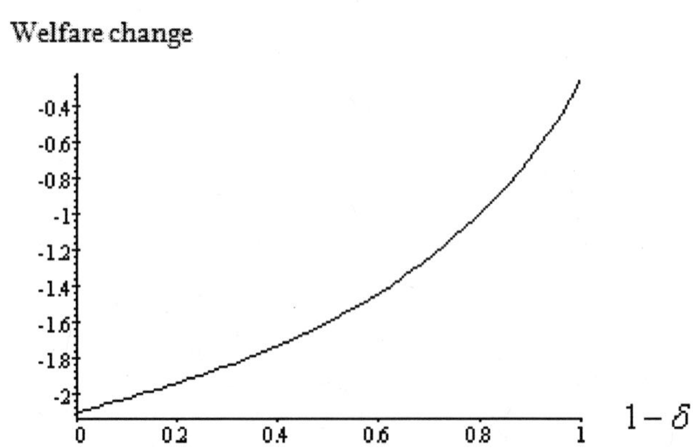

Figure 5. Differential welfare changes and the share of row materials.

Finally, figures 4 and 5 illustrate numerically the influence of the share of imported raw materials in the Northern production technology. In this case, we set $\sigma = 0.3$ in the base case and we plot the exchange rate changes and the welfare differentials after the Northern relative monetary shock as a function of the possible values of $1-\delta$. In those figures, one can see that the increase in that share, by reducing the worsening of the Northern terms of trade, leads both to smaller depreciation of the Northern currency and to smaller beneficial effect favorable to the South. In fact, from $1-\delta = 0.3$ (following Campa and Goldberg, 2006), we find that an increase of 1 percent of $1-\delta$ becomes smaller the Northern currency depreciation in 0.014 percent. In turn, this leads to reduce the utility differential in 0,17 percent.

CONCLUSION

In the framework of the classical North-South trade, the main finding of the model we developed in this chapter is that the low substitutability of the imported raw materials in the Northern production technology is a source of exchange rate volatility as well as of unequal distribution of welfare of a Northern permanent relative monetary expansion. In fact, it is obtained than the lower substitutability, the higher the Northern currency depreciation and the greater the beneficial effect of the South respect to the North. We have focused in this result because of the increasing importance of the imported raw materials from the South for the growth of the Northern new high tech industry.

APPENDIX

Log-Linearized Equations

$$\frac{dY_{It}^{*}}{\overline{Y}_{I0}^{*}} = \frac{dL^{*}}{\overline{L}_{0}^{*}} \qquad (1A)$$

$$\frac{dY_{Tt}}{\overline{Y}_{T0}} = \delta \frac{dL_t}{\overline{L}_0} + (1-\delta)\frac{dI_t}{\overline{I}_0} \qquad (2A)$$

$$\frac{dY_{It}^{*d}(z^{*})}{\overline{Y}_{I0}^{*}} = \frac{dI_t}{\overline{I}_0} \qquad (3A)$$

$$\frac{dY_{Tt}^{d}(z)}{\overline{Y}_{T0}} = \frac{dC_t^{W}}{\overline{C}_0^{W}} \qquad (4A)$$

$$\frac{dP_t}{\overline{P}_0}=\frac{dE_t}{\overline{E}_0}+\frac{dP_t^*}{\overline{P}_0^*} \qquad (5A)$$

$$\frac{dP_{It}}{\overline{P}_0}=\frac{dE_t}{\overline{E}_0}+\frac{dP_{It}^*}{\overline{P}_{I0}^*} \qquad (6A)$$

$$\frac{dC_{t+1}}{\overline{C}_0}=\frac{dC_t}{\overline{C}_0}+\frac{\overline{r}}{1+\overline{r}}\frac{dr_t}{\overline{r}} \qquad (7A)$$

$$\frac{dC_{t+1}^*}{\overline{C}_0^*}=\frac{dC_t^*}{\overline{C}_0^*}+\frac{\overline{r}}{1+\overline{r}}\frac{dr_t}{\overline{r}} \qquad (8A)$$

$$\frac{dM_t}{\overline{M}_0}-\frac{dP_t}{\overline{P}_0}=\frac{dC_t}{\overline{C}_0}-\frac{1}{\overline{r}}\frac{dP_{t+1}}{\overline{P}_0}+\frac{1}{\overline{r}}\frac{dP_t}{\overline{P}_0}-\frac{1}{1+\overline{r}}\frac{dr_t}{\overline{r}} \qquad (9A)$$

$$\frac{dM_t^*}{\overline{M}_0^*}-\frac{dP_t^*}{\overline{P}_0^*}=\frac{dC_t^*}{\overline{C}_0^*}-\frac{1}{\overline{r}}\frac{dP_{t+1}^*}{\overline{P}_0^*}+\frac{1}{\overline{r}}\frac{dP_t^*}{\overline{P}_0^*}-\frac{1}{1+\overline{r}}\frac{dr_t}{\overline{r}} \qquad (10A)$$

$$\frac{dP_{It}^*(z^*)}{\overline{P}_{I0}^*(z^*)}=\frac{dW_t^*}{\overline{W}_0^*} \qquad (11A)$$

$$\frac{dP_t(z)}{\overline{P}_0(z)}=\delta\frac{dW_t}{\overline{W}_0}+(1-\delta)\frac{dP_{It}}{\overline{P}_{I0}} \qquad (12A)$$

$$\frac{dW_t}{\overline{W}_0}-\frac{dC_t}{\overline{C}_0}-\frac{dP_t}{\overline{P}_0}=\frac{dL(i)_t}{\overline{L}_0} \qquad (13A)$$

$$\frac{dW_t^*}{\overline{W}_0^*}-\frac{dC_t^*}{\overline{C}_0^*}-\frac{dP_t^*}{\overline{P}_0^*}=\frac{dL^*(i^*)_t}{\overline{L}_0^*} \qquad (14A)$$

$$\frac{dI_t}{\overline{I}_0}=\frac{dL_t}{\overline{L}_0}+\sigma\left(\frac{dW_t}{\overline{W}_0}-\frac{dP_{It}}{\overline{P}_{I0}}\right) \qquad (15A)$$

$$\frac{d\vec{C}_t}{\overline{C}_0}=\frac{1}{\left(1-\frac{(\vartheta-1)(1-\delta)}{\vartheta}\right)}\left(\frac{d\overline{Y}_{Tt}}{\overline{Y}_{T0}}-\frac{(\vartheta-1)(1-\delta)}{\vartheta}\left(\frac{d\overline{I}_t}{\overline{I}_0}+\frac{d\overline{R}_t}{\overline{R}_0}\right)+\overline{r}\frac{d\overline{B}}{2\overline{C}_0^W}\right) \qquad (16A)$$

$$\frac{d\vec{C}_t^*}{\overline{C}_0^*} = \frac{d\overline{Y}_{It}^*}{\overline{Y}_{I0}^*} + \frac{d\overline{R}_t}{\overline{R}_0} + \bar{r}\frac{\vartheta}{2(\vartheta-1)(1-\delta)}\frac{d\overline{B}^*}{\overline{C}_0^W} \tag{17A}$$

$$\frac{dB_t}{\overline{C}_0^W} = 2\left[\frac{dP_t(z)}{\overline{P}_0(z)} + \frac{dY_{Tt}(z)}{\overline{Y}_{T0}} - \frac{dP_t}{\overline{P}_0} - \frac{(\vartheta-1)(1-\delta)}{\vartheta}\left(\frac{dI_t}{\overline{I}_0} + \frac{dR_t}{\overline{R}_0}\right) - \left(1 - \frac{(\vartheta-1)(1-\delta)}{\vartheta}\right)\frac{dC_t}{\overline{C}_0}\right] \tag{18A}$$

$$\frac{dB_t^*}{\overline{C}_0^W} = \frac{2(\vartheta-1)(1-\delta)}{\vartheta}\left(\frac{dP_{It}^*(z^*)}{\vec{P}_{I0}(z^*)} + \frac{dY_{It}^*}{\overline{Y}_{I0}^*} - \frac{dP_t^*}{\overline{P}_0^*} - \frac{dC_t^*}{\overline{C}_0^*}\right) \tag{19A}$$

REFERENCES

Akin, Ç. and M.A. Kose, 2007, "Changing Nature of North-South Linkages: Stylized Facts and Explanations", *IMF Working Paper 280*

Arora, V. and A.Vamvakidis, 2006, "The Impact of U.S. Economic Growth on the Rest of the World: How Much does it Matter?", *Journal of Economic Integration*, 21, 21-39.

Betts, C., and M.B. Devereux, 2000, "Exchange Rate Dynamics in a Model of Princing-to-Market", *Journal of International Economics*, 50, 215-244.

Campa, J.M. and L.S. Goldberg, 2006, "Distribution Margins, Imported Inputs, and the Sensitivity of the CPI to Exchange Rates", NBER working paper 12121

European Commission, 2010, "Critical Raw Materials for the EU", *Raw Materials Initiative.*

Findlay, R., 1980, "The Terms of Trade and Equilibrium Growth in the World Economy", *American Economic Review*, 10, 291-299.

Garcia-Cebro, J.A. and R. Varela-Santamaria, 2004, "Vertically Integrated North-South Trade and the Redux Model", *Review of International Economics*, 12, 643-661.

Garcia-Cebro, J.A. and R. Varela-Santamaria, 2007, "Raw Materials Price Changes and Exchange Rates in a Small Open Economy", *Economics Letters*, 95, 132-139.

Hau, H., 2000, "Exchange Rate Determination: The Role of Factor Price Rigidities and Nontradables", *Journal of International Economics*, 50, 421-448.

Hummels, D., J. Ishii, and K-M. Yi, 2001, "The Nature and Growth of Vertical Specialization in World Trade", *Journal of International Economics,* 54, 75-96.

Humphries, M.. 2010, "Rare Earth Elements: The Global Chain", *CRS Report for Congress,* R41347, *Congressional Research Service.*

Kouparitsas, M.A., 2001, "Evidence of the North-South Business Cycles" *FRBC Working Paper* 96-9.

Obstfeld, M. and K. Rogoff, 1995, "Exchange Rate Dynamics Redux", *Journal of Political Economy*, 103, 624-660.

Rotemberg, J. and M. Woodford, 1992, "Oligopolistic Pricing and the Effects of Aggregate Demand on Economy activity", *Journal of Political Economy*, 100, 1153-1207.

Tille, C., 2001, "The Role of Consumption Substitutability in the International Transmission of Monetary Shocks", *Journal of International Economics*, 53, 421-444.

In: Exchange Rates: Policies, Effects and Fluctuations
Editor: Natalie B. Perkins, pp. 99-113
ISBN: 978-1-61209-505-9
© 2011 Nova Science Publishers, Inc.

Chapter 5

FOREIGN EXCHANGE RATE EXPOSURE OF CHINESE FIRMS IN THE NEW EXCHANGE RATE REGIME

Aline Muller[1], Robin Luo[2*] and Alireza Tourani-Rad[3]
[1] HEC Management School, University of Liège, Belgium
Nijmegen School of Management, Radboud University, The Netherlands
[2] Department of Research & Development, China Chengxin International Credit Rating Co., Ltd., China
[3] School of Business, Auckland University of Technology, New Zealand

ABSTRACT

The purpose of this chapter is to investigate the foreign exchange rate exposure of Chinese firms in the managed floating system after China announced this regime switch on 21st July 2005. The sample includes 1,448 Chinese listed firms in the Shanghai Stock Exchange (SHSE) and Shenzhen Stock Exchange (SZSE) during the period of 22nd July 2005 – 18th October 2006. In addition to the analysis of the foreign exchange exposure on the firm level, we intend to shed more light on the cross-sectional distributions of exchange rate exposures of Chinese firms by share classes and ownership structures.

JEL Classifications: C32, G14, G15

Keywords: China, Exchange Risk, Exposure, Renminbi.

[*] Corresponding author: Professor Robin Luo, FRM
Department of Research & Development, China Chengxin International Credit Rating Co., Ltd.
12th Floor, Tower D, Beijing Merchants International Financial Center, No.156 Fuxingmennei Avenue, Beijing, 100031, China.
Phone: Tel: +86 10 66428877. Fax: +86 10 6642 6100. E-mail: robin.h.luo@gmail.com

1. INTRODUCTION

It has been more than three years since China reformed her exchange rate regime on July 21, 2005, by moving into a managed floating exchange rate regime based on market supply and demand with reference to a basket of currencies. The exchange rate of the Renminbi (RMB) against the U.S. dollar was adjusted to 8.11 yuan per US dollar at the announcement day and it would no longer be pegged to the U.S. dollar. The change from a highly stable exchange rate regime to a managed floating regime was associated with an increase in exchange rate variability. RMB has been appreciated over 15% during 2005-2008 since the announcement released on 21st July 2005. This regime swift motivates us to study the time-varying relationship between exchange rate and stock price at the individual firm level in the Chinese equity markets. It also provides us a good event window to undertake this analysis as the de facto fixed RMB exchange rate between 1994 and 2005 made it an impossible mission.

Unlike what happened in China, the adoption of floating exchange rate by many countries after 1970s led to enlarging exchange rate volatility. As recent international financial events have demonstrated, an exchange rate crisis could be induced in some emerging markets that adopted the floating exchange rate regime recently and it can expand quickly into a broader financial and economic crisis. The rapid expansion of exchange crises reflects the importance of the exchange rate to firm profitability and its stock value. Exchange rate volatility affects firms' value through many ways. First, it affects directly those firms with financial assets and debts denominated in foreign currencies and those with foreign operational cash flows. Moreover, it influences the value of firms with no foreign currency revenues through its impact on domestic macroeconomic conditions. Therefore, a relatively wide range of firms could be exposed to the movements in foreign exchange rates, regardless of their direct transactional and operational exposure.

As a major source of macroeconomic uncertainty affecting firms, the exchange rate volatility and the impact of foreign currency exposure on the firm value have been studied extensively in a large number of theoretical literature for several decades. (Shapiro, 1975; Hodder, 1982; Adler and Dumas, 1984) A decent number of empirical literature has also emerged in the past two decades. Seminal studies include Booth and Rotenberg (1990) and Jorion (1990). Booth and Rotenberg (1990) analyze the relationship between the foreign currency exposure and the Canadian dollar/US dollar exchange rate using a sample of Canadian firms. A decent number of empirical studies examine the sensitivity of US firms to changes in exchange rate. Jorion (1990) investigates the sensitivity of US multinationals to changes in a trade weighted index and provides weak evidence of exchange rate exposure. Other studies however report that neither U.S. multinationals nor the largest U.S. exporters are significantly affected by contemporaneous exchange rate movements (see, e.g. Amihud, 1994; Bodnar and Gentry, 1993; Bartov and Bodnar, 1994).

The only exception among this bunch of studies is Choi and Prasad (1995). One possible explanation for these ambiguous results is the fact that corporations make extensive use of foreign currency derivatives that may have reduced the ability of these studies to identify a significant contemporaneous correlation between stock returns and exchange rate fluctuations. Bartov and Bodnar (1994) attribute the failure of previous studies to provide strong support for the exchange rate exposure to sample selection procedures and investors' errors in estimating the relationship between contemporaneous exchange rate movements and the changes in firm performance. In a more recent study, Nguyen and Faff (2003) achieve a degree of success in providing empirical evidence in support of the hypothesis that the use of foreign currency derivatives reduces short-term exchange rate exposure of Australian companies. However, foreign currency derivatives appear to be less effective in hedging exchange rate risks in the long run.

The empirical studies on other countries show ambiguous picture. The Australian stock market is analyzed in Loudon (1993), Khoo (1994) and Iorio and Faff (2000). Both Loudon (1993) and Khoo (1994) fail to establish a robust sensitive relationship between the stock returns and changes in the exchange rate. The results are consistent with those reported weak evidence of exchange rate exposure in the US equities market. However, Iorio and Faff (2000) analyze the foreign exchange exposure of the Australian equities market using an augmented market model and found stronger evidence of exposure based on daily data. A stronger lagged response than contemporaneous response and some evidence of significant exchange rate exposures of the predicted sign in several industries have also been observed.

The Japanese stock market has been explored by He and Ng (1998). In a sample of 171 Japanese multinationals they find that about 25 percent of their stock returns experienced economically significant positive exposure effects for the period 1979 to 1993. They also check the determinants of foreign currency exposure. Highly leveraged firms or firms with low liquidity are likely to have smaller exposures. Foreign exposure is found to increase with firm size. Dominguez and Tesar (2003) find a statistically significant and robust level of exposure in their eight-country sample. Those eight industrialized and emerging markets are Chile, France, Germany, Italy, Japan, Netherland, Thailand and UK. They also find that the exposure is more prevalent in small sized firms than in large and medium sized firms and in firms engaged in international activities, although which firms are affected by movements in the exchange rate and the direction of exposure depends on the specific exchange rate. Muller and Verschoor (2006a, 2006b) study 817 European firms quoted in a European stock market and 3,634 Asian firms listed in Hong Kong, Indonesia, South Korea, Malaysia, Philippines, Singapore and Thailand during the period between 1988 and 2002 and report that more than 42 percent of European firms and 61 percent of Asian firms are significantly affected by foreign currency fluctuations in the long-term.

Bodnar, Dumas and Marston (2002) develop a duopoly model of an exporting firm and to explain simultaneously the behavior of the prices of goods and the profits for a firm that competes with a local firm in a foreign market. BDM models define a structural relation between a firm's pass-through decision and its resulting exchange rate exposure and provide a framework for determining if estimates of exposure are sensible. Allayannis and Ihrig (2001) develop a theoretical model that identifies three channels of exposure. These channels are a positive effect through the competitive structure of the destination markets, a positive effect through the interaction of the competitive structure of the export market and a negative effect through the interaction of the competitive structure of the imported input market and the share of production that is imported.

As far as we know, no literature has touched the foreign exchange exposure issue in the Chinese equity market. The major reason is that there is nonsense to conduct such a research within a de facto fixed exchange rate regime which China implemented between 1994 and 2005. The change from a highly stable exchange rate regime to a managed floating regime and the resulting volatile currency movements could be an important source of macroeconomic uncertainty for Chinese public listed firms with foreign trade or financial relationships to the rest of the world. Empirical studies demonstrate that the rise in the volatility of exchange rates – and the subsequent increase in uncertainty and risk - has significant consequences on trade flows.[1] We expect that the increased exchange rate variability in the new managed floating regime altered the trade terms between China and her trading partners. The lesson we have got from the recent financial crises is that currency crişis has led an increase in the observed volatility of financial markets and capital flows around the world. This motivation has led academics and investors to re-evaluate the impact of (increased) exchange rate fluctuations on stock markets.[2]

The contribution of this chapter is as follows. First, we explore the time-varying relationship between the RMB exchange rate and the Chinese stock return at the individual firm level. The empirical analysis investigates whether the enhanced uncertainty about the exchange rate of RMB resulted into an increased stock return variability. We expect an increase of the stock return variability under the new managed floating regime. Using a sample of 1,448 public listed firms, 815 in Shanghai A-share market, 53 in Shanghai B-share market, 525 in Shenzhen A-share market, and 55 in Shenzhen B-share market, we find evidence for the significant foreign currency exposure effects for the managed floating period, which is from 22 July 2005 to 18 October 2006. Second, we compare the exposure patterns of A- and B-shares in both Shanghai and Shenzhen markets. Last but not least, this chapter investigates the relationship between the ownership structure and the exchange exposure of Chinese listed firms.

The remainder of the chapter is organized as follows. Section 2 illustrates the institutional background on the three classes of shares in the China's stock markets and ownership structure of the listed companies. Section 3 describes data and the methodology used in this study. It also provides summary statistics of the data. Section 4 reports and discusses the empirical results. Section 5 offers some concluding remarks.

2. Institutional Background

China's equity markets have attracted investors' attention because of that country's fast development and potential opportunities. China's recent remarkable aggregate economic growth rates, averaging 9% since 1990, have been accompanied by similar growth in its equity markets. However, China's stock markets are unusual in comparison with others in the world due to the complicated share classes and ownership structure.

2.1. Background of A- , B- and H-Shares

A-shares and B-shares are two classes of common shares issued by Chinese firms and listed in both Shanghai Stock Exchange (SHSE) and Shenzhen Stock Exchange (SZSE).[3] In the early years of A-shares being traded on both markets, China's government intended to

---

[1] Rahmatsyah, Rajaguru and Siregar (2002) provide an extensive discussion of this literature.

[2] For example, see Bartov et al. (1996), Chen and So (2002), Chang (2002), Bin, Blenman and Chen (2004).

[3] The Shanghai Stock Exchange (SHSE) and the Shenzhen Stock Exchange (SZSE) began operations at 19 December 1990 and 3 July 1991, respectively.

insulate the A-share prices from the influence of foreign capital while meeting the demand of foreign exchange for local firms. Therefore the government established the B-share market especially for foreign investors in February 1992. The trading activity and liquidity of B-shares had been much lower than that of A-shares until the restriction on B-share market was removed in February 2001. China Securities Regulatory Commission (CSRC) introduced the Qualified Foreign Institutional Investor (QFII) in 2002 and QFIIs are allowed to invest the A-shares within a certain quota. A-shares are domestic shares priced in RMB in both SHSE and SZSE. B-shares in the SHSE are denominated in the U.S. dollar while the B-shares in the SZSE are priced in the Hong Kong dollar. Chinese investors have been permitted to trade B-shares in either the U.S. dollar in the SHSE or the Hong Kong dollar in the SZSE since the China Securities Regulatory Commission (CSRC) removed the restriction in February 2001.

One additional class of common shares is H-share. A limited number of the listed companies issue H-shares to Hong Kong investors and H-shares are traded on the Hong Kong Stock Exchange (HKSE) subject to the Hong Kong listing rules. Although the three classes of shares are entitled to exactly the same voting and dividend rights and obligations, they follow the different accounting standards. The annual reports for A-shareholders follow the Chinese GAAP while the companies issuing B-shares or H-shares are also required to prepare another set of reports based on International Accounting Standards (IASs) for B-shareholders and H-shareholders. They had been traded at significantly different prices with a substantial price discount for B- and H-shares before 2000. (Zhang and Zhao, 2003).

2.2. Background of Ownership Structure

Chinese listed firms have a rather complicated ownership structure in which the shares are classified into state-owned shares, legal-person shares, and tradable shares. All shares carry the same voting rights but the first two categories are not traded in the equity markets. Tradable shares are accounting for about one-third of total shares in issue and are divided into A-shares, B-shares and shares listed in the overseas market. State-owned shares are normally held by government agencies or wholly state-owned enterprises (SOEs). The wholly state-owned enterprises are the firms in which the state totally controls. Normally SOEs are owned by the central, provincial, district, or county government. Legal-person shares are further broken down into domestic legal-person shares, foreign legal-person shares and other legal-person shares. Both state-owned shares and legal-person shares were not tradable before 2005. Chinese government has recently allowed some companies to convert their nontradable shares through the state and institutions to become tradable shares, hoping to unify the fragmented Chinese market and have one type of shares that are gradable. In August 2005, The CSRC encouraged all nontradable shares in listed companies on the stock exchanges to change into tradable shares.[4] The reforms allow the Chinese government to reduce its shareholdings to facilitate further privatization.

[4] See Financial Times, August 22, 2005.

3. Data and Methodology

3.1. Data and Summary Statistics

We use daily stock returns for 1,448 Chinese firms traded on the Shenzhen Stock Exchange (SZSE) and the Shanghai Stock Exchange (SHSE) over the period of July 2005 to October 2006. Returns data were obtained from Datastream and CSMAR database.[5] CSMAR is also used to determine the firm's share classes, industry classification, and the ownership

Table 1. Daily average stock price returns and foreign exchange rate changes during the July 2005 – October 2006 period

Industry (code)	N	Mean	S.D.	Min	Max
Panel A: All Firms					
Finance (1)	10	0.001803	0.049366	-0.321580	0.219084
Utilities (2)	108	0.001048	0.043355	-0.39416	0.872909
Properties (3)	47	0.001742	0.044759	-0.37318	0.159126
Conglomerates (4)	244	0.001601	0.050806	-0.58603	0.352668
Industrials (5)	929	0.001696	0.051839	-0.682131	0.826136
Commerce (6)	109	0.00179	0.046691	-0.353154	0.612705
Not specified (0)	1	0.001177	0.02087	-0.19477	0.054822
Total	1448	0.001644	0.050549	-0.682131	0.872909
Panel B: Shanghai Stock Exchange					
Finance (1)	7	0.001877	0.025972	-0.321580	0.219084
Utilities (2)	67	0.001081	0.026368	-0.39416	0.872909
Properties (3)	25	0.001767	0.027319	-0.37318	0.097202
Conglomerates (4)	172	0.001032	0.025635	-0.58603	0.097815
Industrials (5)	531	0.001754	0.028933	-0.682131	0.826136
Commerce (6)	65	0.001855	0.027525	-0.353154	0.612705
Not specified (0)	1	0.001177	0.02087	-0.19477	0.054822
Total	868	0.001688	0.028501	-0.682131	0.872909
Panel C: Shenzhen Stock Exchange					
Finance (1)	3	0.00163	0.080959	-0.121192	0.190362
Utilities (2)	41	0.00992	0.061768	-0.273149	0.190140
Properties (3)	22	0.001714	0.058585	-0.202971	0.159126
Conglomerates (4)	72	0.001545	0.082237	-0.453385	0.352668
Industrials (5)	398	0.001619	0.071803	-0.392979	0.370966
Commerce (6)	44	0.001694	0.065433	-0.193701	0.214781
Not specified (0)	0	N/A	N/A	N/A	N/A
Total	580	0.001579	0.071858	-0.453385	0.370966
Panel D: Foreign exchange rate and market indexes					
MSCI world		0.000509	0.005634	-0.01823	0.020724
SHSE A		0.001724	0.012042	-0.05509	0.041951
SHSE B		0.002306	0.018242	-0.08619	0.092132
SZSE A		0.001955	0.013191	-0.06057	0.043565
SZSE B		0.001491	0.016169	-0.05872	0.077251
Exchange Rate ($\times 10^{-4}$)		-0.08276	0.508138	-1.53965	2.543017

[5] Datastream is an online database distributed by Datastream International and is updated daily. CSMAR is a database of financial data and marketing data of China's capital market, which was developed by GTA information technology according to the international standards of database.

Table 2. The ownership structure statistics

Panel A: share outstanding			
		Number	Percentage
Number of non-negotiable shares / Total number of shares	0 - 25%	12	0.87%
	25% - 50%	228	16.55%
	50% - 75%	1059	76.85%
	75% - 100%	79	5.73%
Number of negotiable A shares / Total number of negotiable shares	0 - 25%	43	3.12%
	25% - 50%	51	3.70%
	50% - 75%	25	1.81%
	75% - 100%	1259	91.36%

	Mean	**S.D.**	**Min**	**Max**
Panel B: Number of shareholders				
Number of shareholders / Total number of shares ($\times 10^{-4}$)	0.138478	0.115283	0	2.329348
Number of shareholders / Total number of negotiable shares ($\times 10^{-4}$)	0.138511	0.115459	0	2.334786
Number of A shareholders / Total number of negotiable A shares ($\times 10^{-4}$)	0.38606	0.30253	0	5.905453
Number of B shareholders / Total number of negotiable B shares ($\times 10^{-4}$)	0.004383	0.02521	0	0.234083
Panel C: Largest shareholders				
Year-end shareholdings of ten largest shareholders / Total year-end shareholdings	0.04944	0.06653	0	0.589711
Year-end shareholdings of three largest shareholders / Total year-end shareholdings	0.031138	0.056337	0	0.586426

structure. The middle exchange rate for the Chinese currency, Renminbi (RMB), against the U.S. dollar published by the People's Bank of China (PBC) was obtained from the State Administration of Foreign Exchange (SAFE).

Based on the firms' industry affiliation, Table 1 shows the industry sub-samples in both SZSE and SHSE. The summary statistics of foreign exchange and market index movement are also reported in Table 1. CSMAR database categorizes the Chinese listed firms into six main industries. They are finance, utilities, properties, conglomerate, industrials, and commerce. 26 firms were not specified the industry out of 1,378 firms with the ownership structure data available. Overall the individual firm stock returns and the SHSE and SZSE stock indexes illustrate a persistent upward trend through the sample period. The China's stock market performed much better than the average of the rest of the world while the exchange of Renminbi displayed a strong appreciating pattern.

Table 2 reports some statistics of the ownership structure in the China's stock market. The vast majority of the Chinese listed firms have 25% - 75% shares which are not tradable. And most of the firms' negotiable shares are A-shares. According to the number of A shareholders / Total number of negotiable A shares and the number of B shareholders / Total number of negotiable B shares, the A-share market in China is dominated by small or individual investors while the large or institutional investors play a major roll in the B-share market.

3.2. Methodology

The firm-specific exchange rate sensitivity, called *firm-specific exposure*, is defined as the effect of exchange rate changes on the value of a firm in excess of the global market's reaction to foreign exchange rate movements. Following Jorion (1990) and other, it is empirically estimated by the following model:

$$R_{it} = \alpha_i + \beta_i R_{mt} + \gamma_i \theta_t + \varepsilon_{it} \qquad (1)$$

where R_{it} designates the total return of firm i in period t, R_{mt} is the local stock market return – the Shanghai and Shenzhen Stock Exchange return – in period t, β_i is firm i's return sensitivity to market fluctuations, θ_t is the movement in the bilateral U.S. dollar / Chinese Renminbi exchange rate[6], γ_i is firm i's exposure to the exchange rate index independent of the effect these currency movements have on the overall market[7], and ε_{it} denotes the white noise error term. Hence γ_i describes the sensitivity of stock returns to unanticipated changes in exchange rates. Since the bilateral exchange rate has been defined as units of Chinese Renminbi per U.S. dollar, an appreciation of the Chinese Renminbi makes exporting goods more expensive in terms of U.S. dollars, and this may lead to a fall in foreign demand and foreign sales revenue. On the other hand, the importing firm will benefit from an appreciation of the Chinese Renminbi, as its imports become cheaper in terms Chinese Renminbi. Thus, the γ_i coefficient should be negative for net-exporters and positive for net-importers.[8] Similarly, Chinese multinationals with net exposed foreign denominated liabilities will gain with a strengthening Chinese currency, while firms with net exposed foreign denominated assets lose.

---

6 The exchange rate is defined as the price of one U.S. dollar in units of Chinese Renminbi. An appreciation (depreciation) of the Renminbi will, thus, produce a negative (positive) value for X_t.

7 A zero exposure doesn't imply, thus, that the firm is not affected by currency movements. It rather means that the firm value reacts to exchange rate movements to the same degree as the market portfolio.

8 Note that the sign of the exchange rate exposure coefficient becomes less distinct for a company that imports as well as exports. See, for example Adler and Dumas (1984) and He and Ng (1998) for their suggestion that the sensitivity of the firm value to exchange rate fluctuations depends on the elasticity of the firm's demand for foreign goods relative to the elasticity of the foreign market's demand for the firm's goods.

The implicit assumption made in the above-mentioned model (1) is the hypothesis of constant variance. This assumption is often rejected for common financial weekly time series - like exchange rate and stock return series.[9] As the presence of heteroskedasticity invalidates the test statistics of the ordinary least squares regression, we test whether the residuals ε_{it} exhibit time-varying heteroskedasticity. We use the test Engle derived from the Lagrange multiplier principle to check the validity of the null hypothesis that the error terms of Eq. (1) ε_{it} present no heteroskedasticity. If we do not reject the null hypothesis, we perform an ordinary least squares regression. Otherwise we add a GARCH(1,1) process[10] to the initial augmented market model to incorporate conditional variance into the system (Bollerslev, Chou and Kroner, 1992). Thus, the regression model becomes:

$$R_{it} = \alpha_i + \beta_i R_{mt} + \gamma_i \theta_t + \varepsilon_{it}$$

with

$$\varepsilon_{i,t} = \mu_{i,t} * (h_{i,t})^{1/2} \qquad h_{i,t} = \delta_i + \tau_i \varepsilon^2_{i,t-1} + v_i h_{i,t-1} \qquad (2)$$

where $h_{i,t}$ denotes the conditional variance of the residuals; δ_i, τ_i *and* v_i are unknown parameters[11]; and $\mu_{i,t}$ represents the white noise error term.

4. Empirical Results

The empirical findings of this study are reported in the following tables. Table 3 shows the foreign exchange exposure of all firms in the SHSE and SZSE based on Eq. (1) during the entire study period. For the entire sample during the first 15 months in the new exchange rate regime, the average exposure coefficient is -4.2539 in the SHSE and -5.0305 in the SZSE. Nearly half of the firms in the SZSE, 47.43% or 277 of 584 firms, experience statistically significant exposure to the foreign exchange movement, while 39.22% of 877 firms in the SHSE show the same pattern. The sign of foreign exchange exposure is negative indicating adverse impact of foreign exchange rate on firm value.

In terms of the foreign exchange exposure of A- and B-shares in the SHSE and SZSE, more B-shares than A-shares experience statistically significant exposure, 62.96% versus 37.67% in the SHSE and 69.09% versus 45.18% in the SZSE. There may be two interpretations for such a high proportion of B-shares exposed to the foreign exchange movement. First, B-shares are denominated in the foreign currencies. B-shares in the SHSE are denominated in the US dollar and B-shares in the SZSE are denominated in the Hong Kong dollar. A second interpretation may be that the B-shares are invested mainly by the foreign investors or local residents with foreign currencies, while the A-shares are invested by the local residents in the Chinese Renminbi.

[9] See, for example Bollerslev, Chow and Kroner (1992), and Nieuwland, Verschoor and Wolf (1994).

[10] The choice of a GARCH(1,1) specification is supported by many empirical studies which show that the GARCH(1,1) specification is valuable for modeling the variance generating process of financial time series.

[11] The parameters are estimated by maximum-likelihood and generated using the Berndt et al. (1974) algorithm.

Table 3. Chinese Foreign exchange risk exposure

		mean	median	Q_1	Q_3	*N**	*N*
		Shanghai Stock Exchange					
constant	α	0.0009 0.0000	0.0008 0.0001	0.0002	0.0017		
market index	β	1.0977 0.0093	1.1123 0.0117	0.9261	1.2773		
US$/RMB exchange rate	γ	-4.2539 0.1280	-4.2748 0.1604	-6.5696	-1.8069	*344* *39.22%*	*877*
constant	δ	0.0004 0.0000	0.0003 0.0000	0.0002	0.0005		
arch	τ	0.3469 0.0348	0.2021 0.0436	0.0777	0.3344		
garch	ν	0.1658 0.0189	0.1825 0.0237	0.0118	0.3532		
		Shenzhen Stock Exchange					
constant	α	0.0008 0.0001	0.0008 0.0001	0.0000	0.0017		
market index	β	1.0473 0.0117	1.0739 0.0147	0.8956	1.2288		
US$/RMB exchange rate	γ	-5.0305 0.1714	-4.9725 0.2148	-7.3663	-2.3641	*277* *47.43%*	*584*
constant	δ	0.0004 0.0000	0.0003 0.0000	0.0002	0.0004		
arch	τ	0.3212 0.0289	0.2001 0.0362	0.1101	0.3446		
garch	ν	0.2105 0.0174	0.2299 0.0218	0.0497	0.3363		

The numbers are summary statistics of the cross-sectional distribution of the ordinary least squares parameter estimates of Eq. (1), respectively the maximum likelihood (using the Berndt, Hall, Hall and Hausman (1974) algorithm) parameter estimates of Eq. (2). Q1 and Q3 represent the first and third quartiles of the distribution, respectively. N* is the number of firms with a documented significant exchange rate exposure at the 5% level at least. N is size of the total sample.

Table 3 reports cross-sectional summary statistics of the parameters estimated by the following regression model:

$$R_{it} = \alpha_i + \beta_i R_{mt} + \gamma_i \theta_t + \varepsilon_{it} \quad (1)$$

where R_{it} designates the total return of firm i in period t, R_{mt} the orthogonalized local stock market return in period t, β_i firm i's return sensitivity to market fluctuations, θ_t the movement in the bilateral US$ / RMB exchange rate, γ_i firm i's exposure to the exchange rate and ε_{it} the white noise error term.

If, for firm i, the homoscedasticity of the returns is rejected, the previous model is extended to:

$$R_{it} = \alpha_i + \beta_i R_{mt} + \gamma_i \theta_t + \varepsilon_{it}$$

with

$$\varepsilon_{i,t} = \mu_{i,t} *(h_{i,t})^{1/2} \qquad h_{i,t}= \delta_i + \tau_i \varepsilon^2_{i,t-1} + \nu_i h_{i,t-1} \quad (2)$$

where $h_{i,t}$ denotes the conditional variance of the residuals; δ_i, τ_i *and* ν_i unknown parameters; and $\mu_{i,t}$ represents the white noise error term.

Table 4. Foreign exchange risk exposure: Comparison between A- and B-Shares

		A-Shares			B-Shares		
		mean	median	*N**	mean	median	*N**
Shanghai Stock Exchange							
constant	α	0.0009	0.0008		0.0012	0.0013	
		0.0000	0.0001		0.0001	0.0002	
market index	β	1.1037	1.1180		1.0059	1.0335	
		0.0098	0.0122		0.0266	0.0333	
US$/RMB exchange rate	γ	-4.1801	-4.1421	*310 / 823*	-5.3777	-5.0478	*34 / 54*
		0.1344	0.1685	*37.67%*	0.3169	0.3971	*62.96%*
constant	δ	0.0004	0.0003		0.0003	0.0002	
		0.0000	0.0000		0.0000	0.0000	
arch	τ	0.3471	0.1918		0.3396	0.2800	
		0.0358	0.0449		0.0967	0.1212	
garch	ν	0.1675	0.2076		0.1102	0.1014	
		0.0193	0.0242		0.0896	0.1123	
Shenzhen Stock Exchange							
constant	α	0.0008	0.0007		0.0010	0.0010	
		0.0001	0.0001		0.0001	0.0002	
market index	β	1.0581	1.0909		0.9432	0.9734	
		0.0126	0.0158		0.0251	0.0315	
US$/RMB exchange rate	γ	-5.0608	-4.9413	*239 / 529*	-4.7395	-5.2622	*38 / 55*
		0.1849	0.2318	*45.18%*	0.3888	0.4873	*69.09%*
constant	δ	0.0004	0.0003		0.0003	0.0002	
		0.0000	0.0000		0.0000	0.0000	
arch	τ	0.3247	0.1939		0.2915	0.2703	
		0.0320	0.0401		0.0370	0.0463	
garch	ν	0.2119	0.2299		0.1986	0.2366	
		0.0191	0.0239		0.0308	0.0385	

The numbers are summary statistics of the cross-sectional distribution of the ordinary least squares parameter estimates of Eq. (1), respectively the maximum likelihood (using the Berndt, Hall, Hall and Hausman (1974) algorithm) parameter estimates of Eq. (2). Q_1 and Q_3 represent the first and third quartiles of the distribution, respectively. N* is the number of firms with a documented significant exchange rate exposure at the 5% level at least. N is size of the total sample.

Table 4 reports cross-sectional summary statistics of the parameters estimated by the following model:

$$R_{it} = \alpha_i + \beta_i R_{mt} + \gamma_i \theta_t + \varepsilon_{it} \quad (1)$$

where R_{it} designates the total return of firm i in period t, R_{mt} the orthogonalized local stock market return in period t, β_i firm i's return sensitivity to market fluctuations, θ_t the movement in the bilateral US$ / RMB exchange rate, γ_i firm i's exposure to the exchange rate and ε_{it} the white noise error term.

If, for firm *i*, the homoscedasticity of the returns is rejected, the previous model is extended to:

$R_{it} = \alpha_i + \beta_i R_{mt} + \gamma_i \theta_t + \varepsilon_{it}$

with

$\varepsilon_{i,t} = \mu_{i,t} *(h_{i,t})^{1/2}$ $\qquad$ $h_{i,t} = \delta_i + \tau_i \varepsilon^2_{i,t-1} + \nu_i h_{i,t-1}$ (2)

where $h_{i,t}$ denotes the conditional variance of the residuals; δ_i, τ_i *and* ν_i unknown parameters; and $\mu_{i,t}$ represents the white noise error term.

Table 5 displays that the ownership structure tends to be an important determinant of exchange exposure of Chinese listed firms. The following patterns are reported: the more firms' shareholding is concentrated, the less they are exposed to foreign exchange movement; the higher the proportion of non-negotiable shares, the more the firms are exposed to the currency exposure; the number of directors over the total number of directors, supervisors and executives also has the positive impact on the foreign exchange exposure.

Table 5. Chinese foreign exchange risk exposure and ownership structure

Variable	Coefficient	Std. Error	t-Statistic	Prob.	Adj R-sq	D-W stat
Shanghai Stock Market						
C	9.602118	1.362676	7.046518	0		
LARG	-2.41527	2.098406	-1.151	0.2501		
NBSH	-0.01818	0.009448	-1.92473	0.0546		
NONNEG	3.734509	1.398275	2.670797	0.0077		
DIRE	-7.23359	2.280805	-3.17151	0.0016		
					0.702678	1.895691
Shenzhen Stock Market						
C	11.47919	2.236693	5.132217	0		
LARG	-2.43405	4.683437	-0.51971	0.6035		
NBSH	-0.07323	0.027974	-2.61772	0.0091		
NONNEG	7.073513	2.076848	3.405889	0.0007		
DIRE	-9.38973	3.66968	-2.55873	0.0108		
					0.708004	1.862952

Table 5 reports the determinants of Chinese foreign exchange risk exposure estimated by the following regression model:

$$\gamma_i = \alpha_i + \beta_{1i} LARG_i + \beta_{2i} NBSH_i + \beta_{3i} NONNEG_i + \beta_{4i} DIRE_i + \varepsilon_i$$

where γ_i denotes firm *i*'s average exposure to the exchange rate, $LARG_i$ the percentage of year-end shareholdings of ten largest shareholders out of the total year-end shareholdings of firm i, $NBSH_i$ the number of shareholdings per shareholder of firm i divided by 1000, $NONNEG_i$ .the percentage of non-negotiable shares out of total share of firm i, $DIRE_i$ the number of directors over the total number of directors, supervisors and executives.

CONCLUSION

This chapter examines the exposure of 1,448 Chinese firms traded on the SHSE and SZSE under the new exchange rate regime to movements in the foreign value of the Renminbi using GARCH procedures. Our results identify a reliable relation between contemporaneous stock returns and unanticipated Renminbi fluctuations. The relation appears to be stronger for the B-shares in both SHSE and SZSE. Furthermore, ownership structure tends to be an important determinant of exchange exposure of Chinese listed firms. The following patterns are reported: the more firms' shareholding is concentrated, the less they are exposed to foreign exchange movement; the higher the proportion of non-negotiable shares, the more the firms are exposed to the currency exposure; the number of directors over the total number of directors, supervisors and executives also has the positive impact on the foreign exchange exposure.

BIBLIOGRAPHICAL DETAILS

Professor Aline Muller holds the Ethias Chair in Risk & Asset Management at the HEC Management School of the University of Liège (Belgium). She is as well part-time appointed at the Nijmegen School of Management of the Radboud University (Netherlands) and is visiting professor at the Luxembourg School of Finance (Luxembourg). Aline's work on Foreign Exchange Risk Exposure has been published in various academic journals like the Journal of Empirical Finance, Journal of Japanese and International Economies, Emerging Markets Review, European Financial Management, etc.

Professor Robin Luo, FRM, is the Director of Department of Research & Development at China Chengxin International Credit Rating Co., Ltd., the largest credit rating agency in China. He also holds the professorship in Wuhan University and Zhongnan University of Economics and Law. He taught and researched at La Trobe University in Australia, Auckland University of Technology in New Zealand, Nanyang Technological University in Singapore, and a couple of other tertiary institutions in Asia. Robin's research is focused on risk management, asset pricing, market efficiency, international finance, and Asia-Pacific financial markets. He has published in Economics Modelling, Applied Financial Economics, Investment Management and Financial Innovations, and Applied Economics Letters.

Professor Alireza Tourani-Rad is the Chair Professor and Head of Department at Auckland University of Technology (AUT), New Zealand. Prior to joining AUT, he was a Professor of Finance at the Waikato University, New Zealand, and Associate Professor of Finance, Maastricht University, the Netherlands. He is currently a member of Australian-New Zealand Shadow Financial Regulatory Committee, and a fellow of Financial Services Institute of Australasia. He had been a Senior Research Fellow at the Maastricht Research School of Economics of Technology and Organizations, and the Executive Vice President of the European Financial Management Association. Professor Tourani-Rad sits on the editorial board of several finance journals. He has published extensively, in excess of 65 refereed articles, covering financial markets, corporate finance and governance, investment analysis, and mutual fund performance. Professor Tourani-Rad was recently named one of the most prolific authors in finance, ranked among the top 2% worldwide ["Prolific Authors in the Finance Literature: A Half Century of Contributions", 2005, Journal of Finance Literature].

REFERENCES

Adler, Michael, and Bernard Dumas, 1984, Exposure to Currency Risk: Definition and Measurement, *Financial Management* Summer, 41-50.

Allayannis, G. and J. Ihrig, 2001. Exposure and Markups, *Review of Financial Studies*, 14(3), 805-835.

Amihud, Y., 1994. Evidence on Exchange Rates and Valuation of Equity Shares. Amihud, Y., and Levich, R.M. (Eds.), *Exchange Rate and Corporate Performance. Irwin Professional*, New York, pp. 49-59.

Bartov, E., G.M. Bodnar and A. Kaul, 1996. Exchange Rate Variability and the Riskiness of U.S. Multinational Firms: Evidence from the breakdown, Journal of Financial Economics, 42, 105-132.

Bartov, E. and G.M. Bodnar, 1994. Firm Valuation, Earning Expectations, and the Exchange Rate Exposure Effect, *Journal of Finance 49*, 1755-1785.

Bodnar, G.M., Dumas, B. and R.C. Marston, 2002. Pass-through and Exposure, Journal of Finance, 57, 199-231.

Bodnar, Gordon M. and William M. Gentry, 1993, Exchange-rate exposure and industry characteristics: Evidence from Canada, Japan, and the U.S.A., Journal of International Money and Finance, 12, 29-45.

Bodnar, G.M., and Wong, M.H.F. 2000. Estimating Exchange Rate Exposure Some 'Weighty' Issues. *NBER working paper* 7497

Bollerslev, T., R. Chou and K.F. Kroner, 1992. ARCH Modelling in Finance: A Review of the Theory and Empirical Evidence, Journal of Econometrics, 52, 5-59.

Booth, L., and W. Roteberg, 1990. Assessing Foreign Exchange Exposure: Theory and Applications using Canadian Firms. *Journal of International Financial Management and Accounting*, Spring 2(1), 1-23.

Choi, Jay Jongmoo., and Anita M. Prasad, Exchange risk sensitivity and its determinants: A firm and industry analysis of U.S. multinationals, Financial Management, 25, 77-88.

Dalziel, Paul and Lattimore, Ralph, 2001. *The New Zealand Macroeconomy: A Briefing on the Reforms and their Legacy*, 4th edition, Oxford University Press

Dominguez Kathryn M.E., Linda L. Tesar, 2003. Exchange Rate Exposure. *NBER working paper*

Dumas, Bernard, 1978. The Theory of the Trading Firm Revisited, *Journal of Finance 33*, 1019-1029.

Froot, Kenneth, David Scharfstein, and Jeremy Stein, 1993. Risk Management: Coordinating Corporate Investment and Financing Policies, *Journal of Finance 48*, 1629-1658.

Griffin, John, and Rene Stulz, 2001. International Competition and Exchange Rate Shocks: A Cross-Country Industry Analysis of Stock Returns, *Review of Financial Studies*, Spring, 215-241.

He, Jia, Lilian K. Ng, 1998, The Foreign Exchange Exposure of Japanese Multinational Corporations, *Journal of Finance 53*, 733-753.

Hodder, J., 1982. Exposure to Exchange Rate Movements. *Journal of International Economics 13*, 375-386.

Iorio, Amalia Di, and Robert Faff. An Analysis of Asymmetry in Foreign Currency Exposure of the Australian Equities market. *Journal of Multinational Financial Management 10*, 133-159.

Jorion, P., 1990. The Exchange Rate Exposure of Multinationals, *Journal of Business 63*, 331-342.

Khoo, A., 1994. Estimation of Foreign Exchange Exposure—An Application to mining Companies in Australia. *Journal of International Money and Finance 13*, 342-363.

Loudon, G., 1993. The Foreign Exchange Operating Exposure of Australian Stocks. *Accounting and Finance 32*, 19-32.

Muller, A. and W.F.C. Verschoor, 2006a, European Exchange Rate Exposure, *European Financial Management*, 12, 195-220.

Muller, A. and W.F.C. Verschoor, 2006b, Asian Foreign Exchange Risk Exposure, Journal of the Japanese and International Economies, forthcoming.

Nance, Deana R., Clifford W. Smith Jr., and Charles W. Smithson, 1993, One the Determinants of Corporate Hedging, *Journal of Finance 48*, 391-405.

Nguyen, Hoa and Robert Faff, 2003, Can the use of foreign currency derivatives explain variations in foreign exchange exposure? Evidence from Australian companies, *Journal of Multinational Financial Management*, 13, 193-215.

Nieuwland, F.G.M.C., W.F.C. Verschoor and C.C.P. Wolf, 1994, Stochastic Trends and Jumps in EMS Exchange Rates, *Journal of International Money and Finance*, 13, 699-727.

Shapiro, A. 1975. Exchange Rate Changes, Inflation, and the Value of Multinational Corporation. *Journal of Finance 30*, 485-502.

Zhang, Yimin and Ronald Zhao, 2003, Risk Under "One Country and Two Systems": Evidence from Class A, B and H Shares of Chinese Listed Companies, *Review of Pacific Basin Financial Markets and Policies*, 6(2), 179-197.

In: Exchange Rates: Policies, Effects and Fluctuations
Editor: Natalie B. Perkins, pp. 115-129
ISBN: 978-1-61209-505-9
© 2011 Nova Science Publishers, Inc.

Chapter 6

EXCHANGE-RATE FLUCTUATIONS AND MONETARY POLICY REACTION: THE ROLE OF ASYMMETRIC INFORMATION*

Marcelo Sánchez†
European Central Bank, Frankfurt, Germany

Abstract

This paper compares the link between exchange rates and interest rates under full information and a simple alternative asymmetric information approach, in which shocks are not known to any agents in the economy at the time of the monetary policy decision. The latter approach can be seen as incorporating, in a discrete-time context, the notion that there is an institutional constraint in the timing of interest rate decisions relative to the higher frequency of shocks and changes in prices, output and exchange rates. We also distinguish between cases of expansionary and contractionary depreciations. We find that full information results are not robust to the presence of the informational friction here considered. For economies exhibiting expansionary or strongly contractionary depreciations, such friction leads to an optimal deviation from the full information outcome, namely, that the monetary authority does not react on impact to shocks. In the case of mildly contractionary deprec iations, our asymmetric information model predicts a lack of response of the central bank to aggregate demand shocks, as opposed to an offsetting movement in interest rates under full information. Optimal policies are thus found to depend on the degree of informedness in the economy.

Keywords: Transmission mechanism; Emerging market economies; Exchange rate; Monetary policy; Imperfect information

JEL Classification: E52, E58, F31, F41

---

*I gratefully acknowledge comments received from seminar participants at the ECB and the Third Workshop on Emerging Markets organised by Banco de España. Comments from Alfredo Schclarek Curutchet and Antonio Millaruelo are gratefully acknowledged. The views expressed here do not necessarily reflect those of the ECB. The usual disclaimer applies.

†E-mail address: marcelo.sanchez@ecb.int. Correspondence to:. European Central Bank. Kaiserstrasse 29. D-60311. Frankfurt. Germany. Tel: +49 69 1344 6531; fax: +49 69 1344 7062.

Introduction

The important role played by interest rates and exchange rates in influencing macroeconomic developments justifies the considerable research attention recently attracted by how the two variables relate to each other. The literature on exchange rate movements and monetary policy reactions has mostly been conducted under the assumption that agents have full information about the state of the economy. Standard models tend to show that adverse real and financial shocks lead to a weakening in the exchange rate and a rise in interest rates. The assumptions involved in these analyses include that an exchange rate weakening has a positive impact on economic activity. One area that has recently been investigated concerns how the model results are affected by variations in the responsiveness of aggregate demand to the exchange rate. Detken and Gaspar (2003) and Eichengreen (2005) assess the situation of adverse balance sheet effects as eliciting a lower response of aggregate demand to exchange rates. In this case, they find that there is less of a case for raising interest rates in the face of adverse risk premium shocks. As a result, the exchange rate ends up depreciating by a larger amount. Eichengreen (2005) also finds that, in the face of an adverse real shock, the exchange rate will also depreciate by more (and in this case interest rates be further lowered), the smaller the responsiveness of output to exchange rates. Another set of results is reported by Eichengreen (2005) and Sánchez (2005), who explicitly analyse situations under which a weakening in domestic currencies could lead to contractions in economic activity (that is, "contractionary devaluation" scenarios).[1] The former author shows that the covariance between exchange rates and interest rates, conditional on adverse risk premium and net export shocks, is negative for expansionary depreciations and positive for strongly contractionary ones. Sánchez (2005) confirms these findings, but deviates from Eichengreen (2005) in reporting that the positive comovements between exchange rates and interest rates also obtain under mildly contractionary depreciations. The latter result arises from the introduction of forward-looking behaviour in the foreign exchange market, which also raises the issue of whether non-fundamental factors play a role in determining the solution to the model in the case of mildly contractionary depreciations.[2]

One conceptual point in common between all the studies discussed in the previous paragraph is the interpretation of their results as involving optimal monetary policy. More concretely, exchange rate smoothing by means of interest rates is thus shown to originate in optimal policy under flotation. The emphasis on optimal policy distinguishes this literature, at least from a terminological point of view, from other analyses commonly describing similar comovements between interest rates and exchange rates as "fear of floating" - as also

[1]They do so by allowing for an overall negative effect of weaker real exchange rates on output in the aggregate demand schedule. One reason behind this non-standard effect, namely the presence of balance sheet effects arising from liability dollarisation, has attracted most attention in the recent literature (Chang and Velasco, 2001; Céspedes et al., 2003 and 2004; and Morón and Winkelried, 2005). However, it is worth mentioning that there is a large number of rationales for contractionary devaluations and depreciations: Caves et al. (2002) report ten such effects in their celebrated textbook!

[2]It is worth mentioning that, although all studies discussed in this paragraph have in common the use of full information frameworks, they also present some modeling specificities. For instance, Detken and Gaspar's (2003) model displays forward-looking features concerning goods and financial markets, while Eichengreen's (2005) is basically a backward-looking model. Sánchez's (2005) model is somewhere in between, sharing with Detken and Gaspar (2003) the forward-looking features concerning financial markets, while displaying like Eichengreen (2005) backward-lookingness in the goods market.

discussed in Edwards (2002).[3]

The distinction between expansionary and contractionary depreciations is necessary if one wishes to address the relation between interest rates and exchange rates in a general fashion, that is, for the cases of both advanced and developing countries. Authors such as Calvo (2001), Calvo and Reinhart (2001 and 2002) and Eichengreen (2005) have insisted that there are a number of important differences between advanced economies and EMEs. The latter are seen as being prone to exhibiting liability dollarisation, credibility problems, a high degree of exchange rate pass-through and non-stationarities in the inflationary process. The literature normally finds that these specificities of EMEs are responsible for a relatively small degree of exchange rate flexibility in these economies - what Calvo and Reinhart (2002) label "fear of floating".[4] In particular, liability dollarisation is believed to allow exchange rate depreciations to give rise to contractionary balance sheet effects by raising the domestic-currency real value of external liabilities. That the sources of contractionary devaluations may be broader than this is highlighted by the fact that the empirical literature has generally found that weaker currencies tend to induce contractions in EMEs, even after including a number of different controls (see Ahmed, 2003, and the references cited therein). In this context, the work of Eichengreen (2005) and Sánchez (2005) is an attempt to rationalise the lack of exchange rate flexibility by looking at interest rate reactions aimed at dampening variability in foreign exchange markets. Sánchez (2007) studies an asymmetric information context in which - as in Gerlach and Smets (2000) - foreign market participants are aware of the disturbances hitting the economy, with the central bank being able to infer some of the new information - that is not directly available to it - through the analysis of exchange rate developments (asymmetric information with signal extraction).

In contrast with the literature's focus on full information models, this paper compares the link between exchange rates and interest rates under full information and a simple alternative asymmetric information approach, in which shocks are not known to any agents in the economy at the time of the monetary policy decision.[5] In doing so, I start by setting up a simple full information model, which draws from the way the recent literature has formulated small open economy frameworks under flexible exchange rates.[6] I use backward-looking inflationary expectations and forward-looking financial markets. Follow-

[3]Economic models permit us to go beyond reduced-form characterisations of interest rates and exchange rates in terms of comovements. Pending deeper structural empirical analyses, Sánchez (2005) analyses some case studies among EMEs that do not provide us with an entirely clear picture. It appears however to be the case that, in response to adverse risk premium shocks, the exchange rate has tended to depreciate on impact, thereafter strengthening alongside interest rate hikes. The situation is less clear-cut when it comes to shocks characterised by an exogenous fall in net exports, which have, in the cases analysed by the author, taken place at the same time as adverse shocks to risk premia.

[4]This means that, despite the recently proclaimed switch to floating exchange rates, the evidence seems to suggest a reversion to some degree of exchange rate management, albeit one which seems to be less tight than before the crisis. In this regard, some analysts have found considerable discrepancies between the *de jure* exchange rate classifications and *de facto* regimes (see *e.g.* Reinhart and Rogoff, 2004).

[5]In real life agents do not have access to real-time information about all relevant economic data, and that some agents are better informed about the evolution of the economy than others. In particular, policymakers do not afford the luxury of an error-free assessment of current market conditions at the time of taking their decisions.

[6]The model is closest to Sánchez (2007). The related literature also includes Ball (1999 and 2002), Svensson (2000), Taylor (1999), McCallum and Nelson (1999 and 2000), Galí and Monacelli (2005), Gerlach and Smets (2000) and Sánchez (2005).

ing Sánchez (2005 and 2007), I distinguish between cases when depreciations are expansionary and contractionary, while also incorporating the role of exchange rate pass-through into domestic prices. I extend the basic full information framework by deriving results also under the assumption of imperfect information. Unlike Sánchez (2007), whose asymmetric information model postulates that foreign market participants know the shocks hitting the economy, here we assume that disturbances are not known to any agents at that point in time, which does not open the possibility for the central bank to deduce real-time properties of the new data (asymmetric information without signal extraction).

The type of informational friction introduced in this paper aims at capturing one possible way in which a relevant disturbance is hitting the economy in relation to the period during which interest rates are set by the central bank. In our use of asymmetric information without signal extraction, the central bank is assumed not to have access to contemporaneous information. Moreover, at the time interest rate decisions are taken the current disturbances have not yet occurred. It is thus not possible in this case to allow monetary policy decisions to indirectly embody inputs from other, better informed economic agents. This approach can be rationalised as incorporating the notion that the relevant shocks take place right after interest rates have been set.

The results of this paper show that full information outcomes do not appear to be robust to the presence of informational frictions. More concretely, three important differences arise between full information and the imperfect information models analysed here. For economies exhibiting expansionary or strongly contractionary depreciations, such frictions are responsible for two optimal deviations from full information outcomes: i) under asymmetric information with signal extraction, the realisation of a relatively less frequent shock (in the present case, a net export shock) leads the central bank to behave as if a more likely disturbance (a risk premium disturbance) had instead taken place; and ii) under asymmetric information without signal extraction, the monetary authorities does not react on impact to shocks hitting the economy. The latter difference also implies that, for expansionary depreciations, a lower responsiveness of output to exchange rates, which has an impact on comovements between interest rates and exchange rates under full information, instead fails for any shock to affect interest rates on impact under asymmetric information without signal extraction. Finally, in the case of mildly contractionary depreciations, both asymmetric information models predict a lack of response of the central bank to aggregate demand shocks, as opposed to an stabilising movement in interest rates under full information.

The structure of the rest of the paper is as follows. Section 2 presents a simple small open economy model which assumes full information. Section 3 describes the results for the type of informational imperfections used here. Section 4 discusses the similarities and differences with respect to the full information approach of section 2. Finally, section 5 concludes.

1. A Simple Model

In order to investigate the link between interest rates and exchange rates, let us consider a simple small open economy model.[7] I allow for depreciations to be either expansionary or

[7] For a more detailed description of the full information setup, see Sánchez (2005 and 2007).

contractionary. The economy specialises in the production of a single good. The behaviour of the private sector is described in the following equations:

$$\pi_t = E_{t-1}\pi_t + \alpha\left(y_t - \varepsilon_t^S\right) - \gamma(e_t - E_{t-1}e_t) \quad (1)$$

$$y_t = -\beta r_t - \delta e_t + \varepsilon_t^D \quad (2)$$

$$r_t = -E_t e_{t+1} + e_t + \varepsilon_t^f \quad (3)$$

$$r_t = R_t - E_t \pi_{t+1} \quad (4)$$

where all variables, except the interest rate, are in logarithms and expressed as deviations from steady state values. All parameters are assumed to be positive, with the exception of δ, which can adopt any real value. The value of δ is negative in a contractionary depreciation and positive in an expansionary depreciation. All shocks are of the zero-mean, constant variance, type, and are uncorrelated with each other.

Equation (1) is an aggregate supply schedule that relates inflation (π_t) to the output gap (y_t) term and an exchange-rate pass through term. An increase in the real exchange rate (e_t) denotes an appreciation. Expression (2) states that aggregate demand is decreasing in the real interest rate (r_t). Output is also allowed to depend positively or negatively on the real exchange rate. Equation (3) is an uncovered interest parity condition, while (4) is the Fisher equation.

The monetary authority's problem consists in minimising an intertemporal loss function that penalises deviations of output from its potential level, $y_t - \varepsilon_t^S$, and deviations of inflation from the target (or objective), $\pi_t - \tilde{\pi}_t$:

$$E_t \sum_{i=0}^{\infty} \rho^i L_{i+1}$$

$$\text{where } L_t = \alpha^2 (y_t - \varepsilon_t^S)^2 + \chi(\pi_t - \tilde{\pi}_t)^2 \quad (5)$$

The model is solved under the assumption of *full information*, in the sense that the central bank, producers and foreign exchange market participants all observe current output, prices and nominal exchange rates. Moreover, there is discretion on the part central bank and expectations are rational. As a result, I obtain $E_{t-1}\pi_t = E_{t-1}\tilde{\pi}_t$, that is, expected inflation equals expected targeted inflation. Using this, and assuming that the inflation target adopts a fixed and credible value of $\tilde{\pi}$, the optimal inflation rate, π_t^{opt}, is found to follow:

$$\pi_t^{opt} = \tilde{\pi} - (1 - \varphi)\gamma(e_t - E_{t-1}e_t) \quad (6)$$

where $\varphi \equiv \chi/(1+\chi)$. The central bank thus chooses an inflation rate equal to the term capturing the effect of unexpected exchange rate fluctuations on prices, plus a weighted average of the private sector's expectations of the inflation target and the actual inflation target.

Concerning the model's disturbances, I assume that the risk premium shock, ε_t^f, and the excess demand shock, ε_t^{xd}, both follow first-order autoregressive processes with uncorrelated disturbances. In consequence, I can write: $\varepsilon_t^f = \rho_f \varepsilon_{t-1}^f + \xi_t$, in the former case, and $\varepsilon_t^{xd} = \rho \varepsilon_{t-1}^{xd} + \eta_t^{xd}$ in the latter. In consequence, I obtain:

$$e_t = (1-\omega) E_t e_{t+1} - \frac{\theta\varphi\gamma}{\alpha}(e_t - E_{t-1}e_t) + \theta\varepsilon_t^{xd} - (1-\omega)\varepsilon_t^f \quad (7)$$

Examination of (7) leads to the conclusion that the model has a forward solution for the case when $\mid 1-\omega \mid< 1$, and a backward solution for the case when $\mid 1-\omega \mid> 1$. In the rest of the section, I solve for each case in turn.

1.1. Forward Solution for Case when $\mid 1-\omega \mid< 1$

The condition $\mid 1-\omega \mid< 1$ amounts to two different ranges for the values of δ, namely, $\delta \in (-\infty, -2\beta) \cup (0, \infty)$. The forward solution to expectational difference equation (7) in the absence of bubbles can be expressed in terms of the real exchange rate and the real interest rate as:

$$e_t = \frac{1}{\beta(1-\rho)+\delta}\left[\varepsilon_t^{xd} - (1-\sigma)\eta_t^{xd}\right] - \frac{\beta}{\beta(1-\rho_f)+\delta}\left[\varepsilon_t^{f} - (1-\sigma)\xi_t\right] \tag{8}$$

$$r_t^{opt} = \frac{1}{\beta(1-\rho)+\delta}\left[(1-\rho)\varepsilon_t^{xd} - (1-\sigma)\eta_t^{xd}\right] + \frac{1}{\beta(1-\rho_f)+\delta}\left[\delta\varepsilon_t^{f} + \beta(1-\sigma)\xi_t\right] \tag{9}$$

where $\sigma \equiv \alpha/(\alpha+\theta\varphi\gamma)$. From (9), the central bank raises interest rates in response to a positive excess demand shock and an unfavourable risk premium shock.

The workings of the model are shown here by resorting to simulations. I attach numerical values to the parameters, following calibrations used in previous work for small open economies. For key parameter δ, the baseline value is chosen to equal 0.2, as in Ball (1999). I consider three other values for δ: a) $\delta = 0.1$ to assess the impact of balance sheet effects in an economy still displaying overall expansionary depreciations; b) $\delta = -1.5$, a large negative value for simulations in the present subsection satisfying $\delta < -2\beta$ (strongly contractionary depreciations); and c) $\delta = -0.1$, a small negative value for the study of mildly contractionary depreciations in the next subsection. [8] All other parameters are kept unchanged throughout the analysis. The values of α, β and γ are taken from Ball (1999) to equal 0.4, 0.6 and 0.2, respectively. In addition, I draw from McCallum and Nelson (1999 and 2000) for parameters of shock persistence. The two I use in the present paper are $\rho_f = 0.5$ and $\rho_x = 0$. I also reset McCallum and Nelson's value for ϖ to 0.8 from 0.89, to capture the fact that many small open economies are very open to international trade. Finally, in light of the absence of a similar estimate for small open economies, I use Barro and Broadbent's (1997) estimate for χ, obtained using US data. Their value of $\chi = 2.58$ is recalibrated to 0.41 in the present paper, taking account of the presence of α^2 in (5).

The reaction of interest rates and exchanges rates to shocks is examined by means of impulse responses. We consider two disturbances in turn, one real (a favourable net export shock raising η_t^{xd}) and the other a pure portfolio disturbance shock (an adverse risk premium shock pushing ξ_t up). In the present subsection I run simulations for three of the four cases mentioned before, namely, those of a positive δ (equalling either baseline 0.2 or 0.1) and a rather negative δ ($\delta = -1.5$ satisfying $\delta < -2\beta$).[9] Panel A of Figure 1 shows, for the two alternative positive values of δ, the cumulated impulse responses to both a one percent adverse risk premium shock (top chart) and a one percent favourable net export

[8]The latter value for δ is close to Cavoli and Rajan's (2005) estimate of -0.09 for contractionary-depreciation Thailand.

[9]I leave the study of the remaining possible values of δ for the next subsection.

shock (bottom chart). Panel B of Figure 1 reports the corresponding cumulated impulse responses for $\delta = -1.5$.

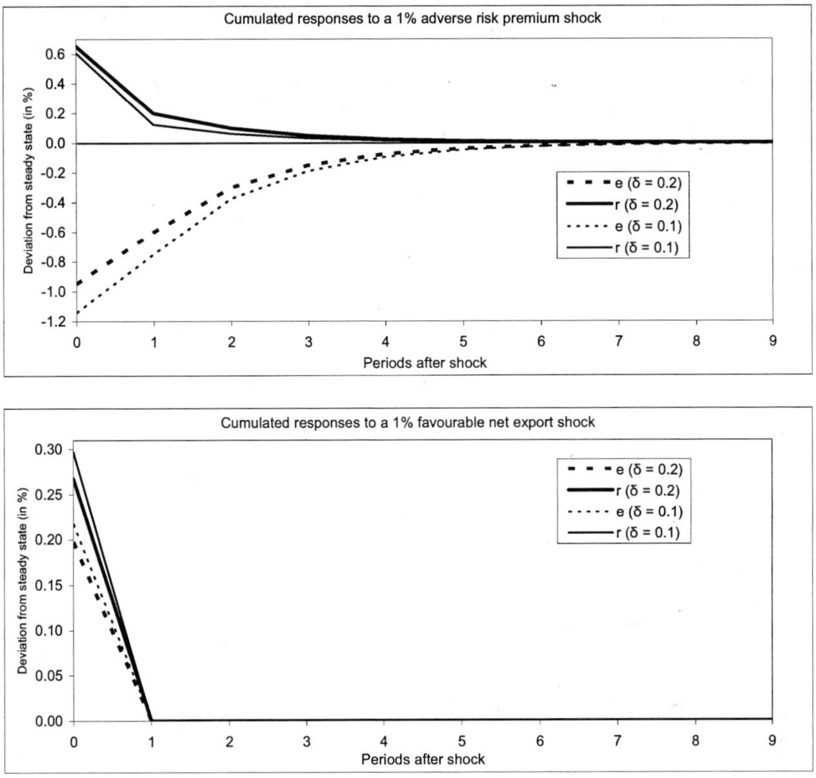

Figure 1. Full information case: Impulse responses of interest rate and real exchange rate.

For an economy exhibiting conventional expansionary depreciations, Figure 1 (panel A, top chart) indicates that an adverse risk premium shock drives the interest rate up and the real exchange rate down. A risk premium disturbance causes a real exchange rate depreciation with consequent inflationary effects via pass-through as well as incipient favourable output effects. In view of the unambiguous inflationary pressures stemming from this shock (via both exchange rate pass-through and output), the monetary authority raises interest rates.

Figure 1 (panel A, bottom chart) shows that a favourable net export shock drives both the interest rate and real exchange rate up. The mix of monetary policy tightening and exchange rate appreciation in turn helps ease excess demand and inflationary pressures.

In panel A of Figure 1 I consider two possible values for δ, namely, $\delta = 0.2$ (baseline) and a value reflecting a smaller responsiveness of output to exchange rates ($\delta = 0.1$). The comparison indicates that, for such smaller value of δ, there is less of a case for raising interest rates in the face of adverse financial shocks as given here by an increase in ε_t^f. In particular, a stronger monetary policy response is needed to stem the consequences of the disturbances on output and inflation when aggregate demand is less responsive to exchange rate developments. A different result holds when the economy is hit by a shock directly affecting the goods market, as given here by an increase in η_t^{xd}. In this case, the lower

δ, the more there is a case for raising interest rates, and the exchange rate thus ends up appreciating by more in real terms. It is worth stressing that, regardless of which of the two shocks is hitting the economy, an adverse disturbance leads to a stronger depreciation, the smaller the responsiveness of aggregate demand to exchange rates.

Finally, let us consider an economy exhibiting large contractionary depreciations ($\delta < -2\beta$). Panel B of Figure 1 (top chart) indicates that an adverse risk premium shock induces both a rise in interest rates and a real exchange rate depreciation. Unlike the case of a positive δ, the shock now induces an incipient contraction in aggregate demand via, say, balance sheet effects. Interest rates are hiked in the present case to a point where exchange rates end up stronger, thereby helping mitigate inflationary pressures and supporting the real side of the economy. Panel B of Figure 1 (bottom chart) shows how a favourable net export shock drives both interest rates and the real exchange rate down. The exchange rate depreciation reduces demand, thus partly offsetting the excess demand conditions in the goods market.

1.2. Backward Solution for Case when $\mid 1-\omega \mid > 1$

The condition $\mid 1-\omega \mid > 1$ refers to mildly contractionary depreciations, that is, a range of $\delta \in (-2\beta, 0)$. In this case, the system is fundamentally backward looking, and the real exchange rate can be expressed as

$$
\begin{aligned}
e_t \;=\; & \left(\frac{1}{1-\omega}\right)^{\tau} e_{t-\tau} - \frac{1}{\beta}\sum_{s=1}^{\tau}\left(\frac{1}{1-\omega}\right)^{s-1} \varepsilon_{t-s}^{xd} + \sum_{s=1}^{\tau}\left(\frac{1}{1-\omega}\right)^{s-1} \varepsilon_{t-s}^{f} + \zeta_t \\
& + \sum_{s=1}^{\tau-1}\left(\frac{1}{1-\omega}\right)^{s-1}\left(\frac{1}{1-\omega} - \frac{\varphi\gamma}{\beta\alpha}\right)\zeta_{t-s} + \left(\frac{1}{1-\omega}\right)^{\tau-1}\frac{\varphi\gamma}{\beta\alpha}\zeta_{t-\tau}
\end{aligned}
\tag{10}
$$

where ζ_t is a sunspot defined by $e_t = E_{t-1}e_t + \zeta_t$. This variable is an error that is purely extrinsic to the economy. In the following, I neglect for simplicity sunspot ζ_t.

Use of (3) and (10), following the reasoning leading to expression (9) in the previous subsection, allows me to characterise the central bank's reaction function in terms of the real interest rate.

Panel C of Figure 1 shows impulse responses of interest rates and exchanges rates to the same two shocks studied in the previous subsection, that is, an adverse risk premium shock and a favourable net export shock. Figure 1 (panel C, top chart) reports that an adverse risk premium shock leaves both the interest rate and real exchange rate unchanged on impact. As with the case of strongly contractionary depreciations, shock ε_t^f induces a rise in interest rates, eventually turning the real exchange rate stronger. This limits inflationary pressures and offsets contractionary forces in place.

In Figure 1 (panel C, bottom chart), a favourable net export shock raises the interest rate, leaving backward-looking real exchange rate unchanged on impact. Starting from the second period, the results are qualitatively the same as those taking place on impact in the case $\delta < -2\beta$, but this time extended over a longer time horizon.

Summarising, the correlation between exchange rates and interest rates, conditional on an adverse risk premium shock, is positive for mildly contractionary depreciations, with both of these variables going up in response to the shock. This result coincides with that found for strongly contractionary depreciations, except that such positive correlation is now delayed to the second period onwards, with both the interest rate and real exchange rate being left unchanged on impact. Turning to the case of a favourable net export shock, the dominant feature still is that of a positive correlation between exchange rates and interest rates, with both going down as a consequence of the shock. One important difference emerges, however, with respect to the case of strongly contractionary depreciations. In the present case, the falls in real exchange rates and interest rates are delayed to the second period onwards, instead of taking place on impact. As analysed in this subsection, in the initial period interest rates are raised and the exchange rate remains at baseline.

2. Imperfect Information without Signal Extraction

In the model of section 2 it was assumed that the central bank could identify the shocks that affected the economy and the exchange rate. In practice, central banks often do not have real-time access to economic information and cannot know the sources of disturbances. In order to analyse the consequences of this real-world feature, in this section I introduce an informational friction two ways by having shocks not to be known to any agent in the model at the time monetary policy decisions are taken. The type of frictions introduced here belongs to the category of asymmetric information. Given that no agent knows the shocks at the time interest rates are set, this type of imperfect information shares some properties with frictions of the common imperfect information variety. More specifically, the model in question can be referred to one of asymmetric information "without signal extraction" (in contrast to that of Sánchez's, 2007, which allows for signal extraction).

In this section I thus examine the other possible case where i) information still becomes available to foreign exchange market participants before it is known to the central bank; but ii) it is not available to any agent in the economy at the time of the monetary policy decision. Item ii) means that, initially, neither the central bank nor the private sector observes current output and prices, and the former cannot thus infer macroeconomic disturbances. To incorporate this possibility into the model, I assume that shocks affecting endogenous variables in period t take place after the central bank forms expectations and takes its decision. The current exchange rate is, like output and prices, unknown to the central bank when setting interest rates.[10] I label expectations formed using the implied limited information set simply by E_t and those of informed agents by E_t^+. After the central bank action is taken, the private sector observes shocks. Producers take decisions on prices and output, and the exchange rate is set to clear the foreign exchange market. All these private sector actions occur too late for the central bank to factor them in during its current period's decision, but they are known to the policymaker at the time of the next monetary policy move.

Nominal exchange rates are to be explicitly handled in order to solve the model. The model still consists of equations (4) and (5). Furthermore, in section 3 I assumed that the central bank could identify the shocks that affected the economy and the exchange rate. It could be argued, however, that the private sector (or at least a part of it) is better informed about developments in the sphere of production. To cope with this possibility, in this sub-

[10]This might seem odd given that information on exchange rates is easily available. The rationale for this setup is that I try to incorporate, in the context of a discrete-time framework, the notion that there is an institutional constraint in the timing of interest rate decisions (such as a fixed time interval between such decisions) as opposed to the higher frequency of shocks and changes in prices, output and exchange rates in real-world situations.

section I explore the implications of informational barriers by assuming that the central bank does not observe current output and prices. Following Gerlach and Smets (2000), I also assume that participants in the foreign exchange market do have information about the current supply and demand shocks.[11] The exchange rate incorporates information about underlying excess demand shocks that is not otherwise available to the central bank. Expectations formed using this information set are denoted E_t^+. In line with these assumptions about information, I rewrite equations (1), (2) and (3) as

$$\pi_t = E_{t-1}\pi_t + \alpha'\left(y_t - \varepsilon_t^S\right) - \gamma'(s_t - E_{t-1}^+ s_t) \qquad (11)$$

$$y_t = -\beta r_t - \delta(s_t + p_t) + \varepsilon_t^D \qquad (12)$$

$$R_t = -E_t^+ s_{t+1} + s_t + \varepsilon_t^f \qquad (13)$$

where s_t is the nominal exchange rate and $\alpha' \equiv \alpha/(1+\gamma)$ and $\gamma' \equiv \gamma/(1+\gamma)$. A comparison with the full information approach of section 2 reveals that nominal exchange rates explicitly show in this subsection's set-up. The reason is that the presence of informational frictions turns necessary to further distinguish between real and nominal variables, the latter being subjected to processes of expectation formation that play an important role in the model.

For the purpose at hand here (namely, a case without signal extraction), the solution needs to incorporate the specific timing of information described above. In particular, the nominal exchange rate s_t needs to be replaced by $E_t s_t$ when it comes to modelling the central bank's expectations and actions. Since the central bank does not observe current prices, I assume that it optimises the objective function by choosing the perceived inflation rate. The contemporaneous inflation perception error is

$$\eta_t \equiv \pi_t - E_t\pi_t = \frac{1}{1+\alpha'\delta}\left[\alpha'\eta_t^{xd} - (\alpha'\delta + \gamma')(s_t - E_t s_t)\right] \qquad (14)$$

Moreover, we have $E_{t-1}\pi_t = \tilde{\pi}$, and, using (4), $r_t = R_t - \tilde{\pi}$.
The equilibrium inflation and output levels equal

$$\pi_t = \tilde{\pi} + \eta_t \qquad (15)$$

$$y_t = \varepsilon_t^S + \frac{\gamma'}{\alpha'}(s_t - E_{t-1}^+ s_t) + \frac{1}{\alpha'}\eta \qquad (16)$$

where I have used the result that $E_t s_t = E_{t-1}^+ s_t$.

I make the same assumptions regarding the stochastic processes driving the shocks to the economy as in section 3. Using (4), (11), (12), (13), (14) and (15), the equilibrium nominal exchange rate can then be found to equal

$$s_t = E_{t-1}^+ s_t - \varepsilon_t^f + \frac{1}{\beta}\left[(\beta - \delta)\,\tilde{\pi} - \delta p_{t-1} + +\rho\varepsilon_{t-1}^{xd} - \delta E_t s_t\right] \qquad (17)$$

Once more, the model has a forward solution for the case when $\mid 1-\omega \mid < 1$, and a backward solution for the case when $\mid 1-\omega \mid > 1$. In the forward solution, the condition

[11] Information about the shocks is widespread among the private sector (except for workers), but the central bank infers some of the properties of the new data only by observing current realisations of the exchange rate.

$\mid 1-\omega \mid < 1$ amounts to two different ranges for the values of δ, namely, $\delta \in (-\infty, -2\beta) \cup (0, \infty)$. The forward solution in the absence of bubbles can be characterised by

$$R_t = \tilde{\pi} + \frac{\delta}{\beta(1-\rho_f)+\delta}\rho_f \varepsilon^f_{t-1} + \frac{1-\rho}{\beta(1-\rho)+\delta}\rho\varepsilon^{xd}_{t-1} \tag{18}$$

$$s_t = -\tilde{\pi} - p_{t-1} - \frac{\beta}{\beta(1-\rho_f)+\delta}\varepsilon^f_t + s_3\xi_t + \frac{\rho}{\beta(1-\rho)+\delta}\varepsilon^{xd}_{t-1} + s_4\eta^{xd}_t \tag{19}$$

where $s_3 \equiv -x/[\beta(1-\rho_f)+\delta]$, $s_4 \equiv [1-(1-\rho)\alpha'(\beta+\delta)]/\{(1-\gamma')[\beta(1-\rho)+\delta]\}$, and $x \equiv \{\delta[1+\alpha'(\beta+\delta)]+\gamma'\beta\}/(1-\gamma')$.

The backward solution obtains when $\mid 1-\omega \mid > 1$. This condition refers to contractionary depreciations of a milder type, that is, the range $\delta \in (-2\beta, 0)$. In the absence of sunspots, the nominal exchange rate is found to be given by

$$\begin{aligned} s_t = {} & \left(\frac{\beta+\delta}{\beta}\right)^{\tau} s_{t-\tau} + \left(\frac{\beta-\delta}{\delta}\right)\left[1-\left(\frac{\beta+\delta}{\beta}\right)^{\tau}\right]\tilde{\pi} + \frac{\delta}{\beta}\sum_{l=1}^{\tau}\left(\frac{\beta+\delta}{\beta}\right)^{l-1} p_{t-l-1} \\ & -\frac{\rho}{\beta}\sum_{l=1}^{\tau}\left(\frac{\beta+\delta}{\beta}\right)^{l-1}\varepsilon^{xd}_{t-l-1} + \sum_{l=1}^{\tau}\left(\frac{\beta+\delta}{\beta}\right)^{l-1}\varepsilon^f_{t-l} \end{aligned} \tag{20}$$

Given that the exchange rate is predetermined in this backward solution, $E_t\eta^{xd}_t = 0$. Under this solution, the system is fundamentally backward-looking. Moreover, underlying the expression for s_t we have that the monetary authorities do not observe the exchange rate, which implies that they ignore the current state of the economy. Finally, equilibrium inflation is again given by (15), while equilibrium output simplifies further from (16) to $y_t = \varepsilon^S_t + \eta_t/\alpha'$.

2.1. Comparison with the Full Information Case

In this subsection I compare the results obtained under imperfect information with those derived under the full information setup. In making this comparison, I relate Figure 1 (the full information case) to Figure 2 (asymmetric information without signal extraction). In addition to the parameter values used for calibration in section 3, simulation analysis under asymmetric information with signal extraction also requires some values for the variances of the shocks. These extra parameter values, taken from McCallum and Nelson (2000), are: $Var(\xi) = 0.04^2$, $Var(\varepsilon^S) = 0.007^2$, $Var(\varepsilon^d) = 0.01^2$ and $Var(\varepsilon^x) = 0$.

Let us the proceed to the comparison between full information and asymmetric information without signal extraction. For the latter case, panel A of Figure 2 (top chart) shows impulse responses for an economy displaying expansionary depreciations to an adverse risk premium shock. The main pattern here is that the interest rate rises and the exchange rate depreciates, qualitatively the same results as obtained under full information (Figure 1, panel A, top chart). The only difference with respect to full information outcomes is circumscribed to the reaction of the interest rate on impact: it does not move under asymmetric information without signal extraction, while it goes up in the case of full information. The bottom chart in panel A of Figure 2 indicates that, in the face of a net export shock, the

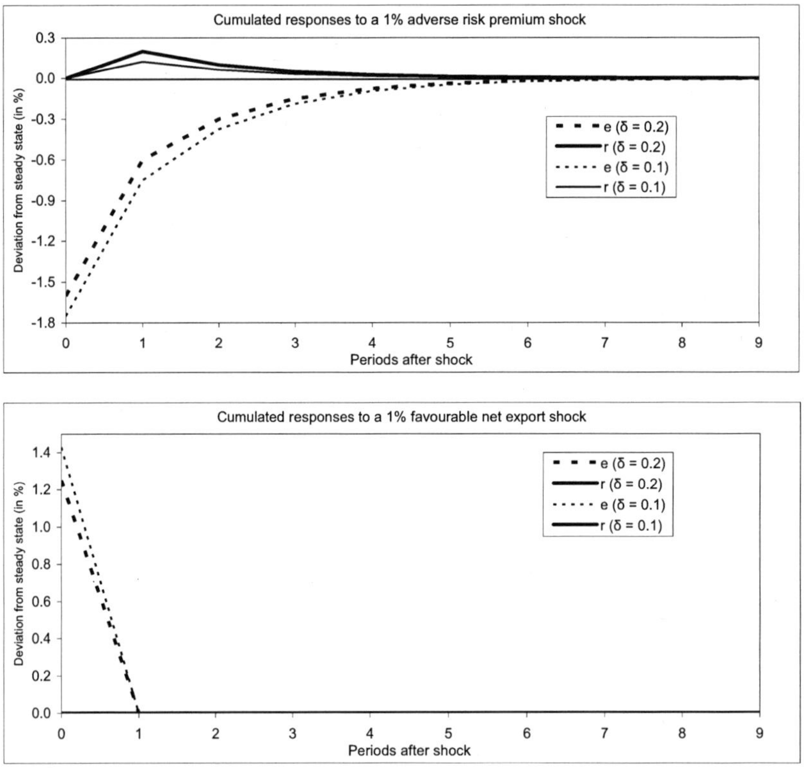

Figure 2. Asymmetric information without signal extraction: Impulse responses of interest rate and real exchange rate.

results mirror those obtained under full information for the real exchange rate, which appreciates in response to the emergence of a positive excess demand for goods. However, the central bank's lack of contemporaneous information implies that interest rate is left unchanged, as opposed to hiked under full information. Finally, for both shocks, assuming that $\delta = 0.1$ instead of $\delta = 0.2$ has, in the present case, a different effect on results for interest rates on impact. More concretely, while changing δ affects the intensity with which the central bank responds to shocks, it has no consequences whatsoever for interest rates in the initial period, which stay at zero under any of the two shocks considered. Other than that, reactions of impulse responses in panel A of Figure 2 to a smaller value of δ are broadly similar to those obtained under full information: a) the exchange rate fluctuates by a wider margin in reaction to either shock; and b) interest rates are, after the initial period, raised by less in the face of adverse financial disturbances and cut by more under real shocks.

For the case of strongly contractionary depreciations, panel B of Figure 2 presents in its top chart the reaction of interest rates and exchange rates to a negative financial disturbance under asymmetric information without signal extraction. Interest rates (after the initial period) go up and the exchange rate strengthens in real terms, the same results obtained under full information (Figure 1, panel B). As with panel A of Figure 2 (top chart), the only difference is circumscribed to the reaction of the interest rate on impact: it is left unchanged in the case of asymmetric information without signal extraction, while it rises under full information. The bottom chart in panel A of Figure 2 indicates that, in the face of a net export shock, the results mirror those obtained under full information for the real exchange rate, which depreciates in response to the emergence of a positive excess demand for goods. Instead, given that monetary authorities lack information about current shocks, the interest rate does not move, as opposed to being cut in the case of full information.

In sum, I find that full information results do not appear to be robust to the presence of the informational friction introduced here. For economies exhibiting expansionary or strongly contractionary depreciations, such friction is responsible for an optimal deviations from the full information outcome, namely, that under asymmetric information without signal extraction the monetary authorities do not react on impact to shocks hitting the economy. This difference in results also implies that, for expansionary depreciations, a lower responsiveness of output to exchange rates, which has an impact on comovements between interest rates and exchange rates under full information, instead fails for any shock to affect interest rates on impact under asymmetric information without signal extraction. Finally, in the case of mildly contractionary depreciations, the asymmetric information model predicts a lack of response of the central bank to aggregate demand shocks, as opposed to an stabilising movement in interest rates under full information.

3. Concluding Remarks

This paper has investigated the link between interest rates and exchange rates in small open economies under flexible exchange rates, comparing situations where information is full with an alternative model of imperfect information. The latter distinction is mostly missing in the previous related literature, despite the obvious real-life feature of economic decisions that they are taken under a less-than-perfect understanding of the current state of affairs. In undertaking this study, I also analyse both economies for which depreciations are expansionary and contractionary. The latter is an attempt to bridge the gap between standard analyses and the empirical evidence commonly found in emerging economies.

The results of this paper allow us to identify the following important differences between full and imperfect information. Full information results are here found not to be robust to the presence of the informational friction here considered. For economies exhibiting expansionary or strongly contractionary depreciations, such friction leads to an optimal deviation from the full information outcome, namely, that the monetary authority does not react on impact to shocks. In the case of mildly contractionary depreciations, our asymmetric information model predicts a lack of response of the central bank to aggregate demand shocks, as opposed to an offsetting movement in interest rates under full information. Optimal policies are thus found to depend on the degree of informedness in the economy.

One last point worth mentioning refers to whether non-fundamental dynamics play a different role depending on the type of informational assumptions used. My conclusion is that there is basically no difference between the three different approaches studied here. The theoretical analyses presented above confirm the potential relevance of non-fundamental behaviour under mildly contractionary depreciations, even after relaxing the assumption of full information. While in my study sunspots are neglected for simplicity, future work would benefit from an assessment as to whether non-fundamental dynamics are empirically relevant and, if so, what specific patterns they adopt in practice.

References

[1] Ahmed, S., 2003. "Sources of Economic Fluctuations in Latin America and Implications for the Choice of Exchange Rate Regimes", *Journal of Development Economics*, **72**, 181–202.

[2] Ball, L., 1999. "Policy Rules for Open Economies". In Taylor, J. (Ed.), *Monetary Policy Rules*, Chicago: University of Chicago Press, 127-144.

[3] Ball, L., 2002. "Policy Rules and External Shocks". In Loayza, N. and Schmidt-Hebbel, K. (Eds.), *Monetary Policy: Rules and Transmission Mechanisms* , Series on Central Banking, Analysis, and Economic Policies, Santiago de Chile, 47-63.

[4] Barro, R. and Broadbent, B., 1997. "Central Bank Preferences and Macroeconomic Equilibrium", *Journal of Monetary Economics,* **39**, 17-43.

[5] Calvo, G., 2001. "Capital Markets and the Exchange Rate. With Special Reference to the Dollarization Debate in Latin America", *Journal of Money, Credit and Banking,* **33**, 312-334.

[6] Calvo, G. and Reinhart, C, 2001. "Fixing for Your Life". In Collins, S. and Rodrik, D. (Eds.), *Brookings Trade Forum: 2000,* Brookings Institution Press, Washington, DC, 1–57.

[7] Calvo, G. and Reinhart, C., 2002. "Fear of Floating", *Quarterly Journal of Economics*, **117**, 379-408.

[8] Caves, R., Frankel, J. and Jones, R., 2002. *World Trade and Payments: An Introduction*, Boston: Addison-Wesley, 9th ed.

[9] Cavoli, T. and Rajan, R., 2005. "Inflation Targeting and Monetary Policy Rules for Small and Open Developing Economies: Simple Analytics with Application to Thailand", *NUS Working Paper* No. **5**.

[10] Céspedes, L., Chang, R. and Velasco, A., 2003. "IS-LM-BP in the Pampas", *IMF Staff Papers*, **50** (special issue), 143-156.

[11] Céspedes, L., Chang, R. and Velasco, A., 2004. "Balance Sheets and Exchange Rates", *American Economic Review,* 94, 1183-1193.

[12] Chang, R. and Velasco, A., 2001. "Monetary Policy in a Dollarized Economy Where Balance Sheets Matter", *Journal of Development Economics,* **66**, 445– 464.

[13] Detken, C. and Gaspar, V., 2003. "Maintaining Price Stability under Free-Floating: A Fearless Way Out of the Corner?", *ECB Working Paper* No. **241**.

[14] Edwards, S., 2002. "The Great Exchange Rate Debate After Argentina", *Working Paper* No. 74, Oesterreichische Nationalbank.

[15] Eichengreen, B., 2004. "Monetary and Exchange Rate Policy in Korea: Assessments and Policy Issues". Paper prepared for a symposium at the Bank of Korea, Seoul.

[16] Eichengreen, B., 2005. "Can Emerging Markets Float? Should They Inflation Target?" In Driver, R., Sinclair, P. and Thoenissen, C. (Eds.), *Exchange Rates, Capital Movements and Policy*, Routledge, London.

[17] Fraga, A., Goldfajn, I. and Minella, A. 2003. "Inflation Targeting in Emerging Market Economies". In Gertler, M. and Rogoff, K. (Eds.), *NBER Macroeconomics Annual*, Washington, DC, 365-400.

[18] Galí, J. and Monacelli, T., 2005. "Monetary Policy and Exchange Rate Volatility in a Small Open Economy", *Review of Economic Studies,* **72**, 707-734.

[19] Gerlach, S. and Smets, F., 2000. "MCIs and Monetary Policy", *European Economic Review,* **44**, 1677-1700.

[20] Leeper, E. and Zha, T., 2003. "Modest Policy Interventions", *Journal of Monetary Economics*, **50**, 1673–1700.

[21] McCallum, B. and Nelson, E., 1999. "Nominal Income Targeting in an Open Economy Optimizing Model", *Journal of Monetary Economics*, **43**, 553-578.

[22] McCallum, B. and Nelson, E., 2000. "Monetary Policy for an Open Economy: An Alternative Framework with Optimizing Agents and Sticky Prices", *Oxford Review of Economic Policy,* **16**, 74-91.

[23] Morón, E. and Winkelried, D., 2005. "Monetary Policy Rules for Financially Vulnerable Economies", *Journal of Development Economics,* **76**, 1-263.

[24] Reinhart, C. and Rogoff, K., 2004. "The Modern History of Exchange Rate Arrangements: A Reinterpretation", *Quarterly Journal of Economics*, 119, 1-48.

[25] Sánchez, M., 2005. "The Link between Interest Rates and Exchange Rates: Do Contractionary Depreciations Make a Difference?", *ECB Working Paper* No. **543**.

[26] Sánchez, M., 2007. "How Does Information Affect the Comovement between Interest Rates and Exchange Rates?", *Rivista Internazionale di Scienze Sociali* , No. **4**, 547-562.

[27] Svensson, L., 2000. "Open-economy Inflation Targeting", *Journal of International Economics,* **50**, 155-183.

[28] Taylor J., 1999. "The Robustness and Efficiency of Monetary Policy Rules as Guidelines for Interest Rate Setting by the European Central Bank", *Journal of Monetary Economics*, **43**, 655–79.

In: Exchange Rates: Policies, Effects and Fluctuations
Editor: Natalie B. Perkins, pp.131-145
ISBN: 978-1-61209-505-9
© 2011 Nova Science Publishers, Inc.

Chapter 7

NOMINAL AND REAL EXCHANGE RATE FLUCTUATIONS OF YEN-DOLLAR RATES

Shigeyuki Hamori*
Faculty of Economics, Kobe University
2-1 Rokkodai, Nada-Ku, Kobe 657-8501, Japan

ABSTRACT

This chapter uses a long-run structural VAR approach to study the sources of real exchange rate fluctuations of yen-dollar rates. We begin by identifying two types of macroeconomic shock (real and nominal), in order to reveal the sources of movements in real exchange rates. The evidence presented indicates that real shocks play a dominant role in explaining the fluctuations of the real exchange rate. Next, we extend the model to identify three types of macroeconomic shock (real supply, real demand, and nominal), again to reveal the sources of movements in real exchange rates. The evidence from the extended model also indicates that real shocks (real demand and real supply) play a dominant role in explaining the fluctuations of the real exchange rate.

1. INTRODUCTION

When modeling exchange rates and studying economic policy, we must measure the relative importance of permanent and temporary shocks on exchange rates. Disequilibrium models of exchange rate determination (e.g., Dornbusch, 1976) mainly attribute variations in real and nominal exchange rates to nominal disturbances of a type likely to have only transitory effects on real exchange rates. Equilibrium models (e.g., Stockman, 1987) rely on permanent, real shocks to explain movements in real and nominal rates. Isolating these sources of variation can assist policymakers in determining the extent of excess variability in exchange rates (Lastrapes, 1992). A thorough understanding of the sources underlying real

* E-mail address: hamori@econ.kobe-u.ac.jp

exchange rate fluctuations is also crucial, given that the real exchange rate reflects the performance and competitiveness of an economy. Movements of the real exchange rate may also influence inflation, output, and the balance of payments.

This chapter investigates the sources of real exchange rate fluctuations between the US dollar and Japanese yen. By constructing a structural VAR model to analyze the sources of real exchange rate fluctuations, we try to identify the dynamics and forces driving the real exchange rate variations since the beginning of the 1980s. Several studies have attempted to investigate the sources of real exchange rate fluctuations since Blanchard and Quah (1989) published their influential work based on a bivariate structural VAR model for output and unemployment. The paper by Bayoumi and Eichengreen (1992) was among the first to analyze exchange rate variations using the Blanchard and Quah (1989) approach. They distinguish between supply shocks and demand shocks by assuming that the former have permanent effects whereas the latter have only temporary effects. Their empirical results, for the G-7 countries, indicate that the shift from the Bretton Woods system of pegged exchange rates to the post Bretton Woods float can be explained by a modest increase in the cross-country dispersion of supply shocks

Lastrapes (1992) carries out a similar analysis for six industrialized countries from 1973 to 1989. He identifies two types of structural disturbance, nominal shocks and real shocks, with the restriction that the former has no long-run impact on the real exchange rate. His results indicate that real shocks account for the major part of both real and nominal exchange rate fluctuations for all six of the countries analyzed.

Enders and Lee (1997) decompose real and nominal exchange rate movements into the components induced by real and nominal factors over the period from 1973 to 1992. They find that nominal shocks have a minor effect on the real and nominal bilateral exchange rates of the Canadian, Japanese, and German currencies against the US dollar.

Chowdhury (2002) investigates sources of fluctuations in the real and nominal US dollar exchange rates of selected emerging market economies by decomposing the exchange rate series into stochastic components induced by real and nominal factors. His analysis focuses on the dynamic effects and relative importance of real and nominal shocks in explaining the behavior of these exchange rates.

Clarida and Gali (1994) extend the bivariate VAR model to the trivariate VAR model and identify three types of structural disturbance: real aggregate supply shocks (those capable of influencing the levels of all three variables in the long run), real aggregate demand shocks (those with no long-run impact on the real output level), and nominal shocks (those that affect only the price level in the long run). According to their empirical analysis for four industrialized countries (Germany, Japan, the UK, and Canada) over the floating period from 1973 to 1992, nominal disturbances explain a substantial amount of the variance in the real exchange rates against the dollar in two of the countries (Germany and Japan: 41% of the variance of the change in the dollar-deutschmark real exchange rate and 35% of the variance of the change in the dollar-yen real exchange rate), whereas the real exchange rate fluctuations in the other two countries are mainly driven by real demand shocks.

According to a five-dimensional structural VAR analysis on a long-term data set (from 1889 to 1992) for the US and UK by Rogers (1999), monetary shocks typically account for nearly one-half of the forecast error variance of the real exchange rate over short horizons. The evidence indicates that monetary shocks are generally very important for real exchange rate movements. This result contradicts the findings by Lastrapes (1992), Clarida and Gali (1994), and Enders and Lee (1997).

These studies set a benchmark for researchers seeking to explain real exchange rate movements. In this study we begin by constructing a bivariate structural vector autoregressive (SVAR) model, following the example of Enders and Lee (1997), in order to assess the relative importance of two types of shocks: real shocks and nominal shocks. The structural VAR decomposition implies that (i) real shocks are expected to influence real and nominal exchange rates in the long-run; and (ii) nominal shocks are expected to have no long-run impact on real exchange rates. Next, we extend the model to a trivariate SVAR model, in order to assess the relative importance of three types of shocks: aggregate supply shocks, aggregate demand shocks, and nominal demand shocks. The structural VAR decomposition implies that (i) only supply shocks are expected to influence the relative output level in the long run; (ii) both supply and demand shocks are expected to influence the real exchange rate in the long run; and (iii) monetary shocks are expected to have no long-run impact on the relative output levels or the real exchange rate.

The chapter is organized as follows. Section 2 explains the data used for empirical analysis. Section 3 shows the empirical techniques and empirical results for the bivariate system. Section 4 shows the empirical techniques and empirical results for trivarite system. Some concluding remarks are summarized in section 5.

2. DATA

The data are taken from the *International Financial Statistics* (IFS) of the International Monetary Fund (IFM). The empirical analysis is carried out using monthly observations from January 1980 to April 2006. We use the exchange rate, consumer price indexes of Japan and the United States, and industrial production indexes (seasonally adjusted value) of Japan and the United States. The exchange rate is expressed per US dollar. The log of the nominal exchange rate (e_t), the log of the real exchange rate (r_t), and the log of the relative output (y_t) are used in the empirical analysis. The log-level real exchange rate, r_t, may be expressed as follows:

$$r_t = e_t + p_t^{US} - p_t^{JAPAN}, \qquad (1)$$

where p_t^{JAPAN} is the logarithm of the price level in Japan); p_t^{US} is the logarithm of the price level in the United states. The real exchange rate thus measures the relative price of goods in Japan in terms of US goods. $y_t(= y_t^{JAPAN} - y_t^{US})$ is the difference between the real income in Japan and the real income in the United States. Figure 1 shows the movements of real and nominal exchange rates over the period. The value of the Japanese currency appreciated sharply against the US dollar during the 1980's.

This chapter uses the augmented Dickey-Fuller (ADF) test (Dickey and Fuller, 1979) to test for the presence of a unit root for each variable in the univariate representations of the log of the nominal exchange rate (e_t), the log of the real exchange rate (r_t), and the log of the relative output (y_t). The null hypothesis of a unit root is not rejected at conventional significance levels for any of the variables. The null hypothesis of a unit root is rejected, however, for the first-differenced for each variable. Thus, e_t, r_t and y_t are each found to be I(1) series.

3. BIVARIATE SYSTEM

3.1. Empirical Techniques

The bivariate VAR model developed by Enders and Lee (1997) will serve as a starting point for our discussion. Consider the following infinite-order vector moving average (VMA) representation:

$$\Delta x_t = C(L)\varepsilon_t, \tag{2}$$

where L is a lag operator, Δ is a difference operator, $\Delta x_t = [\Delta r_t, \Delta e_t]'$ is a (2×1) vector of endogenous variables, and $\varepsilon_t = [\varepsilon_{r,t}, \varepsilon_{n,t}]'$ is a (2×1) vector of structural shocks with covariance matrix Σ. The error term can be interpreted as real shocks and nominal shocks. We assume that the structural shocks have no contemporaneous correlation or autocorrelation. This implies that Σ is a diagonal matrix.

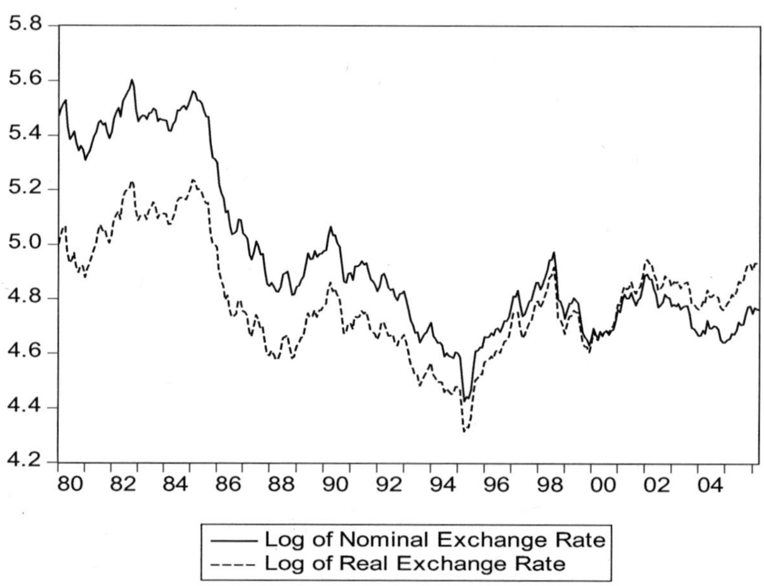

Figure 1. Real and Nominal Exchange Rate Movements.

To implement the econometric methodology, we need to estimate the following finite-order VAR model:

$$[I - \Phi(L)]\Delta x_t = u_t \qquad (3)$$

where $\Phi(L)$ is a finite-order matrix polynomial in the lag operator and u_t is a vector of disturbances. If the stationarity condition is satisfied, we can transfer equation (3) to the VMA representation,

$$\Delta x_t = A(L)u_t \qquad (4)$$

where $A(L)$ is a lag polynomial.

Equations (2) and (4) imply a linear relationship between ε_t and u_t:

$$u_t = C_0\varepsilon_t \qquad (5)$$

C_0 in Equation (4) is a 2×2 matrix that defines the contemporaneous structural relationship that needs to be identified for the vector of structural shocks ε_t in order to be recovered from the estimated disturbance vector u_t. Four parameters are required to convert the residuals from the estimated VAR into the original shocks that drive the behavior of the endogenous variables. Three of the four are given by the elements of $\Sigma = C_0C_0'$, hence we need to add one more identifying restriction. Blanchard and Quah (1989) suggest that economic theory can be used to impose this restriction. By the methodology of Enders and Lee (1997), we thus impose an additional restriction on the long-run multipliers while freely determining the short run dynamics. This restriction is written as follows:

Assumption

Nominal (monetary) shocks have no long-run impact on the real exchange rate;

The long-run representation of equation (2) can be written as:

$$\begin{bmatrix} \Delta r_t \\ \Delta e_t \end{bmatrix} = \begin{bmatrix} C_{11}(1) & C_{12}(1) \\ C_{21}(1) & C_{22}(1) \end{bmatrix} \begin{bmatrix} \varepsilon_{r,t} \\ \varepsilon_{n,t} \end{bmatrix} \qquad (6)$$

where $C(1) = C_0 + C_1 + C_2 + \cdots$ are long-run multipliers of the structural VAR (long-run effect of ε_t on Δx_t). By the method of Enders and Lee (1997), we stipulate that the long-run multiplier C_{12} is equal to zero, thus making $C(1)$ lower triangular matrix.

3.2. Empirical Results

Using the SBIC (Schwarz Bayesian Information Criterion) to choose the optimal lag length of VAR in empirical analysis, we find that the VAR(2) model is the most appropriate.

We present the impulse responses of each of the variables to one standard deviation in each of the fundamental shocks.

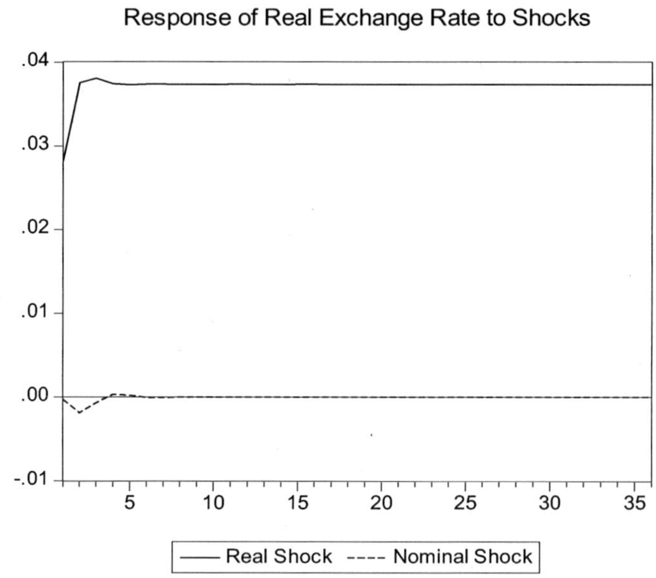

(a) Response of Real Exchange Rate

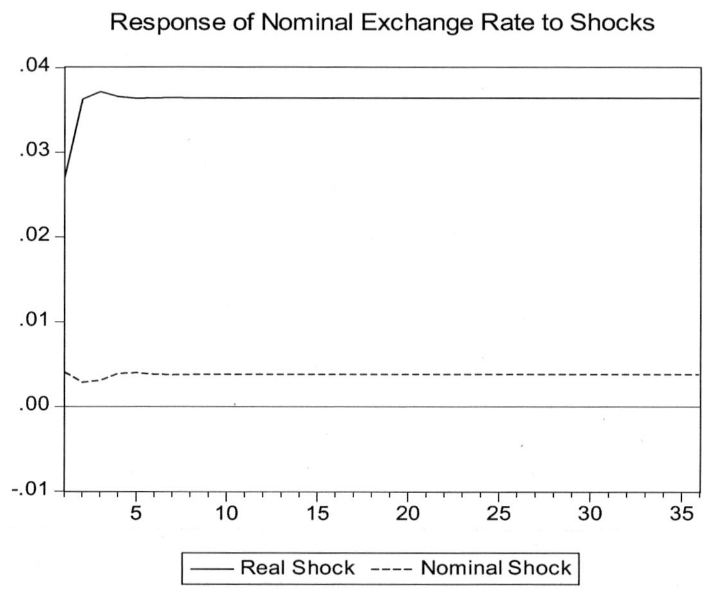

(b) Response of Nominal Exchange Rate

Figure 2. Accumulated Impulse Responses (Bivariate Model).

Figure 2 illustrates the impulse response functions of real and nominal exchange rates to one-standard-deviation structural shocks. Impulse responses are useful for assessing the signs and magnitudes of responses to specific shocks by revealing the dynamic effects of each shock. The results broadly coincide with conventional models of the open economy. Panel (a) shows that real shocks lead to a permanent increase in the real exchange rate. Nominal shocks have smaller effects and leave the long-run real exchange rate unaffected in accordance with the long-run restrictions imposed. Panel (b) demonstrates that a real shock leads a persistent increase in the nominal exchange rate. A nominal shock is associated with a permanent increase in the nominal exchange. Our results show that a real shock induces a jump in the real and nominal rate of nearly the same magnitude. Hence, there is little movement in the price ratio in response to a real shock. We also find that nominal shocks have no long-run effects on real rates. Given that nominal shocks have no effect on relative prices, they can be assumed to affect prices by an equal but opposite amount. These results are consistent with those of Enders and Lee (1997).

To shed light on the question of the sources of real exchange rate fluctuations, we then calculate the forecast error variance decompositions. Variance decomposition is a useful technique to evaluate the relative importance of such shocks to the system. Table 1 shows the fraction of the forecast error variance that can be attributed to each shock at different horizons in the model for each variable. Real shocks account for more than 99% of the variance in real exchange rate throughout the estimation horizons. The less then 1% of variance remaining is attributable to nominal shocks. The estimates imply that real shocks explain a substantial amount of the variance of the real exchange rate.

Table 1. Forecast Error Variance Decomposition (Bivariate System)

(A) Real Exchange Rate

Horizon (month)	Real Shock (%)	Nominal Shock (%)
1	99.991	0.009
3	99.539	0.461
6	99.414	0.586
9	99.413	0.587
12	99.413	0.587
24	99.413	0.587
36	99.413	0.587

(B) Nominal Exchange Rate

Horizon (month)	Real Shock (%)	Nominal Shock (%)
1	97.795	2.205
3	97.849	2.151
6	97.765	2.235
9	97.765	2.235
12	97.765	2.235
24	97.765	2.235
36	97.765	2.235

Forecast error variance decompositions for the variations in the nominal exchange rate show that real shocks explain most of the movements in the nominal exchange rate. Specifically, real shocks account for more than 97% of the variance in the nominal exchange rate movement. Nominal shocks, meanwhile, contribute less than 3% to the fluctuations of the nominal exchange rate. To summarize, real shocks explain most of the forecast error variance of the changes in the real and nominal exchange rates.

4. TRIVARIATE SYSTEM

4.1. Empirical Techniques

Consider the following infinite-order vector moving average (VMA) representation:

$$\Delta x_t = C(L)\varepsilon_t \tag{7}$$

where L is a lag operator, Δ is a difference operator, $\Delta x_t = [\Delta y_t, \Delta r_t, \Delta e_t]'$ is a (3×1) vector of endogenous variables, and $\varepsilon_t = [\varepsilon_{s,t}, \varepsilon_{d,t}, \varepsilon_{n,t}]'$ is a (3×1) vector of structural shocks with covariance matrix Σ. The error term can be interpreted as relative supply shocks, relative real demand shocks, and relative nominal shocks. We assume that the structural shocks have no contemporaneous correlation or autocorrelation. This implies that Σ is a diagonal matrix.

To implement the econometric methodology, we need to estimate the following finite-order VAR model:

$$[I - \Phi(L)]\Delta x_t = u_t \tag{8}$$

where $\Phi(L)$ is a finite-order matrix polynomial in the lag operator and u_t is a vector of disturbances. If the stationarity condition is satisfied, we can transfer equation (8) to the VMA representation,

$$\Delta x_t = A(L)u_t \tag{9}$$

where $A(L)$ is a lag polynomial.

Equations (7) and (9) imply a linear relationship between ε_t and u_t:

$$u_t = C_0\varepsilon_t \tag{10}$$

C_0 in Equation (9) is a 3×3 matrix that defines the contemporaneous structural relationship that needs to be identified for the vector of structural shocks ε_t in order to be recovered from the estimated disturbance vector u_t. Nine parameters are required to convert the residuals from the estimated VAR into original shocks that drive the behavior of the endogenous variables. Blanchard and Quah (1989) suggest that economic theory can be used to impose these restrictions. By the methodology of Clarida and Gali (1994), we thus impose three additional restrictions on the long-run multipliers while freely determining the short-run dynamics. These three restrictions are as follows:

- Assumption (i) Nominal (monetary) shocks have no long-run impact on the levels of output;
- Assumption (ii) Nominal (monetary) shocks have no long-run impact on the real exchange rate;
- Assumption (iii) Real demand shocks have no long-run impact on the levels of output.

The long-run representation of equation (6) can be written as :

$$\begin{bmatrix} \Delta y_t \\ \Delta r_t \\ \Delta e_t \end{bmatrix} = \begin{bmatrix} C_{11}(1) & C_{12}(1) & C_{13}(1) \\ C_{21}(1) & C_{22}(1) & C_{23}(1) \\ C_{31}(1) & C_{32}(1) & C_{33}(1) \end{bmatrix} \begin{bmatrix} \varepsilon_{s,t} \\ \varepsilon_{d,t} \\ \varepsilon_{n,t} \end{bmatrix} \tag{11}$$

where $C(1) = C_0 + C_1 + C_2 + \cdots$ are long-run multipliers of the structural VAR (long-run effect of ε_t on Δx_t). By the method Clarida and Gali (1994), we stipulate that the long-run multipliers C_{12}, C_{13} and C_{23} are equal to zero, thus making the matrix $C(1)$ a lower triangular matrix.

4.2. Empirical Results

Using the SBIC to choose the optimal lag length of VAR in empirical analysis, we find that the VAR(1) model is the most appropriate. We present the impulse responses of each of the variables to one standard deviation in each of the fundamental shocks.

Figure 3 illustrates the impulse response functions of the explanatory variables to one-standard-deviation structural shocks. Panel (a) shows that supply shocks lead to a permanent increase in relative output. Positive real or nominal demand shocks have smaller effects and leave the long-run relative output level unaffected in accordance with the long-run restrictions imposed.

Panel (b) demonstrates that a positive supply shock leads to a persistent decrease in the real exchange rate. A positive real demand shock is associated with a permanent increase in the real exchange rate, while a nominal shock temporarily increases the real exchange rate and is asymptotic to zero in accordance with the long-run restrictions imposed.

Finally, panel (c) shows that the impulse response of the nominal exchange rate drops immediately and permanently after a supply shock. We can also see that demand shocks have positive permanent effects on nominal exchange rates, while nominal shocks have positive permanent effects on nominal exchange rates.

Next, we calculate the forecast error variance decompositions. Table 2 shows the fraction of the forecast error variance that can be attributed to each shock at different horizons in the model for each variable. Supply shocks account for most of the variance in output growth throughout the estimation horizons and represent the most important factor for variation in the forecast errors of relative output. The rest of the variance is attributable to demand and nominal shocks in more or less similar fractions (less than 1%). The estimates imply that real supply shocks explain a substantial amount of the variance of output growth.

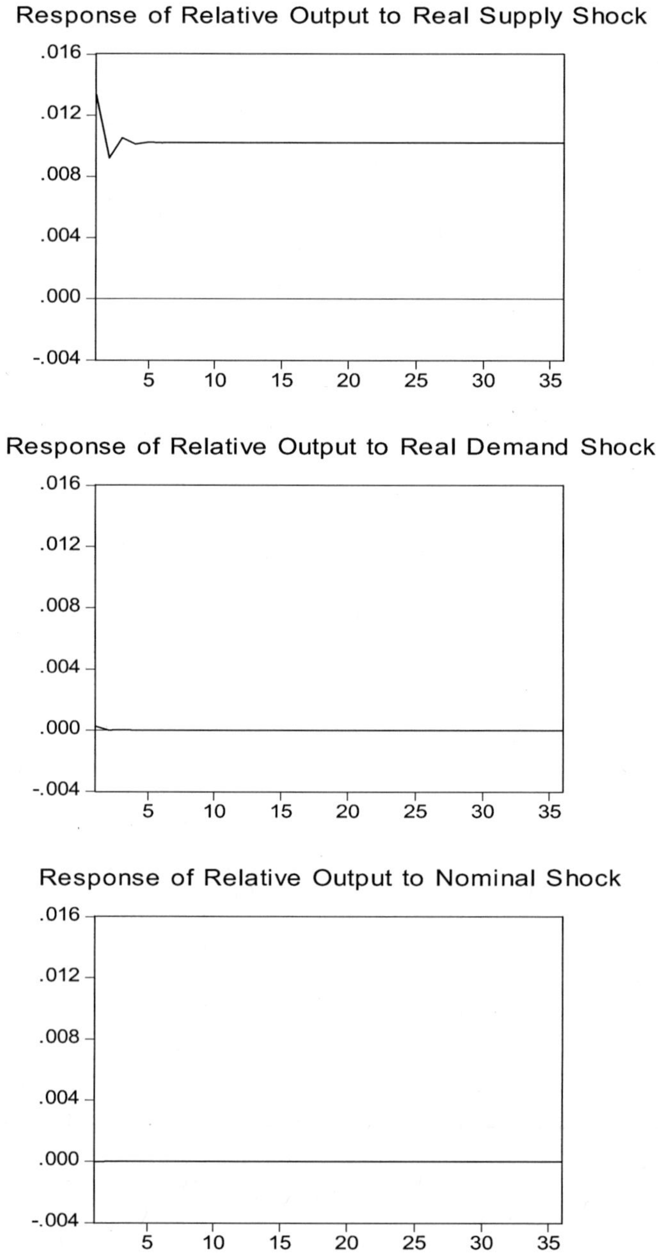

(a) Response of Real Relative Output

Figure 3. Continued on next page.

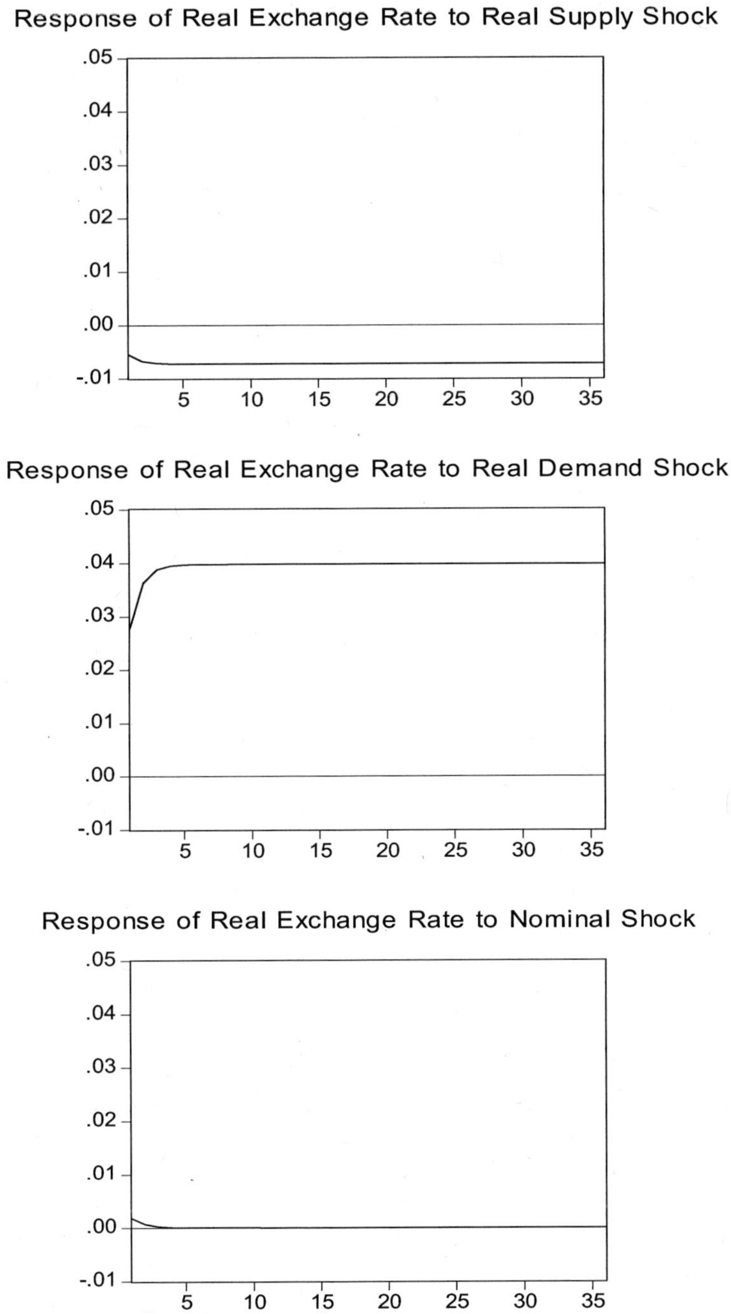

(b) Response of Real Exchange Rate

Figure 3. Continued on next page.

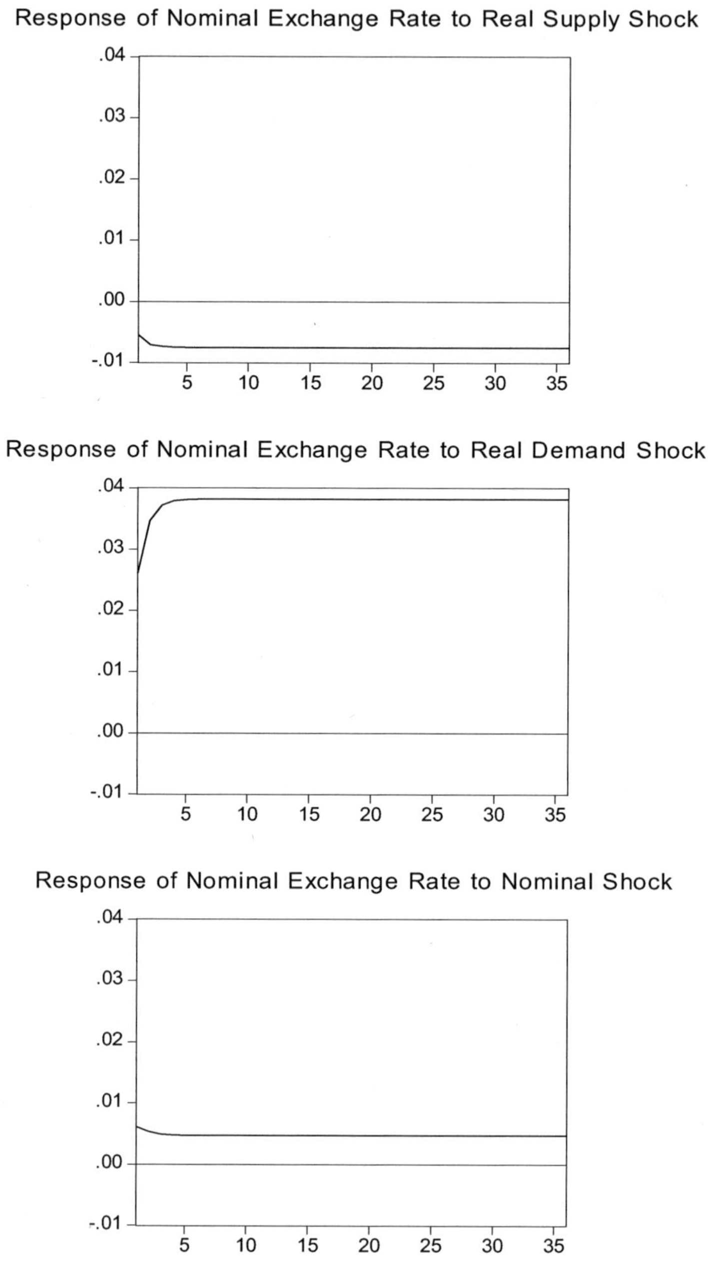

(c) Response of Nominal Exchange Rate

Figure 3. Accumulated Impulse Responses (Trivariate Model).

Forecast error variance decompositions for the variations in the real exchange rate suggest that real demand shocks explain most of the movements in the real exchange rate. Real demand shocks, the most important factors, account for about 95% of the variance in exchange rate movement. Real supply shocks, meanwhile, appear to play a small role in explaining fluctuations in the real in exchange rate, accounting for roughly 3 to 4% of the forecast error variance. The contribution of nominal shocks to the fluctuations of the real of the real exchange rate amounts to about 0.5%. To summarize, a substantial amount of the forecast error variance of the change in the real exchange rate in the yen-dollar rate is due to real demand shocks.

Table 2. Forecast Error Variance Decomposition (Trivariate System)

(A) Real Relative Output

Horizon (month)	**Real Supply Shock (%)**	**Real Demand Shock (%)**	**Nominal Shock (%)**
1	99.965	0.034	0.000
3	99.936	0.064	0.001
6	99.936	0.064	0.001
9	99.936	0.064	0.001
12	99.936	0.064	0.001
24	99.936	0.064	0.001
36	99.936	0.064	0.001

(B) Real Exchange Rate

Horizon (month)	Real Supply Shock (%)	Real Demand Shock (%)	Nominal Shock (%)
1	3.818	95.770	0.411
3	3.654	95.803	0.543
6	3.652	95.802	0.546
9	3.652	95.802	0.546
12	3.652	95.802	0.546
24	3.652	95.802	0.546
36	3.652	95.802	0.546

(C) Nominal Exchange Rate

Horizon (month)	**Real Supply Shock (%)**	**Real Demand Shock (%)**	**Nominal Shock (%)**
1	3.960	91.009	5.031
3	3.888	91.492	4.620
6	3.887	91.494	4.619
9	3.887	91.494	4.619
12	3.887	91.494	4.619
24	3.887	91.494	4.619
36	3.887	91.494	4.619

Finally, forecast error variance decompositions for nominal exchange rates show that more than 90% of the variation in the changes of nominal exchange rates comes from real demand shock. The rest of the variance is attributable to real supply shocks and nominal shocks in similar fractions (less than 5%).

Some Concluding Remarks

This chapter examines the sources of real exchange rate fluctuations of yen-dollar rates using a long-run structural VAR approach. We begin by identifying two types of macroeconomic shocks (real and nominal) by the method of Enders and Lee (1997), and then uncovering the sources of movements in real exchange rates by a technique developed by Blanchard and Quah (1989). The evidence presented indicates that real shocks play a dominant role in explaining the fluctuations of the real exchange rate. Real disturbances account for more than 99% of the forecast error variance of the real exchange rate and more than 97% of the nominal exchange rate. These results are consistent with those of Lastrapes (1992) and Enders and Lee (1997).

Next, we extend the model to identify three types of macroeconomic shocks (real supply, real demand and nominal), in order to reveal the sources of movements in real exchange rates. The evidence presented indicates that real shocks (real demand and real supply) play a dominant role in explaining the fluctuations of the real exchange rate. Real disturbances account for more than 99% of the forecast error variance of the real exchange rate and more than 95% of the nominal exchange rate. These results are consistent with those obtained by the bivariate SVAR model.

The dominant influence of real shocks over real exchange rate fluctuations in yen-dollar rates has some implications for policy management and exchange rate modeling. With regard to exchange rate policy, our results imply that the best approach for policy authorities, in their policymaking to improve competitiveness, is to focus on improvements in the real economy, such as in efficiency, technologies, and productivity. This also calls into question monetary policies which seek to promote competitiveness through currency devaluation.

Acknowledgments

The author is grateful to the Japan Society for the Promotion of Science for providing financial support to the 21st Century Center of Excellence Project.

References

Bayoumi, T. and Eichengreen, B., (1992), Shocking aspects of European Monetary Unification, *National Bureau of Economic Research Working Paper* No. 3949.

Blanchard, O. and Quah, D., (1989), The dynamic effects of aggregate demand and supply disturbances, *American Economic Review,* 79, 655-673.

Chowdhury, I.S., (2004), Sources of exchange rate fluctuations: empirical evidence from six emerging market countries, *Applied Financial Economics*, 14, 697–705.

Clarida, R. and Gali, J., (1994), Sources of real exchange rate fluctuations: how important are nominal shocks? *National Bureau of Economic Research Working Paper* No. 4658.

Dibooglu, S and Kutan, A (2001), Sources of real exchange rate fluctuations in transition economies: the case of Poland and Hungry, *Journal of Comparative Economics*, 29, 257–275.

Dickey, D.A. and Fuller, W.A., (1979), Distribution of the estimators for autoregressive time series with a unit root, *Journal of the American Statistical Association*, 74, 427–431.

Dornbusch, R., (1976), Expectations and exchange rate dynamics, *Journal of Political Economy*, 84, 1161-1176.

Enders, W. and Lee, B.-S., (1997), Accounting for real and nominal exchange rate movements in the post-Bretton Woods period, *Journal of International Money and Finance*, 16, 233-254.

Lastrapes, W.D., (1992), Sources of fluctuations in real and nominal exchange rates, *Review of Economics & Statistics*, 74, 530-9.

Rogers, J.H., (1999), Monetary shocks and real exchange rates, *Journal of International Economics*, 49, 269-88.

Stockman, A.C., (1987), The equilibrium approach to exchange rates, *Economic Review*, Federal Reserve Bank of Richmond, (Mar./Apr), 12-30.

Wang, T (2004) "China: Sources of Real Exchange Rate Fluctuations," *International Monetary Fund Working Paper* No. 04/18.

In: Exchange Rates: Policies, Effects and Fluctuations
Editor: Natalie B. Perkins, pp.147-166
ISBN: 978-1-61209-505-9
© 2011 Nova Science Publishers, Inc.

Chapter 8

EXCHANGE RATE FLEXIBILITY AND REAL ADJUSTMENTS IN EMERGING MARKET ECONOMIES[1]

José García Solanes*

Universidad de Murcia, Departamento de Fundamentos del Análisis Económico
Facultad de Economía y Empresa
Universidad de Murcia. Campus de Espinardo, 30100 Murcia

ABSTRACT

This chapter analyses the extent to which managed floating helps macroeconomic stabilisation and contributes to real adjustment, in the face of real external disturbances in emerging market economies. We find that optimal policy reactions, as opposed to "fear of floating", may explain why nominal exchange rates have exhibited lower variability than nominal interest rates in developing countries along the recent years. We show that for this to occur it is necessary that devaluation affects positively the aggregate demand. Furthermore, we demonstrate that even when the analysis is restricted to a financial context, which seems appropriate when output achieves its long run potential level, some institutional arrangements can be engineered to reduce the destabilising effects of controlled floating.

1. INTRODUCTION

Recent and very comprehensive empirical studies by Reinhart (2000) and Calvo and Reinhart (2002) document that the authorities of emerging market economies frequently intervene to dampen fluctuations in their exchange rates. Consequently, the large majority of

[1] This work was presented in the III Workshop on International Economics held in Málaga, 21-22 November 2003. I wish to thank Angelos Kanas for his helpful discussion in the Workshop, and to Arielle Beyaert for her wise comments. I am also grateful to the Fundación Banco Bilbao Vizcaya Argentaria for its financial support in the frame of the "Primera convocatoria de Ayudas a la investigación en Ciencias Sociales, año 2002".

* E-mail address: solanes@um.es

exchange rate regimes in these countries exhibit much reduced flexibility in the form of dirty floats or soft pegs. This feature has also been outlined by McKinnon and Schnabl (2003) in the case of the East Asian economies, which have pegged their currencies to the US dollar after the crisis of 1977.

According to Calvo and Reinhart (CR), the rationale behind this behaviour lies in the harmful effects that exchange rate flexibility may inflict on the economy when policy credibility is absent and the amount of dollarised debt is huge. The same authors, however, show that the dampening effects are obtained at the cost of raising the level and variability in the domestic interest rate. They remark that these results disturb investment decisions and encourage investors to borrow in foreign currencies. Nonetheless, the above-mentioned analysis is restricted to the financial side of the economy and neglects the role of the exchange rate in dealing with real problems. The most relevant ones have to do with helping adjustments in the real exchange rates in response to external real shocks, which are extremely relevant for developing countries.

Contrary to this view, which regards exchange rate management as "fear of floating", other authors argue that a managed float is a rational choice when dealing with external shocks to improve economic performance. Thus, according to the empirical evidence reported by Edwards (2002), the countries that were regarded as managed floaters during the period 1970-1998 tended to experience higher GDP per capita growth, coupled with (slightly) higher yearly rates of inflation, than other similar economies with fixed exchange rates. On the other hand, Edwards and Levy-Yeyati (2002) found that countries with flexible exchange rates are generally less affected by terms of trade shocks and tend to grow faster than countries with rigid exchange rate regimes.

Our main contention is that the extent to which an exchange rate regime contributes to real adjustment in the face of supply and demand disturbances is particularly crucial in emerging economies, where both the degree of openness to international trade and nominal flexibility are very low. For this reason, one (the main) purpose of this chapter is to provide theoretical and empirical evidence supporting the virtues of a managed floating regime for easing real adjustments. Another objective, and which is tackled first, is to demonstrate that, even in the financial environment described by CR, some institutional arrangements can be engineered to reduce the negative effects of controlled floating; that is, to curtail the increase in interest rates without affecting their variability.

Our work is organised as follows: in section 2 we analyse the financial aspects of managed floating and make some qualifications to the main conclusions of CR. In section 3 we shift to real aspects, and examine the relative advantages and shortcomings of a managed floating in stabilising the economy and adjusting the real exchange rate. In section 4 we test the Balassa-Samuelson hypothesis in a group of developing countries that have adopted some kind of managed floating in recent years. Section 5 provides some concluding remarks and policy implications. Finally, we provide two Appendixes at the end of this work. The first one builds a simple model to demonstrate the effects of monetary policy when the country risk is important; and the second one includes a description of the data sources and the method we used to elaborate some indexes applied in our empirical study.

2. Financial Implications of Exchange Rate Floating

The CR framework refers to a small open developing economy in which authorities try to do their best in an environment characterised by high capital mobility, incomplete markets, imperfect information and dollarised liabilities. Under such conditions, the monetary authorities are exceedingly fearful of exchange rate movements and react with two kinds of intervention to dampen exchange rate swings: first, intervening in the foreign exchange market, and second, setting an optimal level for the domestic interest rate. The main result is that, because of the risk premium, the nominal interest rate is pushed to a high level both in terms of absolute amount and variability.

In the CR model, workers and investors have incomplete information and make decisions at the start of the period, before shocks are realised, on the basis of their expectations concerning the interest rate. The central bank observes the shocks and responds by establishing an optimal interest rate in each period. Its objective function is:

$$W = i\frac{\left(c - \eta i^{e} + \varsigma\right)}{k} - \frac{b}{2}\pi^{2} \qquad (1)$$

where W is the nominal wealth, and i (i^e) stands for the current (expected) nominal interest rate; π is the deviation of the inflation rate from its target (taken to be zero). The parameter k and b are the monetary base multiplier and the social weight attached to inflation stabilisation, respectively. ς is a random shock with zero mean and constant variance. The terms in brackets represent the (log of) demand for money, and the first part of the right hand side is the revenue from seignorage.

Assuming purchasing power and uncovered interest-rate parity conditions and normalising the foreign interest and inflation rates to zero, the objective function is:

$$W = i\frac{\left(c - \eta i^{e} + \varsigma\right)}{k} - \frac{b}{2}(i - \rho)^{2} \qquad (1a)$$

where ρ is the risk premium, assumed to be an i.i.d. variable.

Calvo and Reinhart maximise (1') with respect to the interest rate, under the assumption that the central bank cannot commit to a state-contingent rule (Cournot solution), and obtain the following results for the expected and current interest rates:

$$i^{e} = \frac{c}{bk + \eta} \qquad (2)$$

$$i = \rho + \frac{\varsigma}{bk} + \frac{c}{bk + \eta} \qquad (3)$$

The third term of the right hand side of (3) is the inflation premium in the long run, and is due to a) the presence of seignorage in the objective function, and b) the temptation to generate surprise inflation to obtain extra seignorage. This second element makes the result a third best equilibrium, as is usual when the Cournot solution is coupled to a source of economic distortion (the seignorage revenue). The solution is represented graphically by point A in Figure 1. The position of the indifference curve I is given by the expected interest rate in (2).

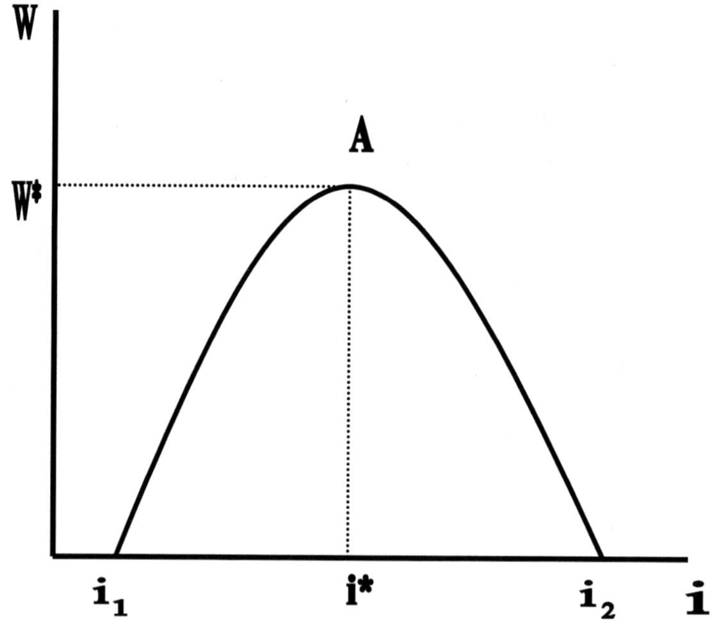

Figure 1. The Calvo and Reinhart model. The central bank acts under discretion.

Let us now see what happens in the CR model if the central bank could commit to a state-contingent rule of the interest rate. In this case, we solve the problem by maximising the expected inflation function:

$$\underset{i_t, i_t^e}{Max}\, E_{t-1}\left\{ i_t \frac{c - \eta i_t^e + \varsigma}{k} - \frac{b}{2}(i_t - \rho)^2 \right\} - \lambda\left(i_t^e - E_{t-1} i_t\right) \tag{4}$$

where λ is the Lagrange multiplier.

Taking first derivatives with respect to i and i^e, and eliminating λ, we obtain:

$$\frac{c - \eta i_t^e + \varsigma}{k} - b(i_t - \rho) + E_{t-1}\left(i_t \frac{-\eta}{k} \right) = 0 \tag{5}$$

Applying expectations in (5), and solving $E_{t-1} i_t$, we get:

$$E_{t-1}i_t = i^e = \frac{c}{2\eta + bk} \qquad (6)$$

Substitution of this value in (5) allows the current interest rate to be obtained:

$$i_t = \rho + \frac{\varsigma}{bk} + \frac{c}{2\eta + bk} \qquad (7)$$

As can be seen, the inflation premium is lower in this case because it is devoid of the part attributed to the central bank's temptation to cheat systematically. The average interest rate, $E_{t-1}i_t$, will equal the desirable inflation rate.

Since the expected interest rate is lower in this solution, the equilibrium is found at a point on the upper solid indifference curve, as represented by point B in Figure 2. However, this solution suffers from time inconsistency as reflected by the fact that the indifference curve has a positive slope at that point. For the expected value of the interest rate attached to curve II, which is known at the beginning of the period, the optimal choice for the central bank is point C. Consequently, commitment to a state-contingent rule appears unfeasible. The literature shows suggested improvements to remove the inflation bias under discretion, and in our case we apply the solution recommended by Walsh (1995) in the context of the Barro-Gordon (1983) model.

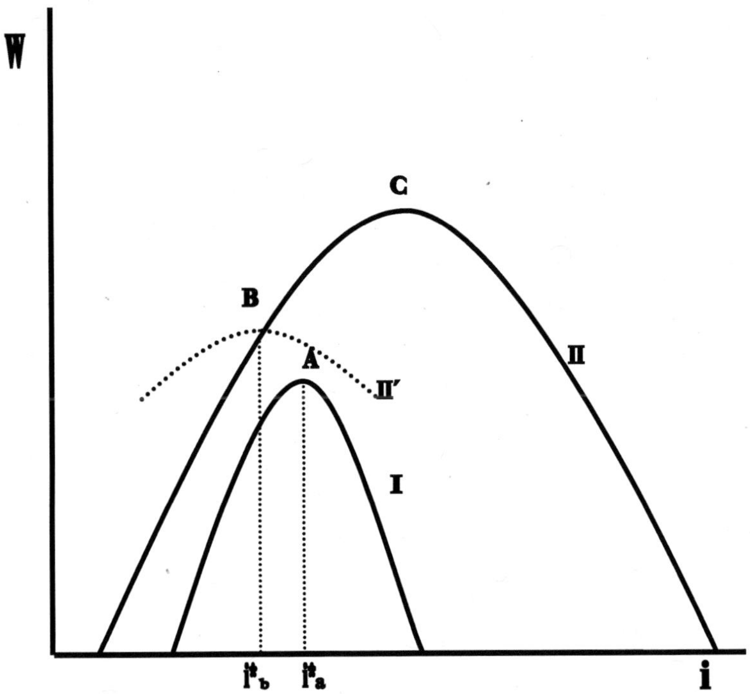

Figure 2. Discretion, commitment and second-best solutions in the CR model.

According to this solution, a simple linear inflation contract is designed in such a way that the central bank is assigned this wealth function:

$$W = \frac{c - \eta i^e - \varsigma}{k} i - \frac{b}{2}(i - \rho)^2 - di \tag{8}$$

where d is a positive parameter which measures the linear interest-penalty imposed to central bank.

Maximisation of this function leads to:

$$i^e = \frac{c - kd}{bk + \eta} \tag{9}$$

$$i = \rho + \frac{\varsigma}{bk} + \frac{c - dk}{bk + \eta} \tag{10}$$

The optimal value of d is that for which the new expected interest rate equals the value given by (6) in order to ensure that the optimal point belongs to the indifference curve II:

$$\frac{c - dk}{bk + \eta} = \frac{c}{2\eta + bk}$$

Resolving d gives:

$$d = \frac{c\eta}{k(bk + 2\eta)} \tag{11}$$

Substituting this value in the wealth function:

$$W = \frac{c - \eta i_t^e + \varsigma}{k} i - \frac{b}{2}(i - \rho)^2 - \frac{c\eta}{k(bk + 2\eta)} i \tag{12}$$

Deriving the first order conditions, and tacking expectations we obtain:

$$i^e = \frac{c}{2\eta + bk} \tag{13}$$

and, substituting in the first order condition:

$$i = \rho + \frac{\varsigma}{k} + \frac{c}{2\eta + bk} \tag{14}$$

This is the same value as that obtained under commitment and is consequently represented by the same point (B) in Figure 2. However, it is time consistent and corresponds to the maximum point of the indifference curve II', which is generated by the new utility function (8). In short, this point is a second best solution that allows the interest rate to be reduced compared with the solution under discretion. Furthermore, this solution does not imply higher variability in the interest rate because since ρ and ζ are assumed to be uncorrelated, for both solutions we have:

$$\sigma_i^2 = \sigma_\rho^2 + \frac{\sigma_\varsigma^2}{b^2 k^2} \tag{15}$$

Combining (14) with the uncovered interest parity condition, we obtain the rate of exchange-rate variation:

$$\varepsilon = \frac{\varsigma}{bk} + \frac{c}{bk + 2\eta} \tag{16}$$

This expression indicates that the linear contract solution also contributes to dampening exchange rate fluctuations.

The general conclusion of this section is that, even if we restrict our analysis to the financial factors and focus our attention on long run equilibrium, as in the CR model, there is still scope to diminish the destabilising effects of managed exchange rate intervention without increasing instability. In the next section our analysis turns to the real side of the economy and to the problems involved in shorter run adjustments.

3. Real Shocks and Exchange Rate Management

In this section we consider a small open country with three important features characteristic of an emergent market economy. First, it has important nominal rigidities, mainly in the downward; second, it is frequently hit by supply real shocks, and third, it suffers a high country risk. Taking into account these characteristics we analyse the extent to which the managed floating regime facilitates a) the stabilisation task of monetary policy, and b) the correct adjustment of the real exchange rate.

For these purposes, we will assume that the authorities adjust the aggregate demand to achieve an appropriate combination of output and inflation in response to shocks, in the same lines, for instance, as Barro and Gordon (1983) model. In that framework, the behaviour of the private sector is summarised by a short run aggregate supply, which is obtained under the assumption that wages are set in advance, based on inflation expectations. Furthermore, the government seeks to minimise a quadratic loss function, which depends on deviations of both inflation and output.

In the following lines we will analyse the way in which the central bank must use the available operating (demand) targets to stabilise the economy and to adjust correctly the real exchange rate. We will assume that a real supply disturbance hits the economy and that the central bank reacts following a two-step strategy. First, it determines the level of the aggregate demand, which enables the optimal combination of output and inflation to be achieved along the supply curve. Second, it decides the appropriate combination of the two operating targets, which are the short-term interest rate and the nominal exchange rate, to obtain the optimum aggregate demand and the new equilibrium value of the real exchange rate. Let us analyse, in turn, this procedure more formally. The results will allow us to derive the relative advantages of a managed float as compared to a strict peg.

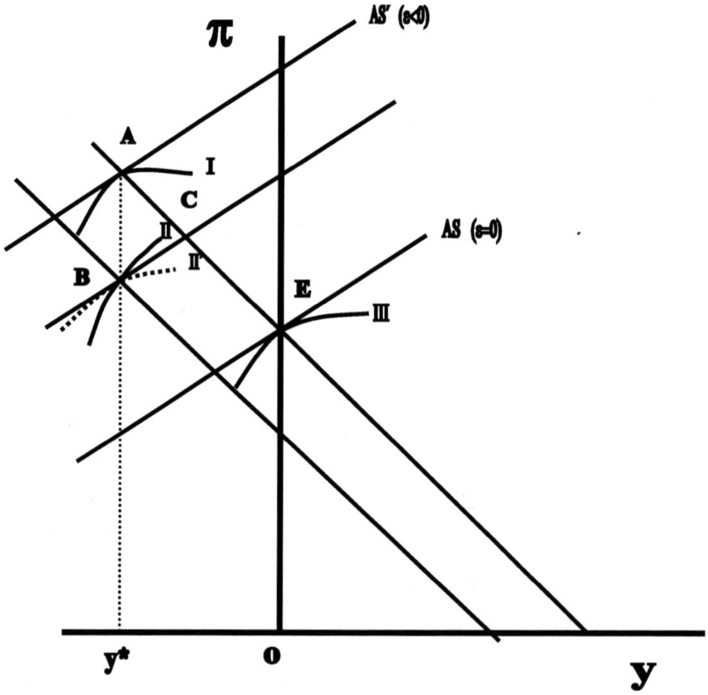

Figure 3. The Barro and Gordon's Model. Discretion, commitment and second best solutions after a negative supply shock.

Suppose that the economy is initially in a long run equilibrium situation as described by point E in Figure 3 and that a negative supply shock occurs that shifts the aggregate supply upwards to the position AS (ε<0)[2]. In a first reaction the central bank will decide an aggregate demand that moves the equilibrium point to C which is at the intersection of the supply curve and the locus of the tangency points (expansion line). We denote this optimal demand AD_t^o, and assume that it depends on an autonomous expenditure $\bar{d}$, which the most important component is the government deficit, the real interest rate (r) and the real exchange rate (q):

---

[2] The level of potential output is normalised to zero.

$$AD_t^o = \bar{d}_t - r_t + \gamma q_t \tag{17}$$

where γ measures the relative effect of variations in the real-exchange rate on the aggregate demand, compared to the coefficient of the real interest rate which we normalise to one. All variables are in logs except for the interest rate. The real exchange rate is defined as the relative price of the foreign good, so that an increase in q indicates a real depreciation of the domestic currency.

Tacking into account the Fisher equation and the fact that the current real exchange rate is equal to the expected level of this variable minus its expected variation, we can write:

$$AD_t^o = \bar{d}_t - i_t + \pi_t + \gamma\left(q_{t+1}^e - \Delta q\right) \tag{18}$$

Denoting s the log of the nominal exchange rate, and its expected change along this period, it is clear that $\Delta q = \Delta s + \pi_t^* - \pi_t$. Consequently:

$$AD_t^o = \bar{d}_t - (i_t - \pi) + \gamma\left(q_{t+1}^e - \Delta s - \pi_t^* + \pi_t\right) \tag{19}$$

Furthermore, uncovered interest parity establishes that:

$$\Delta s + \rho = i_t - i_t^* \tag{20}$$

From equations (19) and (20) we can resolve the nominal interest rate and the expected variation of the nominal exchange rate:

$$i_t = \pi_t - \frac{1}{1+\gamma}\left(AD_t^o - \bar{d}_t - \gamma r_t^* - \gamma\rho - \gamma q_{t+1}^e\right) \tag{21}$$

$$\Delta s = \pi_t - \pi_t^* - \frac{1}{1+\gamma}\left(AD_t^o - \bar{d}_t + r_t^* + \rho - \gamma q_{t+1}^e\right) \tag{22}$$

Equations (21) and (22) indicate how the operating targets can be set simultaneously to achieve the desired level of the (optimum) aggregate demand corresponding to point C. To obtain the current exchange rate that satisfies the targeted variation given by (22), we need an equation for the expected change in the exchange rate. If we adopt, for instance, the mechanism of Dornbusch (1976), the expected exchange-rate change will be:

$$\Delta s = \delta(\bar{s}_t - s_t) \tag{23}$$

were $\bar{s}_t$ is the long run equilibrium value of the nominal exchange rate, and δ is a positive parameter smaller than 1, that measures the speed to which the current exchange rate approaches its long run level. Assuming for now that $\bar{s}_t$ is given, s_t can be solved combining (22) and (23):

$$s_t = \bar{s}_t - \frac{1}{\delta}\left(\pi - \pi^*\right) + \frac{1}{\delta(1+\gamma)}\left(AD_t^o - \bar{d}_t + r_t^* + \rho - \gamma q_{t+1}^e\right) \qquad (24)$$

Equations (21) and (24) indicate that in order to reduce the aggregate demand, as required for going from point E to point C, the central bank must increase the nominal interest rate and appreciate the domestic currency. The short run equilibrium point will change several times before reaching the long run equilibrium represented by point A (Cournot solution) in Figure 3, which output is the new potential level after the shock. If the inflation bias is removed, by signing for instance an inflation contract with the central bank, the final equilibrium point will be B.

Note that, contrary to CR, in our model variations in i_t take place simultaneously as those in s_t, in response to foreign shocks, and are not a strategy to dampen exchange rate swings.

It is worth outlining that the central bank can rely on the exchange rate as a useful lever of stabilisation policy in so far as it ensures normal or conventional effects on the aggregate demand, as we have assumed so far. However, the possibility exists that a devaluation of the domestic currency produces contractionary effects on the aggregate demand. The latter result is specific of some developing countries, which are particularly affected by capital market imperfections and strong balance sheet effects. In Appendix I we derive the necessary conditions for this abnormal result using an IS-LM model, for an open economy, that includes those crucial features of emerging countries[3]. Since the conditions for this result are extreme and not usually met, we will assume that devaluation causes expansionary effects on the aggregate demand, which amounts to saying that the parameter γ in equation (17) is positive.

The nominal exchange rate may also be managed to adjust the real exchange rate (RER) towards the equilibrium level determined by real fundamentals. Let us examine, for instance, what would happen in the case where a deterioration of the terms of trade takes place. The theory of real exchange-rate determination postulates a depreciating effect in the RER (Δq). In terms of the model explained above, this negative real shock implies an increase in both the expected RER for the next period (Δq_{t+1}^e) and the long run equilibrium level of the nominal exchange rate ($\Delta \bar{s}$). As a result, the nominal interest rate will increase (equation (21)). However, the effect on the current nominal exchange rate is undetermined unless we get more information about the parameters γ and δ and the relative adjustments in $\Delta \bar{s}$ and Δq_{t+1}^e in response to the shock. For normal situations in which the variation in $\Delta \bar{s}$ is more intense than, Δq_{t+1}^e the likely result is a current depreciation of the domestic currency (Δs_t).

In any case, if the managed exchange rate level is not in accordance with the equilibrium RER, the current account will serve as the transmission mechanism to bring the exchange rate

[3] For a more elaborated model, based on microfounded decisions, see Céspedes, Chang and Velasco (2002).

into equilibrium. Suppose, for instance, that the exchange rate is overvalued because it has been targeted too low. This situation will cause a current account deficit and increase both foreign indebtedness and the country risk premium. From equation (24) we derive that an increase in $\Delta\rho$ leads the central bank to depreciate its currency (Δs_t)[4].

The contribution of nominal exchange rate variations to adjust the RER is particularly valuable in the depreciating case, because in this situation the alternative way to bring down the RER (Δq), which is by reducing domestic prices, seems very costly or even unfeasible in developing countries.

Equations (21) and (24) provide the rationale for one of the puzzles raised by Calvo and Reinhart (2002) concerning volatilities in interest and exchange rates. These authors found that in developing countries the variability of the first variable is higher than that of the second one. In their opinion this is a striking finding in "declared" flexible exchange regimes, which can only be explained by the fact that central bank uses the interest rate to smooth exchange rate fluctuations[5]. Our model provides scope to analyse this situation distinguishing two kinds of disturbances. In the case of temporary changes in market beliefs and other financial lurches that modify the country risk premium, the flexible exchange rate should react more intensively than the interest rate provided that, as empirical evidence tends to indicate, $\delta < 1/\gamma$. The arguments of CR explaining why the facts show a different pattern for these variabilities, as a result of massive intervention in the foreign exchange market, would be acceptable in this case.

However, when external disturbances are caused by real factors (variations in AD, $\bar{d}$, r^* and q^e in formula (24)), the implied simultaneous adjustments in $\bar{s}$ provide dampening results in s_t. For instance, in the case of a positive real supply shock, the authorities react expanding the aggregate demand to obtain an optimal combination of output and inflation, and this causes a nominal depreciation (Δs_t). But, at the same time, $\bar{s}$ decreases, as a result of the shock, and reduces the net fluctuation of s_t. This cushioning effect could explain why s_t fluctuates less intensively than i_t.

Let us now examine what happens when the authorities fix firmly the exchange rate of its currency with respect to a foreign strong one. In this case, the central bank cannot modify the exchange rate, and the level of the aggregate demand (AD^f) must be derived from equation (22) by imposing $\Delta s=0$ on it:

$$AD_t^f = (1+\gamma)(\pi_t - \pi_t^*) + \bar{d}_t - r_t^* - \rho + \gamma q_{t+1}^e \qquad (25)$$

This equation indicates that the aggregate demand depends on external factors and on the fiscal budget. The implications for policy stabilisation follows directly from this equation:

---

[4] In the case where the exchange rate floats freely, the current account imbalances put in motion portfolio adjustments that modify both interest rates and exchange rates. In turn, these modifications gradually bring the current account to zero, which is its long run equilibrium. Models which account for the stock-flow implications of the current account imbalance include, for instance, the portfolio models of Branson (1977) and Frenkel and Mussa (1988).

[5] This feature was also remarked by Lahiri and Végh (2000).

a) Domestic monetary policy expansions have contractionary effects to the extent to which an increase in the money supply causes a loss of foreign reserves, which in turn pushes up the country risk.
b) Domestic fiscal policy expansions have a direct positive effect on the aggregate demand, but this effect can be seriously curtailed, or even reversed, by the induced increase in the country risk premium[6].

As can be seen, the presence of the country risk term may substantially change the results of macroeconomic policies, with respect to the propositions of the standard Mundell-Fleming model in a context of fixed exchange rate and perfect capital mobility.

As far as adjustments of the RER are concerned, it seems evident that the fixed exchange rate regime makes those variations slower and/or more costly in terms of output and employment, to the extent that they are channeled through modifications in domestic prices. As explained above, difficulties and costs increase when the required adjustment of the RER implies reductions in domestic prices.

As a general conclusion of the whole section, it should be stressed that managed floating facilitates stabilisation of the economy in the short run, and paves the way for real exchange-rate adjustment, provided that variations in the exchange rate work as conventionally expected. However, if devaluation affects the aggregate demand abnormally, the country would do better by firmly pegging his currency to a strong foreign one or by joining a monetary union. The relative advantage of a managed peg increases with the frequency of negative real shocks because the downwards adjustment of prices, which are the only way to lower the real value of the domestic currency under a fixed rate system, is particularly costly and painful in developing countries.

4. Real Exchange Rates and Productivity Differentials[7]

Since the managed exchange rate regime makes adjustment easier in the real exchange rate towards its equilibrium level, one would expect the theories of real exchange-rate determination to be more easily fulfilled in economies which have adopted this exchange-rate regime[8]. For the particular case of economies that are predominantly affected by real supply disturbances, the Balassa-Samuelson hypothesis (BSH) would go a long way to explaining medium-run real exchange rate changes. To test this proposition empirically we applied the BSH to a group of Latin American countries that have adopted some kind of exchange rate flexibility in recent years[9].

[6] Ortiz and Rodríguez (2002) build an IS-LM model with country risk to explain the results of some fiscal measures implemented in Argentina under the currency board regime.

[7] This section has been written with the research assistance provided by Fernando E. Torrejón.

[8] Since in a regime of managed floating the exchange rate can jump quickly to restore equilibrium, it is reasonable to think that misalignments will be short lived, in contrast with the pegged exchange rate where the shadow or equilibrium exchange rate is potentially different from the actual observed exchange rate.

[9] In accordance with the exchange rate arrangements declared to the International Monetary Fund, the eleven countries which we include in the empirical analysis adopted managed flexibility, ranging from crawling pegs to independent floating, throughout most of the years of our sample. The fixed exchange rate regime was the exception, and is found in very few countries and years: Nicaragua (1991), Ecuador (1992, 2000, 2001), and Venezuela (1994, 1995). In all of these cases, the countries adopted a currency board with respect to the US Dollar.

According to the BSH, labour productivity differentials between tradable and non-tradable sectors determine the price of non-tradables relative to tradables (named the "relative price" hereafter). Under Cobb-Douglas technology in both sectors, it can easily be seen that:

$$ln\, RP_{it} = ln\left(\frac{a_i^T}{a_i^N}\right) + ln\left(\frac{\vartheta_{i,t}^T}{\vartheta_{i,t}^N}\right) \tag{26}$$

where *RP* is the relative price and a^T, a^N are the labour shares in value added in the tradable and non-tradable goods sectors, respectively. Labour productivity in tradable and non-tradable sectors is represented by ϑ^T and ϑ^N, respectively. Subscripts *i* and *t* denote country and date.

Assuming that technical parameters do not change, and grouping the terms corresponding to the relative price and the productivity of the non-tradable sector in the left-hand side for empirical purposes, we obtain this transformed expression:

$$ln\, RP_{it} + ln\,\vartheta_{i,t}^N = b_i + ln\,\vartheta_{i,t}^T \tag{27}$$

We interpret Eq. (27) as a restriction on the long-run trends in the relative price and the labour productivity in each sector. In the following lines we will test whether $(ln RP_{it} + ln\,\vartheta_{i,t}^N)$, which we call the "composite variable", and $\ln \vartheta_{i,t}^T$ are cointegrated and whether the cointegrating slope is one. We will also explore the possibility that the cointegration relationship holds with a trend.

We use annual data from Bolivia, Chile, Colombia, Costa Rica, Ecuador, México, Nicaragua, Paraguay, Peru, Uruguay and Venezuela, and construct indexes for prices and labour productivity in each sector. In Appendix II we describe the sources and the procedure followed to calculate aggregate sector indexes from the raw data provided by individual branches of activity. The period covered is imposed by the availability of data for the whole set of countries, and corresponds to the years 1991-2001. Since the individual series are not sufficiently long for time series analysis in each country, we work with panel data and apply Pedroni (1999)'s panel method, which was expressly designed to deal with this problem.

First of all, we examined the trend in behaviour of each series in the panel by applying the method suggested by Levin and Lin (1993) to ascertain the integration order of each series. We applied the test to both filtered and not filtered series, and considered alternatively the possibility of one or two lags[10]. Since we could not reject the null hypothesis of non-stationarity, and found evidence against two-order integration, we concluded that each series has a unit root. In a second stage, we proceeded to look at cointegration relationships. We began with the hypothesis that, in the long run, the log of the composite variable and the log of the productivity in the tradable sector are cointegrated.

Table 1 contains the results of Pedroni's panel test assuming that the null hypothesis is that the two variables are not cointegrated. The statistics Panel-t (PT) and Panel-t (P) reject

[10] A higher number of lags would not be reasonable account taken of the size of our sample.

the null hypothesis at the 5% and 1% level, respectively. Consequently, the panel test provides strong evidence that relative prices and relative productivities are, in fact, cointegrated as the Balassa-Samuelson model predicts. However, the point estimates of coefficient $\hat{a}$, presented in the bottom column of Table 1, are generally distinct from one, and even negative in four cases. For this reason, we tested the stronger prediction of the BS model that the slope in the cointegration relationship is 1.0.

Table 1. The Balassa-Samuelson model. Cointegration test with the Pedroni (1999) Method for panel data

Regression: $(lnRP + ln\vartheta^N)_{i,t} = \gamma_i + \beta ln\vartheta^T_{i,t} + \varepsilon_{i,t}$

11 Latin American countries 1991-2001

Pedroni (1999) test. Period 1991-2001		
Statistics		**p-value**
Panel-υ	48.52	0.17
Panel-ρ	-29.58	0.6
Panel-t (PT)	-8.84	0.05
Panel-t (P)	-128.8	0.00
Estimated value of β		
Countries		
Bolivia		0.898552
Chile		0.535975
Colombia		0.658681
Costa Rica		-0.109722
Ecuador		1.215595
Mexico		-0.126483
Nicaragua		0.038861
Paraguay		1.296599
Peru		-0.060837
Uruguay		0.790096
Venezuela		-0.220163

1) The null hypothesis is Ho: the estimated residuals of all individuals of the panel have a unit root (no cointegration). According to the statistics 1υ and 3t, Ho is rejected at 1% of significance.
2) Estimates of β were obtained with OLS with fixed effects for a balanced panel of data.
3) γ_i is the specific parameter for fixed effects.

In order to verify that the slope is equal to 1.0, we performed a unit root test for the variable $(lnRP + ln\vartheta^N - ln\vartheta^T)_{i,t}$, which we denote "$d_{i,t}$", applying the Levin and Lin (1993) and the Im-Pesaran and Shin (2002) tests for panel data. The null hypothesis is that $d_{i,t}$ has a unit root as opposed to being stationary. If the null is rejected we accept the stronger version of the BSH for this group of Latin American countries taken as a whole. In Table 2 we report the results for the whole set of countries.

As it is apparent from Table 2, the adjusted statistics of Levin and Lin (1993) indicate that the null hypothesis is rejected when we include both one and two lags. In the case of model 1, which has no independent term and shows no trend, the null hypothesis is rejected at 1% for one and two lags. In the case of model 2 the null hypothesis is rejected at 5% when one lag is included.

Table 2. Unit root test on stationarity of $(lnRP + ln\vartheta^N - ln\vartheta^T)_{i,t}$

Method of Levin and Lin (1993) to test that $\beta = 1$

11 Latin American countries 1991-2001

	Model 1		**Model 2**	
	One lag	**Two lags**	**One lag**	**Two lags**
Filtered series				
t-statistics of $\hat{\rho}$	-3.06	-3.20	-6.06	-6.13
t*-statistics of $\hat{\rho}$	-2.93	-3.07	-2.14	-1.23
p-value	0.0017**	0.0011**	0.0162*	0.1096
Non filtered series				
t-statistics of $\hat{\rho}$	-3.09	-2.74	-6.67	-4.77
t*-statistics of $\hat{\rho}$	-2.97	-2.64	-1.97	1.40
p-value	0.0015**	0.0042**	0.024*	0.92

1) The null hypothesis is Ho: each of the panel members has a unit root, as opposed to the alternative H_1: all of the individuals of the panel are stationary.
2) Model 1 does not include an independent term or any trend in the autoregressive equation. Model 2 includes an independent term.
3) (*), (**) indicate 5% and 1% significance, respectively.

Table 3 reports the results obtained with the IPS test. The null hypothesis is rejected again at 5% when the model includes a trend and a constant. These results do not change when the series is filtered. Overall, the results lend support to the strong version of BSH in the set of countries taken as a whole. The relative price and the relative productivity appear to be cointegrated, and the coefficient relating both variables is close to one. However, the results are not so clear for countries considered individually, since the Pedroni's test provides negative point estimates of coefficient β for four countries (Table 1).

Table 3. Unit root test on stationarity of $(lnRP + ln\vartheta^N - ln\vartheta^T)_{i,t}$

Method of Im-Pesaran and Shin (2002) to test that $\beta = 1$
11 Latin American countries 1991-2001

	Model 1	**Model 2**
	Without lags	**Without lags**
Non filtered series		
t-bar NT	-1.63	-2.80
Critical value	-1.93	-2.74*
Filtered series		
t-bar NT	-1.83	-2.92
Critical value	-1.93	-2.74*

1) The null hypothesis is Ho: each of the panel members has a unit root, as opposed to the alternative H_1: some members of the panel are stationary and some are not.
2) Model 1 includes an independent term. Model 2 includes an independent term and a trend.
3) The critical values correspond to N= 10, and T= 10.
4) (*) indicates 5% significance.

CONCLUDING REMARKS

The choice of an appropriate exchange rate regime for developing countries has been the object of intense scrutiny and policy debate in recent years[11]. Some authors have focused their attention on the financial aspects of the problem and found that, by intervening in the foreign exchange and domestic money markets, the authorities of these countries are pursuing a sub-optimal course of action and introducing destabilising forces in investment decisions and output variations. We demonstrate that even in the financial framework of Calvo and Reinhart (2002), which seems appropriate when output has achieved its long run level, there is scope for reducing the level of the domestic interest rate without increasing its volatility and, consequently, for dampening the destabilising effects of managed floating. A simple linear contract with the central bank concerning the level of the interest rate is a useful device for this purpose.

Paradoxically, the above authors do not include these "real" investment and output consequences in the welfare function of their models. Instead, they neglect real shocks and consider that full employment and purchasing power parity are normal assumptions for these countries. We believe that the virtues and failures of exchange rate regimes must be evaluated within the general framework of economic policy, where stabilisation and exchange rate adjustments play an important role. This is particularly relevant in countries suffering high unemployment rates and frequent and variable real disturbances. For this reason, a substantial

[11] See E. C. B. (2003) for a systematic overview of the different arguments and theoretical positions.

part of this chapter has been devoted to showing the positive effects of exchange rate management in this field.

We find that the advantages of managed floating increase with the frequency of asymmetric real shocks and the presence of nominal rigidities. For this to occur, which is also evident in the theory of optimal currency areas, it is necessary for a devaluation to affect the aggregate demand in the normal or conventional way. Since such an effect is not evident in developing countries, we obtain the conditions under which it can be achieved. As in previous work by Céspedes, Chang and Velasco (2001), we show that debt ratios and risk premiums would have to reach unrealistically high steady levels to generate the abnormal case.

Furthermore, we show that optimal policy reactions, in the face of real external shocks, as opposed to "fear of floating", may explain why nominal exchange rates have exhibited lower variability than nominal interest rates in developing countries along the recent years.

In the empirical part of the work we obtain evidence to support the Balassa-Samuelson hypothesis in eleven Latin American countries that have adopted some kind of managed exchange-rate regime in recent years. Although this result, obtained for the period 1991-2001, cannot be taken as direct or immediate proof of the advantages of managed floating, it does constitute a good and favourable sign that this system makes adjustments in the real exchange rates quicker and less painful.

The results of this chapter are in the same line as Ball (1999) and Ades (2002), who demonstrated that many countries try to stabilise their economies by following a Taylor rule for an open economy and take into consideration the real exchange rate when conducting monetary policy. If this is the case, the efforts of these economies to manage floating should be regarded as a symptom of a "fear of fixing" rather than a "fear of floating."

APPENDIX I

The Effects of Exchange Rate Variations on the Aggregate Demand

Let us consider the following IS-LM model for a small open and developing country:

$$Y = Y\left(\overset{-}{i},\overset{+}{D},\overset{+}{X},\overset{+}{S}\right) \tag{I.1}$$

$$i = i^{*} + z\left(\overset{-}{S}\right) + \rho\left(\overset{+}{D},\overset{+}{S}\right) \tag{I.2}$$

$$M = L\left(\overset{-}{i},\overset{+}{Y}\right) \tag{I.3}$$

The signs above variables indicate the sign of the corresponding partial derivatives. Equation (I.1) is a standard IS equation indicating that the aggregate demand Y depends negatively on interest rate i, and positively on government deficit D, autonomous net exports X, and exchange rate S, defined as the price of the foreign country. Variables i and S are nominal and real since in this kind of models it is assumed that the expected rate of inflation is zero.

Equation (I.2) is the uncovered interest parity condition. In an economy with a managed exchange rate, international capital mobility implies that the domestic interest rate is equal to the sum of world interest rate i^*, the expected variation in the exchange rate z, and a risk premium ρ. We assume that, ceteris paribus, a higher S today means a lower expected depreciation[12]. The function ρ contains the main novelty of this model, which we explain in the following lines.

The extensive literature on country risk indicates that the risk premium grows with government deficit and falls with the net wealth of the residents. In turn, the net wealth decreases when the domestic currency depreciates since developing countries have huge amounts of dollarised debt. The country risk premium measures the imperfections of the international capital market; its sensitivity with respect to the exchange rate (ρ_e) reflects the importance of the "balance-sheet effect". As it will be seen, the last features are crucial for the functioning and results of the model in these countries.

Equation (I.3) is a standard LM function where demand for money depends positively on domestic output and negatively on the domestic interest rate.

Tacking derivatives and solving the model for the three endogenous variations (dY, dM, di), we obtain that an unexpected (managed) devaluation produces the following results on the aggregate demand, the money supply and the interest rate:

$$\frac{dy}{dS} = (z_S + \rho_S)Y_i + Y_S \qquad \text{(I.4)}$$

$$\frac{dM}{dS} = (z_S + \rho_S)(L_i + L_Y Y_i) + Y_S L_Y \qquad \text{(I.5)}$$

$$\frac{di}{dS} = (z_S + \rho_S) \qquad \text{(I.6)}$$

These equations indicate that for very vulnerable economies, that is for countries with a very sensitive risk premium to exchange rate variations ($|\rho_S| > |z_S|$)- as a result of important balance-sheet effects- devaluation may produce contractionary impacts on the aggregate demand (note that the partial derivative, Y_i, has a negative sing). Furthermore, under these circumstances, devaluation also may induce an endogenous contraction in the money supply and an increase in domestic interest rate.

---

[12] This assumption is in accordance with the Dornbusch mechanism of expectations formation adopted in section 3 of this work.

For robust economies, in which $|z_S| > |\rho_S|$, devaluation has expansionary effects in both the aggregate demand and the money supply, and reduces the domestic interest rate.

APPENDIX II

Data Sources and Construction of Some Variables for the Test of Balassa and Samuelson Hypothesis

Main sources: central banks, national institutes of statistics, CEPAL, and Labour International Organisation.

The ranking of the branches of activity was taken from the United Nations Statistical Papers, *Series M, Nr 4/Review 3.* New York, 1990.

Goods were grouped under the headlines of tradables and non-tradables according to the general criteria accepted in the literature and the extent of data availability. In the group of tradables we included manufactures, transports, storage and communications, and mining and quarrying. Within the group of non-tradables we included electricity, gas and water, construction, wholesale and retail commerce, motor repairing, home goods, hotels and restaurants, financial intermediation, estate activities, hiring, and other trade activities.

Because lack of data in important aspects such as output and/or employment, the following activities and goods were excluded: education, health and social work, other social service activities, home services, non-governmental organisations, agriculture, forestry, hunting and fishing, and public administration.

For each sector we constructed indexes for prices and average labour productivity. As far price indexes are concerned, we obtained them dividing the aggregate nominal output by the real aggregate output in the sector. Aggregate outputs were obtained as a weighted sum of outputs of individual branches.

To calculate the average labour productivity in each sector we measured previously total employment as a weighted sum of employment in individual branches. Then we divided real production by employment in each sector.

REFERENCES

Ades, A. (2002), “Taylor Rules in Emerging Markets”, in *Goldman Sachs Emerging Market Strategy,* 02, 12 (July).

Ball, L. (1999), “Policy Rules for Open Economies”, in J. B. Taylor (Ed) *Monetary Policy Rules,* University of Chicago Press.

Barro, R. J. and Gordon, D. B. (1983), “Rules, Discretion and Reputation in a Model of Monetary Policy”, *Journal of Monetary Economics*, 17 (1): 101-122.

Branson, W. (1977), “Asset Markets and Relative Prices in Exchange Rate Determination”, *Sozialwissenschaftliche Annalen,* Vol. 1: 69-89.

Calvo, G. amd C. Reinhart (2002), “Fear of Floating”, *Quarterly Journal of Economics*, Vol. CXVII, (May): 379-408.

Céspedes, L. F., R. Chang, and A. Velasco (2002), "IS-LM-BP in the Pampas", *Working Paper* 9337, NBER.

Dornbusch, R. (1976), "Expectations and exchange rate dynamics", *Journal of Political Economy,* 84: 1161-1176, December.

European Central Bank (2003), "Exchange rate regimes for emerging economies", *Monthly Bulletin*, February, 53-66.

Edwards, S. (2002), "The great exchange rate debate after Argentina", *North American Journal of Economics and Finance,* 13:237-252.

Edwards, S. And E. Levy-Yeyati (2002), "Flexible Exchange Rates as Stock Absorbers: An Empirical Investigation", *UCLA Working Paper.*

Frenkel, J. and M. Mussa (1988), "Exchange Rates and the Balance of Payments", in R. Jones and P. Kennen (eds), *Handbook of International Economics*, North Holland, Amsterdam.

Im, Pesaran and Shin (2002), "Testing for Unit Roots in Heterogeneous Pannels", Mimeo.

Lahiri, A., and C. A. Végh (2001), "Living with the Fear of Floating: An Optimal Policy Perspective", in *Preventing Currency Crisis in Emerging Markets*, S. Edwards and F. Frankel (eds), Chicago: University of Chicago Press for the National Bureau of Economic Research.

Levin, A. and Lin, C. F. (1993), "Unit Roots Test in Panel Data: New Results", Department of Economics, University of California at San Diego, Discussion Paper.

McKinnon R. and Schnabl (2003), "The East Asian Dollar Standard, Fear of Floating, and Original Sin", Stanford University Working Paper 03-001.

Ortiz, J. and C. Rodríguez (2002), "Country Risk and the Mundell-Fleming Model Applied to the 1999-2000 Argentine Experience", *Journal of Applied Economics,* Vol. 2 (November): 327-348.

Reinhart, C. (2000), "Mirage of Floating Exchange Rates", *American Economic Review*, Vol. 90, Iss. 2 (May): 65-70.

Pedroni, P. (1999), "Critical Values for Cointegration Tests in Heterogeneous Panels with Multiple Regressors", in A. Banerjee (edt) *Special Issue of the Oxford Bulletin of Economics and Statistics*, Oxford.

Walsh, C. E. (1995), *"Optimal Contracts for Central Bankers*", *American Economic Review*, 85 (1): 150-167.

INDEX

2

A

B

C

D

E

F

G

H

I

Q

R

S

Y

Z